power
programming...

MOTIF

ERIC F. JOHNSON
KEVIN REICHARD

ADVANCED COMPUTER BOOKS

MIS: PRESS

First Printing
ISBN 1-55828-059-6
Library of Congress Catalog Card Number 90-26693

Printed in the United States of America

For information about our audio products, write us at:
Newbridge Book Clubs, 3000 Cindel Drive, Delran, NJ 08370

TRADEMARKS

AIX is a registered trademark of IBM
A/UX is a trademark of Apple Computer, Inc.
Amiga and AmigaDOS are trademarks of Commodore Business Machines, Inc.
Aviion is a trademark of Data General, Inc.
Cray Y-MP is a trademark of Cray Research, Inc.
DEC VAX and VMS are trademarks of Digital Equipment Corp.
Esix is a trademark of Everex
HP-UX is a trademark of Hewlett-Packard, Inc.
Interactive UNIX and Interactive 386/ix are trademarks of Interactive Systems
Macintosh is a registered trademark of McIntosh Laboratory, licensed to Apple Computer, Inc.
Motif and OSF/Motif are trademarks of the Open Software Foundation
Open Desktop is a trademark of Santa Cruz Operation, Inc.
Open Look and UNIX are trademarks of AT&T
PC Xview is a trademark of Graphic Software Systems, Inc.
PC Xsight is a trademark of Locus Computing, Inc.
SunOS and SPARCStation are registered trademarks of Sun Microsystems, Inc.
X Window System is a registered trademark of the Massachusetts Institute of Technology

This book is dedicated to those struggling to make sense of the X Window System, Motif, and everything a graphical interface has to offer. It's always been a standard rule that graphical interfaces are easy to use but dreadfully hard to program. With this book, we hope, in our own little way, to ease the burden of writing Motif applications. Good luck.

Also dedicated to Penny Johnson Reichard and Geisha, two irreplaceable soulmates.

Special thanks goes to the Santa Cruz Operation and Jim Boulware.

Contents

Contents

Contents

SECTION II. MORE MOTIF WIDGETS

Contents

SECTION III. USING RESOURCES

SECTION IV. FOLLOWING THE MOTIF STYLE

SECTION VI. APPENDICES

Introduction

This book introduces Motif programming and the Motif interface. After finishing this book, you should have a good working knowledge of programming Motif applications and a good knowledge of how to go further.

As in previous books (*X Window Applications Programming* and *Advanced X Window Applications Programming*), we've concentrated on the nuts and bolts of writing Motif programs. This book is not a full reference work and will not describe in boring detail every Motif function call and data type. Instead, we hope to present the most important topics you'll need to get started writing Motif applications in the C language.

Just about every chapter has a sample Motif program. We strongly believe that working source code examples are a powerful tool to help learn a new subject, especially one as complex as Motif.

After reading this book, you should be ready to start writing Motif applications—in fact, you'll develop a number of applications as you go through these pages. Figure 0-1 shows some Motif applications.

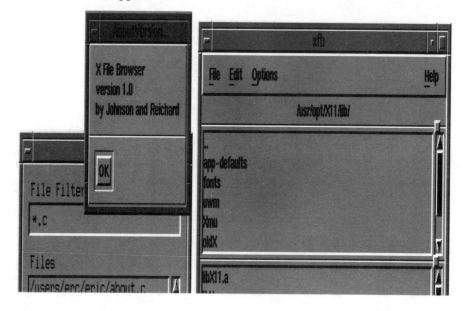

Figure 0-1. Some Motif Applications.

WHAT IS MOTIF?

Motif is a graphical interface, a style guide for providing application consistency, a window manager, and a programmer's toolkit library. In this book we'll spend most of our time on the programmer's library.

The Motif library allows you to create programs with a graphical interface that can run on a wide variety of platforms, including systems based on Digital Equipment, Hewlett-Packard, IBM, Sun, and 386 clone architectures.

Motif is a software product of the Open Software Foundation, an organization that includes IBM, DEC, and HP among its members, so it promises to be a standard for user interfaces.

Motif is based on the X Window System.

WHERE DOES MOTIF SIT IN RELATION TO X?

Figure 0-2 shows the Xt-based toolkits.

Motif	Athena Xaw	Open Look/OLIT	Open Look/ XView
Xt Intrinsics			
X Library			
Inter-Process Communication or Networking Library			

Figure 0-2. Xt-Based Toolkits.

The Motif toolkit sits on top of the Xt Intrinsics toolkit, which is part of the X Window System. That means Motif uses many of the Xt features and functions. Motif does have a set of functions of its own, and Motif has its own widget set with their own look and feel. The Xt Intrinsics provide some basic mechanism for many widget sets to sit on top of (you'll find a lot of this mechanism stuff as you read about X). The Xt Intrinsics in turn sit on top of the X library, or Xlib, which is the low-level X Window application programmer's interface (which often uses the acronym API).

Underneath the X library sits the X network protocol. Since X is network-based, you can distribute applications over a network.

WHAT IS THE X WINDOW SYSTEM?

The X Window System is a network-based graphical windowing system that runs on a wide variety of architectures, including UNIX, VMS, AmigaDOS, Macintosh, and to a limited extent, MS-DOS-based systems.

X is based on network technology, which means you can run programs on one system, say a Cray supercomputer, and display the output from the workstation on your desk. X uses the concepts of client/server computing but reverses the standard terminology. With X, the X server runs on the workstation on your desk. The X server controls your physical monitor, mouse, and keyboard. The server actually draws the dots on the screen.

3

X client programs can run on a host computer and display their windows on the screen controlled by the X server on your workstation, as long as the two are connected with a network. In addition, X client programs can run on your workstation (provided it has a multitasking operating system).

The primary advantage of X is its near-universal adoption by all the major players in the computer industry. You can get an X implementation for just about any UNIX workstation or high-end PC. X also runs on other operating systems, like VMS and AmigaDOS.

X also tries to provide the mechanism to create graphical interfaces, but with no single policy. What this means is that you can choose to layer just about any type of graphical interface on top of X. Motif is one such interface and Open Look is another.

MOTIF AND OPEN LOOK

As of this writing the two primary X interfaces with the most effort behind them are Motif and Open Look. Open Look is provided by Sun and AT&T. Contrary to popular opinion, since both Motif and Open Look are based on the X Window System, you can easily run Motif programs on an Open Look system and vice versa. You won't have the full look and feel of Motif without the Motif window manager, mwm, but you can still run Motif programs just fine. What this means is that you as users are insulated to some degree from the Motif/Open Look controversy.

WHY USE MOTIF?

Controversy aside, why should you want to learn and use Motif?

1) Motif provides a standard interface with a consistent look and feel. Your users will have less work to do in learning new Motif applications, since much of the work learning other Motif applications will translate directly to your applications.

2) Motif provides a very high-level object-oriented library. You can generate extremely complex graphical programs with a very small amount of code. The whole idea of using a toolkit is to reuse the functions in the toolkit and save valuable time when writing applications.

3) Motif has been adopted by many of the major players in the computer industry. Many of your customers are probably using Motif right now. You'll do a better job selling to them if your applications are also based on Motif.

THIS BOOK'S APPROACH TO MOTIF

This book provides an introduction to programming Motif applications. We've included a sample program in just about every chapter, based on the idea that working source code really helps when learning Motif. The book is divided into five sections.

Section I introduces Motif programming. Chapter 1 starts with a beginning Motif program. Each chapter in Section I builds on the last, adding features like menu bars, pulldown menus, and text entry that you will need in every Motif application you write.

Section II introduces more advanced Motif widgets and techniques. This section covers scrolled lists of items, how to select items from a list, the scale widget and how to use the libraries that sit under Motif—the Xt Intrinsics and the X library—from within Motif programs.

Section III covers resources and resource files. By setting resources in resource files, you can change the appearance of your Motif programs without making any code changes.

Section IV introduces the *OSF/Motif Style Guide*, the arbiter of the Motif look and feel. Your Motif applications should strive to fo llow the *OSF/Motif Style Guide*. Section IV concentrates on Motif standards for pull-down menus and dialogs.

Section V wraps up the first four sections by presenting a working Motif application.

Section VI is the appendices. The appendices include information on what you need to run Motif, where you can order Motif, a Unix Makefile, and additional reading material.

WHAT YOU SHOULD KNOW

To get the most out of this book, you should have a background in C programming, as all the sample programs are written in C. We won't be teaching C, so if you're a newcomer to C, you may want to pick up a C tutorial, such as *Teach Yourself C* (MIS Press, 1989)

WHAT YOU'LL NEED

You'll need a system that runs X Window and Motif programs. In addition, you'll need a C/X Window/Motif developer's package, including the OSF/Motif documentation with the Motif and X Window libraries, as well as a C compiler.

If you cannot run the X Window System, you won't get very far, since Motif programs are really X programs under the hood. If you do not have the X and Motif libraries, you won't be able to compile and run the sample programs in this book.

Introducing Motif

S ection I introduces Motif programming and provides a jump-start to creating real Motif programs. This section discusses the basic widgets and initial steps you'll need to go through in creating your Motif applications. It also introduces the concept of X and Motif toolkit programming. Chapters 1 through 7 show you how to set up a Motif application and progressively add container widgets, dialogs for user interaction, menu bars, pulldown menus, and text entry fields.

Section I focuses on the most common widgets and functions you'll need in order to build real applications. Key topics include creating widgets, modifying widget values and adding callback functions.

After reading Section I, you should be able to program simple Motif applications using the most common Motif widgets. You'll then have no trouble using the Motif reference manuals to find out more about other widgets or to discover how to customize the widgets you already know.

A First Motif Program

This chapter lays out the basic structure of the Motif programming environment. By the time you reach the end of this chapter, you'll be a full-fledged Motif applications programmer. Before you go out and celebrate though, note that there is a reason for the rest of this book.

It's simply not very easy to write Motif applications. This book is going to show how it's done in as straightforward a manner as possible, but Motif and the X Window System (upon which Motif is built) are very complex. Since we believe that the best way to learn something is to do it, we'll start out slowly with a small Motif program. Even though the program is small, it will introduce most of the basic and necessary Motif concepts.

Motif is many things. This book treats it as a programmer's toolkit and a certain interface style (a look and feel, to use the popular terminology). As a toolkit, Motif builds upon the X Window foundation that we discussed in the introduction. Motif uses the Xt Intrinsics library directly from the X Window System—in this sense, it can be viewed as a widget set that sits on top of the Xt toolkit. This concept is depicted graphically in Figure 1-1.

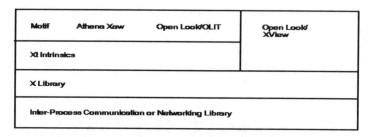

Motif	Athena Xaw	Open Look/OLIT	Open Look/ XView
Xt Intrinsics			
X Library			
Inter-Process Communication or Networking Library			

Figure 1-1. Xt-Based Toolkits.

THE XT INTRINSICS AND MOTIF

To say that the Motif toolkit sits on top of the Xt Intrinsics toolkit means that Motif uses many of the Xt features and functions. The Xt Intrinsics provide a basic mechanism for many widget sets; you'll encounter this mechanism quite often as you read about X. Motif does, however, have a set of functions of its own, and it has its own widget set with its own look and feel.

On one hand, it's great that Motif has to do less work—if you know another Xt-based toolkit, like the Athena widgets, your prior knowledge will help as you learn Motif. But this also means that all Motif applications pay for the added complexity and difficulty (and massive program size) of all Xt-based applications. You win some and you lose some.

BASIC FORMAT OF MOTIF PROGRAMS

We're going to start off quickly with a first Motif program. Don't worry if you don't catch everything right away, as we'll explain all these topics in depth in later chapters. For now, we'll go over the basic format of all Motif programs and then show you a small program that follows this format.

Most Motif programs follow the same basic five-step format:

1) Include the Proper files:
        X11/Intrinsic.h
        X11/StringDefs.h
        Xm/Xm.h
    and widget include files.

2) Initialize Xt Intrinsics with XtInitialize().

3) Create your widgets.

4) Realize the widget hierarchy.

5) Call XtMainLoop().

These steps are the same for other Xt-based applications that use widget sets other than Motif's (including the Athena or Xaw widgets). In fact, this chapter won't even introduce any Motif functions—just Xt Intrinsics functions.

Including the Proper Files

The first step in writing Motif programs is to include the proper files. Almost all Motif source files must include the standard Xt Intrinsics files:

```
#include <X11/Intrinsic.h>
#include <X11/StringDefs.h>
```

All Motif source files also must contain Xm.h, the standard Motif include file:

```
#include  <Xm/Xm.h>
```

These files are included in every source code example file in this book. In addition, you'll need the widget class's include file for each widget class you use. In your first Motif program, you'll only use the pushbutton widget class, so you need Xm/PushB.h:

```
#include  <Xm/PushB.h>
```

Note that the official *OSF/Motif Programmer's Reference Manual* (which should have come with your implementation of Motif) shows what include files are needed for each widget class. We'll also show which include files are needed for each of the example source files provided in this book and each of the widgets we use.

Initializing the Xt Intrinsics with XtInitialize()

The next step is to initialize the Xt Intrinsics library, using XtInitialize(). XtInitialize() sets up a connection to an X server and also creates a top-level shell widget. This top-level widget is used mainly as a parent widget to the next level of widgets you want to create.

11

Widgets come in a hierarchy, or tree. That is, you start out with one parent—the shell widget returned by XtInitialize()—and then create the next level of child widgets—your application's top-level widgets. Some of your widgets may have child widgets underneath them, and so on. To keep matters simple in this first chapter, you'll just create one widget underneath the main shell widget.

The basic idea here is that before you can create any fun Motif widgets, you must call XtInitialize(). Here's the formal description :

```
String                    shell_name;
String                    application_class;
XrmOptionDescRec          xrm_options[];
Cardinal                  number_of_xrm_options;
Cardinal                  *pointer_to_argc;
String                    argv[];

Widget XtInitialize( shell_name,
      application_class,
      xrm_options,
      number_of_xrm_options,
      pointer_to_argc,
      argv );
```

In real life, you'll call XtInitialize() in this style:

```
main( argc, argv )

int      argc;
char     *argv[];

    {
    ...

    /*
     * Initialize the X Toolkit
     * Intrinsics.
     */
    Widget parent;

    parent = XtInitialize( argv[0],        /* program name */
                    "First",               /* app class*/
                    NULL,                  /* no options */
                    0,                     /* option count = 0 */
                    &argc,                 /* number args */
                    argv );                /* cmd-line args */

    ...
    }
```

Normally, you pass `argv[0]`—the name of your program—as the Xt shell name. (At least, this is the long-held convention among X Window folks.) You use the application class to name the type of application you have. This is especially important for X resource files, which we'll cover in Section III.

You pass a pointer to `argc` (the number of command-line arguments passed originally to your program's `main()` function), and then `argv` (the actual command-line arguments). `XtInitialize()` searches these command-line arguments for special Xt options that modify the way your program behaves.

If you have some exposure to Motif or X programming through a course or a book, you may have run across the `XrmOptionDescRec` structure. We consider the `XrmOptionDescRec` structure and all its complexity too advanced for a beginning Motif programming book. There's simply too much to cover. Check out an Xt Intrinsics manual for more information on this subject.

`XtInitialize()` returns a parent widget to be used for the next level in your widget hierarchy. This parent widget is used mainly as a parent for other Motif widgets.

WHAT IS A WIDGET?

Since we've been bandying about the term "widget" for so long, we should define it. According to the *X Toolkit Intrinsics: C Language Interface ROM* (see Appendix D for more information on this document), a widget is:

> •An object providing a user-interface abstraction (for example, a scrollbar widget).

Each widget has a class that is defined as:

> •The general group to which a specific widget belongs, otherwise known as the type of the widget.

Basically, widgets are what you call the things you place on the screen in your application, such as labels, pushbuttons, and scroll bars. Most widgets have an associated window on the X display that holds the user-interface elements of the widget. As a result, Motif programs create a great many windows on your X server.

Some widgets, like the parent shell widget described above, contain other widgets called child widgets or just plain children.

When you're planning out your applications, you'll need to choose the type and number of widgets that you want to use. We've found that it's best to start at the top and plan out the widget hierarchy working from the top down. This approach makes it a lot easier to test and debug Motif applications.

X11 Release 4

With Release 4, the designers of the Xt Intrinsics are trying to phase out the use of XtInitialize(). Instead, they advise using XtAppInitialize(), which handles more options than XtInitialize(). As of this writing, few X vendors have delivered Release 4 implementations, so a great many people don't have this new function. When you upgrade to Motif 1.1 or higher, you may want to start using XtAppInitialize(). It's a tough choice, however, since the designers of X changed something that had been used by a great many people.

On one hand, you're getting a better toolkit. On the other hand, your customers may not have the newest release of X and, if you have to port your Motif applications to a number of platforms, you're stuck with special options or the least common denominator. For this book, we've decided to stay with XtInitialize(), since that's what the Motif 1.0 documentation uses (and most Motif programmers are still using 1.0 as of this writing). When you choose to upgrade to XtAppInitialize(), it won't be that difficult.

The first thing you need to do in order to use a widget is to create it. XtInitialize() took care of that for your parent widget. Now you'll need to create at least one more widget, or else you'll have a very boring program. In the program called first, below, you'll be creating a pushbutton widget that is simply a quit button. Click the first mouse button in the quit widget and the program quits.

Creating a Widget and Managing It

You can use a number of functions to create widgets. The simplest is XtCreateManagedWidget():

```
String          name;
WidgetClass     widgetclass;
Widget          parent;
ArgList         args;
Cardinal        number_args;

Widget XtCreateManagedWidget( name,
            widgetclass,
            parent,
            args,
            number_args );
```

XtCreateManageWidget takes care of creating and managing your widgets, so you can avoid an extra step. Motif comes with a set of functions that create each class of Motif widgets. In some cases, these functions are easier to use than creating your own, especially for the more complex Motif compound widgets. In this case, however, XtCreateManagedWidget() is the simplest way to go.

In the file `first.c`, below, you'll use `XtCreateManagedWidget()` to create a pushbutton widget:

```
Widget        parent; /* Returned by XtInitialize() */
Widget        quit_widget;
Arg           args[ 10 ];
int           n = 0;

quit_widget=XtCreateManagedWidget("quit",    /* widget name */
        xmPushButtonWidgetClass,             /* widget class */
        parent,                              /* parent widget */
        args                                 /* arguments */
        n );                                 /* number args */
```

The name "quit" is the name of your new widget. This name will be used in resource files (see Section III). As a default for a pushbutton widget, this name appears as the text string displayed with the pushbutton when you realize the widgets. You'll see a 3D "button" with the word "quit" inside. The idea is that if you click (using mouse button 1) on the "quit" button, then the program will quit.

The class is `xmPushButtonWidgetClass`, which is a constant defined in `Xm/PushB.h`. This is one reason why you need to include a special file for each widget class you use.

The parent in this case is the parent widget returned by `XtInitialize()`. If you create a child of another widget, you must pass the proper parent.

The `Arg` type is a tricky structure used to change the default resources of a widget. Each widget comes with a set of default resources—data and functions that influence the way the widget behaves—and generally you have to change at least one of these resources to get the widget to do anything useful. This process is easy to use, but hard to explain. `XtSetArg()`, usually implemented as a very complex macro, sets up these options.

Changing Default Widget Values and Behavior

Anyway, getting back to the program: You pass the `ArgList` (or array of type `Arg`), to `XtCreateManagedWidget()`, with the number n equal to the number of options in the `Arg` array.

There's a convention on how you use `XtSetArg()`, and this book tries to follow that convention:

```
int       n;
Arg       args[10];      /* 10 or however many you need */
n = 0;
XtSetArg( args[n], XmNwidth, 100 ); n++;
XtSetArg( args[n], XmNheight, 100 ); n++;
```

Note that `XtSetArg()` sets up one option in the `Arg` array. Since `XtSetArg()` is most often implemented as a macro that accesses the value of n more than once, you never want to increment n inside of the `XtSetArg()` parameters. Normally, it's not considered good practice to have two C statements on one line, but with `XtSetArg()` it's easiest to call `XtSetArg()` and then increment your counter, n. This way, you can comment out or add in any of these lines, without worrying if the value in n is set up correctly.

This stylized method of using `XtSetArg()` was implemented mainly to avoid errors, so we advise you to follow along in the style. It looks weird at first to type:

```
XtSetArg( args[n], XmNwidth, 100 ); n++;
```

but you'll get used to it.

`XtSetArg()` takes three parameters:

```
Arg           arg,
String        name;
XtArgVal      value;

XtSetArg( arg, name, value )
```

The `Arg` type is defined as:

```
typedef struct
    {
    String          name;
    XtArgVal value;
    } Arg;
```

`XtArgVal` is usually set up as (in `X11/Intrinsic.h`):

```
typedef long XtArgVal;
```

`XtArgVal` should be able to hold a long, function, or `caddr_t` (character) pointer. You'll note that the Xt Intrinsics are playing tricks with C types here.

The name parameter to `XtSetArg()` is really a text string, such as "width"; in fact that's what `XmNwidth` is defined as in `Xm/Xm.h`. No one uses the string name, though; a constant, like `XmNwidth`, is always used. Most of these string constants begin with `XmN` and then contain the actual value of the text string:

•`XmNwidth` evaluates to the text string "width."

The basic idea is to use `XtSetArg()` to set up any resources or options to be used by a widget. You use an element of an array of `Arg` type and pass the name of the resource you want to change, and then the proper value—be it an integer, a string, a data pointer, or a function pointer. You really don't want to know exactly how this macro works. You just want to use `XtSetArg()`.

To put it all together, here's how to create a pushbutton widget:

```
Arg        args[10];
int        n;
Widget     parent; /* Returned by XtInitialize() */
Widget     quit_widget;

/*
 * Set up resource values
 * for our quit button. We
 * could allow the user to
 * customize these by using
 * a resource file instead.
 *
 * Set up size for quit button
 */
n = 0;
XtSetArg( args[n], XmNwidth, 100 ); n++;
XtSetArg( args[n], XmNheight, 100 ); n++;

/*
 * Create the quit-button widget
 */
 quit_widget = XtCreateManagedWidget( "quit",    /* widget name */
    xmPushButtonWidgetClass,                      /* widget class */
    parent      /* parent widget */
    args,                                         /* arguments */
    n );                                          /* number args */
```

Once you've set up a pushbutton widget, your next step is to get the widget to do something when you push the button (in this case, click mouse button 1 over the quit widget). To do this, you need to set up a callback function.

SETTING UP A CALLBACK FUNCTION

A callback function is a function that is called back from some part of the Motif (or Xt Intrinsics) toolkit at the proper time. Until the time it is called back, a callback function doesn't do anything.

You use XtAddCallback() to register your function as a callback function for the pushbutton widget you created above:

```
Widget          widget; /* widget to set up the callback for */
String          callback_name; /* which callback */
XtCallbackProc  callback_function;  /* function to call */
XtPointer       client_data;/* any extra data you want passed */
```

continued...

...from previous page

```
XtAddCallback( widget,
        callback_name,
        callback_function,
        client_data );
```

The widget is the one for which you want the callback set up. Many widgets don't have any publicly accessible callbacks. Your quit pushbutton widget, however, has an activate callback that you will set up below.

The `callback_name` is another text string—in this case, the name of the callback you want to set up. Some widgets, like the drawing area widget, have many callbacks you can set up. The names are usually text strings defined in the widget's include file or `Xm/Xm.h`. These names usually begin with `XmN`, as shown above. In this case, the activateCallback's defined name is `XmNactivateCallback`. That is:

• `XmNactivateCallback` is defined as the text string "activateCallback."

The `callback_function` is the special function you want to be called. In this case, you want the function `quit_callback()` to be called whenever the user activates (clicks in) the quit pushbutton.

The `client_data` is a pointer to any extra data you want to pass to your callback. In this case, you don't have any extra data—this is the simplest way to go, since passing data to a callback can be kind of tricky. We'll show examples of that in later chapters.

For now, here's how you set up a callback function in the file `first.c`:

```
Widget    quit_widget;

    XtAddCallback( quit_widget,   /* widget */
    XmNactivateCallback,          /* what type of call-back */
    quit_callback                 /* function to call */
    NULL );                       /* extra client data to pass */
```

Now that you've set up your pushbutton widget, the next step is to write the callback function.

Writing the Callback Function

Most callback functions have this format:

```
void quit_callback( widget, client_data, call_data )

Widget widget;
caddr_t client_data;          /* our data, if any */
```
continued...

...from previous page

```
caddr_t call_data;              /* data passed from   */
                                /* other Motif widgets, if any */


{               /* function quit_callback */
}               /* function quit_callback */
```

Widget, in this case, is the "calling" widget; that is, the widget you passed to
`XtAddCallback()`. The `client_data`—the data you can pass to the callback, is
NULL, since that's what you set up in `XtAddCallback()`. In this case, you don't
worry about any `call_data`. In some widgets, though, this `call_data` is in the
format of a pointer to some special Motif structure. Most callbacks have no return value.

Passing Data to a Callback Function

The easiest and most common mistake to make when passing data to callback
functions is to reverse `client_data` and `call_data`. Usually, you'll figure out
that something is wrong right away, but it's often hard to determine exactly what's
wrong.

The trick is remembering that `client_data` is your data while `call_data`
comes from the Motif or Xt toolkit. Many callbacks provide a specialized structure
with information useful to your functions. Those structures are always in the
`call_data` parameter. Any data you pass from `XtAddCallback()` is passed as
the `client_data` parameter, as shown in the callback function below:

```
void generic_callback( widget, client_data, call_data )

Widget widget;
caddr_t  client_data;           /* our data, if any */
caddr_t  call_data;             /* data passed from */
                                /* other Motif widgets, if any */
    { /* function generic_callback */
    } /* function generic_callback */
```

If your callback doesn't seem to work properly, always check that the parameters are
correct. This is an easy error to make and even easier to correct.

MAKING WIDGETS REAL

After you've set up all your widgets and managed them, it's time to make them real.
`XtRealizeWidget()` takes care of all the initializations necessary for a widget
and all of its managed children. Note that when you created the pushbutton widget,

you used `XtCreateManagedWidget()` to both create and manage the pushbutton. `XtRealizeWidget()` takes one parameter: a high-level widget to be realized. Normally, this is the widget returned from `XtInitialize()`:

```
Widget  parent;

XtRealizeWidget( parent );
```

Until you call `XtRealizeWidget()`, none of your child widgets will appear on the screen. For those who've programmed with Xlib before, this create-then-"realize" process is a lot like the X library's create-then-"map" process for windows. In both cases, you won't see the items you're creating until the full realization (or mapping) is complete. Sometimes, `XtRealizeWidget()` takes a long time to execute. Expect this. After calling `XtRealizeWidget()`, most applications let the Xt Intrinsics take over and loop awaiting events.

LETTING XT TAKE OVER

After realizing your widget tree, or hierarchy, most programs call `XtMainLoop()`.

`XtMainLoop()` takes no parameters and basically loops forever:

```
XtMainloop();
```

> ### X11 Release 4
>
> `XtMainLoop()` is replaced by `XtAppMainLoop()` in Release 4 of the X Window System. We'll use `XtMainLoop()`, which still exists in R4, just as we use `XtInitialize()` instead of `XtAppInitialize()`.

`XtMainLoop()` doesn't seem very fun, but it lets the Xt Intrinsics handle most of the work of an X application for you. With `XtMainLoop()`, the Xt Intrinsics essentially take over your application. That's one of the prices you pay for using a Xt-based toolkit: the toolkit takes over. `XtMainLoop()` loops, checking for things the toolkit needs to do, including handling timeouts, work procedures (both covered later), and handling input from the X server (including user input).

You won't regain control of your program until the point at which the user clicks a mouse button (usually button 1, or the left button) in your Quit widget. When this happens, `quit_callback()` gains control. That is, Xt (through the Motif functions) calls `quit_callback()`.

In `quit_callback()` (or in most any callback), you can do what you want. Sometimes your callbacks will need to execute completely in a very short amount of time (i.e. the millisecond range). But for now you can do what you want.

What you want to do in this case is quit your application. After all, that is what a button labeled "Quit" should do, isn't it?

To quit an Xt-based application, you first should call `XtCloseDisplay()`. `XtCloseDisplay()` trashes all your carefully crafted widgets and closes the connection to the X Window server. Then you can call `exit()` to quit the program. You could just call `exit()` and assume that your underlying operating system (probably a variant of UNIX, but it may be VMS, AmigaDOS, the Macintosh operating system, or something else entirely) cleans up after you. We've found that at least making an effort to be nice to X and Xt is a good idea. Besides, it gives us a chance to document a few more Xt functions.

`XtCloseDisplay()` takes one parameter: the `Display` pointer:

```
    Display *display;

    XtCloseDisplay( display );
```

`Display` pointers identify connections to X servers, so if you have connections to many X servers, you'll have many `Display` pointers. (Since that statement opens some rather tough issues, we'll just refer you to our previous book, *Advanced X Window Applications Programming* (MIS: Press, 1990). All the programs in this book will deal with just one display connection at a time—Motif is too complex without further confusing the issue.) If you've written Xlib programs before, the `Display` pointer will be old hat.

Before you can call `XtCloseDisplay()`, you need to get a `Display` pointer:

```
    Display     *display;
    Widget      widget;

    display = XtDisplay( widget );
```

Few Xt and Motif functions ever use a `Display` pointer (which is nice, since the widget interface hides those low-level details from you). So you need to call `XtDisplay()` to get your current `Display` pointer. `XtDisplay()` takes one parameter— a valid widget— and returns the `Display` pointer associated with that widget. (The `Display` pointer is the same for all your widgets in a program, since you have only one display connection.)

Now that you know how to quit the application, you need to put together a proper callback function:

```
    void quit_callback( widget, client_data, call_data )
```

continued...

...from previous page

```
Widget      widget;
caddr_t     client_data;    /* our data, if any */
caddr_t     call_data;      /* data passed from other Motif widgets,
                            *if any */

{               /* quit_callback */
            Display *display;

            /*
             * Get our current display
             * pointer.
             */
            display = XtDisplay( widget );

            /*
             * Close out display connection,
             * this will trash all widgets
             */
            XtCloseDisplay( display );

            exit( 0 );

}               /* quit_callback */
```

This callback function, which was discussed earlier, is the one you passed to
XtAddCallback() in the main part of our program. The only parameter you need
is the widget passed to most Xt-based callbacks.

SOURCE CODE FOR FIRST.C

Here's the full source code to your first Motif program, called first. It should only
take you about five minutes to type this in:

```
/*
 *      first.c
 *      A first Motif program, which
 *      creates a quit button.
 *
 *      Written for Power Programming Motif
 *
 */

/*
 *      Most Motif source files
 *      need two Xt include files
 */
#include <X11/Intrinsic.h>
```
continued...

...from previous page
```
#include <X11/StringDefs.h>

/*
 *      Xm.h is the basic Motif
 *      include file
 */
#include <Xm/Xm.h>

/*
 *      You'll also need to include
 *      a file for each Motif widget
 *      class you use. In this case,
 *      PushB.h is the include file
 *      for the PushButton widget
 *      class.
 */
#include <Xm/PushB.h>

void quit_callback( widget, client_data, call_data )

Widget      widget;
caddr_t     client_data;       /*our data, if any */
caddr_t     call_data;         /*data passed from other Motif widgets,
                               * if any */

/*
 *      quit_callback() is the callback for the
 *      Motif quit button. This function
 *      terminates the program by calling exit().
 */

{       /* quit_callback */
        Display *display;

        /*
         * Get our current display
         * pointer.
         */
        display = XtDisplay( widget );

        /*
         * Close out display connection,
         * this will trash all widgets
         */
        XtCloseDisplay( display );

        exit( 0 );

}       /* quit_callback */
```
continued...

...from previous page

```
main( argc, argv )

int      argc;
char     *argv[];

{         /* main */
          Widget                    parent, quit_widget;
          Arg                       args[ 10 ];
          int                       n;

          /*
           * Initialize the X Toolkit
           * Intrinsics.
           */
          parent = XtInitialize( argv[0],      /* program name */
                          "First",     /* app class */
                          NULL,        /* no options */
                          0,           /* option count = 0 */
                          &argc,       /* number args */
                          argv );      /* cmd-line args */

          /*
           * Set up resource values
           * for our quit button. We
           * could allow the user to
           * customize these by using
           * a resource file instead.
           *
           * Set up size for quit button
           */
          n = 0;
          XtSetArg( args[n], XmNwidth, 100 ); n++;
          XtSetArg( args[n], XmNheight, 100 ); n++;

          /*
           * Create the quit-button widget
           */
          quit_widget = XtCreateManagedWidget( "quit",    /* widget name */
                  xmPushButtonWidgetClass,                /* widget class */
                  parent,                                 /* parent widget */
                  args,                                   /* arguments */
                  n );                                    /* number args */

          /*
           * Set up a call-back function:
           * whenever the quit button is
           * "activated", call our function.
           */
```

continued...

...from previous page

```
        XtAddCallback( quit_widget,    /* widget */
            XmNactivateCallback,       /* what type of call-back */
            quit_callback,             /* function to call */
            NULL );                    /* extra client data to pass */

        /*
         * Bring the top-level widget
         * (and all its children) to
         * reality, that is map the windows.
         */
        XtRealizeWidget( parent );

        /*
         * Process events forever
         */
        XtMainLoop();

}       /* main */

/* end of file */
```

COMPILING AND LINKING MOTIF PROGRAMS

In order to get `first.c` to compile on most X Window installations, you'll need to link in three libraries: the Motif library, the Xt Intrinsics library, and the Xlib library. Usually these are the Xm, Xt, and X11 libraries. You'll need these libraries in every program in this book. On UNIX-based systems, something like this should suffice:

```
        cc -o first first.c -lXm -lXt -lX11
```

If the X Window System and Motif libraries are located in an area other than the standard `/usr/lib`, you may need to pass a `-L` option specifying where these libraries are. The Data General Aviion, for example, often places the X and Motif libraries in the `/usr/opt/X11/lib` directory. In such a case, you'll need a command something like:

```
        c -o first first.c -L/usr/opt/X11/lib -lXm -lXt -lX11
```

We've added a `Makefile` in Appendix C, so that once you've set up the proper options, you can simply type:

```
        make first
```

or

```
        make all
```

This will compile all the example sources. From now on, we'll assume you know how to compile and link Motif programs, so use this first example to work all the glitches out of the process. If you cannot compile and link this program, you'll have many problems in the rest of the book.

Compiling and Linking on SCO Open Desktop

If you're running SCO's Open Desktop, things get a bit more complex. We've found that in order to get Xlib to link properly the following three additional libraries are needed: tlisock, socket, and nsl_s. You'll also need to define LAI_TCP, SYSV and i386. This command should work:

```
cc -o first first.c -DLAI_TCP -Di386 -DSYSV -lXm -lXt -lX11 \
      -ltlisock -lsocket -lnsl_s
```

On Interactive's 386 UNIX, you may need to link in the inet library:

```
cc -o first first.c -lXm -lXt -lX11 -linet
```

In general, check with the Motif documentation that came with your system for the proper method to compile and link Motif programs. We've found that it's easiest to figure out all the options for first.c and then set up the Makefile properly for your system. That way you'll be spared typing the long command lines each time you modify a program.

RUNNING THE FIRST PROGRAM

After compiling and linking, you can run first without any command-line parameters:

```
first
```

The first program displays a quit button, as shown in Figure 1-2.

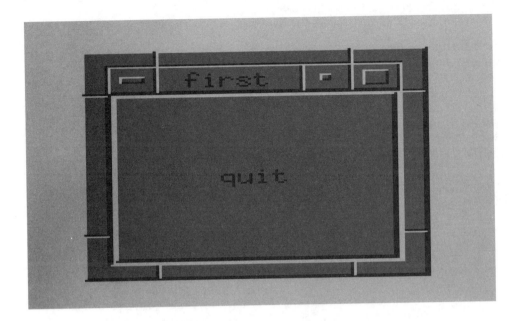

Figure 1-2. The First Motif Program.

You can resize the window, move it around, and generally do what you want with it. A resized window appears in Figure 1-3.

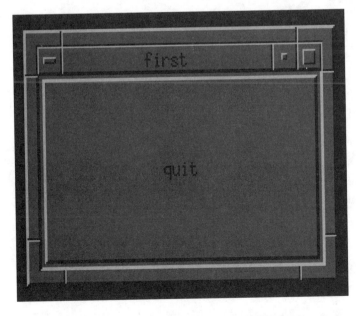

Figure 1-3. A Resized First Program's Window.

Move the mouse pointer cursor on top of the quit button and click mouse button 1 (usually the left mouse button, but if you're left-handed, you may have reversed that). The first program should quit. Pretty simple, right?

X TOOLKIT FUNCTIONS AND MACROS INTRODUCED IN THIS CHAPTER

The following is a list of X Toolkit functions and macros that were introduced in this chapter.

```
XtAddCallback()
XtCloseDisplay()
XtCreateManagedWidget()
XtDisplay()
XtInitialize()
XtMainloop()
XtSetArg()
```

You should be familiar with these functions and macros before you move on to Chapter 2.

SUMMARY

Now you're a Motif programmer. It wasn't too hard, was it? That's one of the main ideas behind Motif (and the other X toolkits, too). You have a large body of code that your applications can reuse again and again as you create user interfaces. If only it wasn't so complex....

This chapter introduced the concepts of widgets, callbacks, and modified widget values. We'll use these concepts often in the rest of the book.

If you've noticed, we didn't even make any Motif function calls in our first Motif program. (How's that for truth in advertising?) That's because Motif makes heavy use of the Xt Intrinsics and inherits as many features of Xt as possible. Don't worry, though, in later chapters you'll learn more Motif function calls than you probably want to handle.

In the next chapter, we'll go into more depth about widgets and show you a few more classes of widgets.

# Chapter 2

What is a Widget?

T his chapter provides more basic information about widgets. It also introduces Motif's label widget and describes Motif's method for storing text strings. Widgets are a generic abstraction for user interface components in the Motif toolkit. They are used for scroll bars, pushbuttons, and dialogs. Each widget has a data structure that is dynamically allocated at creation time. This structure contains the widget's resources and pointers to the functions, such as callbacks. Each widget is of a certain class. The class also defines a set of functions and resources that apply to every widget of that class.

If this looks suspiciously like object-oriented programming, you're catching on. There is a whole hierarchy of widget classes: a widget class, like label, inherits features of all ancestor classes. In this case, the label widget inherits from the Core classes of Object, RectObj, and WindowObj, and from the XmPrimitive class. Other classes, like the pushbutton class described in Chapter 1, inherit from the label widget class.

In general you really don't care which widgets inherit from what. What you really need is a list of a widget's resources, including the resources inherited from ancestor widgets. You'll usually find these lists in the *OSF/Motif Programmer's Reference Manual* that should have come with your implementation of Motif. You'll use this manual a lot.

Some widgets display graphics on the screen, while others serve as container widgets. Container widgets group other widgets, called child widgets. There are two widget hierarchies, and they differ from one another quite a bit. The first Motif widget hierarchy is the tree of widget classes. The label widget class is a subclass of the primitive class (called XmPrimitive). The second hierarchy is the hierarchy of widget instances that you create when you program a Motif application. For example, in the hello program, you'll create a widget hierarchy that looks like:

> * Top-Level Shell
>   * Label Widget

This program-created hierarchy is a hierarchy of widget instances, not classes. The distinction is important.

There are a host of Motif widget classes from which to choose. Throughout the rest of this book, we'll cover the most common widget classes and show you how to use Motif reference manuals to understand the other Motif widget classes.

WIDGET STANDARDS

For each Motif widget class, there is a special function to create an instance of that class (what we generally call a widget). Usually this function has the name of XmCreatewidget-name(), i.e. XmCreatePushButton() to create a pushbutton widget or an instance of an XmPushButton widget.

Notice how most Motif functions and definitions start with Xm. Most widget classes have names, too, i.e. XmPushButton for the pushbutton widget class. When you call XtCreateManagedWidget() you'll need to pass the proper class pointer, which is usually something like:

```
xmwidget-nameWidgetClass
```

Note the lower-case xm. The pushbutton widget class, XmPushButton, uses a class pointer of:

```
xmPushButtonWidgetClass
```

As you can tell, these Motif-style names can get quite long. The class pointer is usually defined in the widget's include file (in this case, Xm/PushB.h).

Widget Include Files

For each widget, you'll usually need to include a widget header file and Xm.h—the standard Motif header file. Each widget has a file in the /usr/include/Xm directory (this is the standard location, but your system may put these files somewhere else). The name of this file is most often the name of the widget class, except for classes with long names.

Take a look at the files in /usr/include/Xm (or wherever the Motif include files are stored on your system). The listing from SCO Open Desktop 1.0 (using Motif 1.0) is shown in Figure 2-1.

ArrowB.h	DialogSP.h	List.h	RowColumn P.h	Text.h
ArrowBG.h	DrawingA.h	ListP.h	SashP.h	TextInP.h
ArrowBGP.h	DrawingAP.h	MainW.h	Scale.h	TextOutP.h
ArrowBP.h	DrawnB.h	MainWP.h	ScaleP.h	TextP.h
BulletinB.h	DrawnBP.h	MenuShell.h	ScrollBar.h	TextSrcP.h
BulletinBP.h	FileSB.h	MenuShellP.h	ScrollBarP.h	ToggleB.h
CascadeB.h	FileSBP.h	MessageB.h	ScrolledW.h	ToggleBG.h
CascadeBG.h	Form.h	MessageBP.h	ScrolledWP.h	ToggleBGP.h
CascadeBGP.h	FormP.h	PanedW.h	SelectioB.h	ToggleBP.h
CascadeBP.h	Frame.h	PushB.h	SeparatoG.h	XmP.h
CommandP.h	Label.h	PushBG.h	SeparatoGP.h	bitmaps.h
CutPaste.h	LabelG.h	PushBGP.h	Separator.h	mwm.h
CutPasteP.h	LabelGP.h	PushBP.h	SeparatorP.h	mwmP.h
DialogS.h	LabelP.h	RowColumn.h	StringSrcP.h	

Figure 2-1. Listing of Motif Files from SCO Open Desktop 1.0.

You can divide most of the files into four major types:

Xm/widget-whatever.h	Widget include file you use in your applications.
Xm/whateverP.h	Private header file for widget whatever.
Xm/whateverG.h	Gadget include you could use in your applications (see below for more on gadgets).
Xm/whateverGP.h	Gadget private file.

For example, the label widget class, which we will introduce below, has four include files:

Xm/Label.h	The file you'll use in your applications.
Xm/LabelP.h	The label widget class's private header file.
Xm/LabelG.h	The label gadget class file.
Xm/LabelGP.h	The label gadget's private header file.

Unless you're writing your own widgets, you won't need to worry about the private include files.

Gadgets or Windowless Widgets

Most Motif widgets create a window on your X display. For example, the pushbutton widget described in Chapter 1 created a subwindow of the main application window to hold the quit push button. The top-level shell, returned by XtInitiialize(), also created a window on the X display. Even though two windows aren't a lot for an X application, the first program is a very simple application. A complex Motif application, however, creates many windows which use up resources in the X Window server and in your application.

Creating numerous windows also slows down Motif applications. To alleviate performance problems, the designers of Motif use a concept called *gadgets*. Gadgets (windowless widgets) serve to improve the performance of both Motif applications, because they don't use as many system resources (the system being both your application and the X server). Gadgets, if available, work much like widgets. Note, however, that every widget class does not have a corresponding gadget class.

Each gadget class has a creation function. These functions have the same name as the corresponding widget creation functions, but add the word Gadget at the end. For example, the function to create a pushbutton widget is XmCreatePushButton(). The function to create a pushbutton gadget is XmCreatePushButtonGadget(). You may want to try using gadgets in your applications if performance becomes an issue. Note that many gadgets use special gadget functions instead of the normal widget functions to reach their data. This is something to be careful of.

The Label Widget

The label widget provides a message, in text or pixmap graphic, in a window. This is important because most programs need to display some sort of text information to the user. Label widgets are also useful for displaying a company logo if you want to get fancy. In addition, the label widget class is used as a parent for the pushbutton widget class.

For now, we'll concentrate on label widgets that hold text strings. Motif uses a special format for holding most (but not all) text strings. The label widget, for example, needs the message it displays to be formatted as an XmString, not a regular C string.

HOW MOTIF STORES TEXT STRINGS

XmStrings are specially formatted strings that allow for international character sets, and text that goes left-to-right and right-to-left. XmStrings may also cross multiple lines and have multiple fonts. The main idea is that a number of widgets (i.e., the label widget) and a host of Motif functions require the use of XmStrings. So you'll need to convert a plain old C string to an XmString.

The basic functions to create an XmString are XmStringCreate() and XmStringCreateLtoR():

```
    XmString                motif_string;
    char                    *string;
    XmStringCharSet         char_set = XmSTRING_DEFAULT_CHARSET;

    motif_string = XmStringCreate( string,
                                      char_set );

    motif_string = XmStringCreateLtoR( string,
                                      char_set );
```

XmStringCreate() creates a Motif string from a regular C string in the given character set. In this case, you use the default character set, which is what most Motif programs should use.

XmStringCreateLtoR() creates a (potentially) multiline XmString. Wherever there is a C newline character ("\n") in the C string, XmStringCreateLtoR() creates a separator, so that the resulting XmString contains a new line as well. Note that the "LtoR" means left-to-right—programmers using Arabic or Hebrew may not want to use this function. Since we want a number of our messages to have multiple lines (and since we don't know Arabic or Hebrew), we use XmStringCreateLtoR() in this book.

A simple function to hide the details of converting a C string to an XmString could look like:

```
XmString Str2XmString( string )

char      *string;

{         /* Str2XmString */
          XmString          motif_string;

          motif_string = XmStringCreateLtoR( string,
                              XmSTRING_DEFAULT_CHARSET );

          return( motif_string );

}         /* Str2XmString */
```

We've put this handy utility function in the file string.c, and we use it throughout the example programs that appear in the book.

Copying XmStrings

You can copy an XmString with XmStringCopy():

```
XmString                motif_string,motif_string2;

motif_string2 = XmStringCopy( motif_string );
```

Appending Strings

XmStringConcat() appends motif_string2 onto the "end" of motif_string:

```
XmString                motif_string, motif_string2;

motif_string = XmStringConcat( motif_string, motif_string2 );
```

The location of the "end" of motif_string depends on the string order (left-to-right or right-to-left) and how many lines are in motif_string.

Comparing XmStrings

You can compare two XmStrings with XmStringCompare():

```
XmString                motif_string, motif_string2;

if ( XmStringCompare( motif_string, motif_string2 ) == True )
```
continued...

...from previous page
```
        {
        /* both XmStrings are equivalent */
        }
```

Freeing XmStrings

When you're all done with an `XmString`, free the storage with `XmStringFree()`:

```
XmString    motif_string;

XmStringFree( motif_string );
```

You'll want to do this for any `XmString` created with the routines described above. Note that if you use an `XmString` in a widget, such as the label widget, it's a good idea to wait until the widget is created and managed before calling `XmStringFree()`.

Pulling a C String From an XmString

`XmStringGetLtoR()` pulls a plain old C string from an `XmString`:

```
XmString        motif_string;
char            *string;

XmStringGetLtoR( motif_string,
         XmSTRING_DEFAULT_CHARSET,
         &string );

printf( "The string is %s\n", string );
```

`XmStringGetLtoR()` technically returns a Boolean value (`True` or `False`). It returns `True` if `XmStringGetLtoR()` finds a string with the proper character set inside the `XmString`. If you use `XmSTRING_DEFAULT_CHARSET`, it should always return a value of `True`. We'll cover this routine more in `listtest.c`, in Chapter 8. You should free up the memory for the string returned by `XmStringGetLtoR()` when you're done with the string.

Source Code for String.c

The file `string.c` contains a useful function for converting a C string to a Motif string:

```
/*
 *      string.c
 *      Motif utility function to convert a text string
 *      to a Motif compound string.
 *
```
continued...

```
...from previous page
*     Written for Power Programming Motif *
*/

#include  <Xm/Xm.h>

XmString Str2XmString( string )

char *string;

/*
 *    Str2XmString() converts a standard C-style
 *    null-terminated string into a Motif-style
 *    compound string. Newline characters (\n)
 *    in the C string become separators in the
 *    Motif string, because we use
 *    XmStringLtoRCreate().
 */

{     /* Str2XmString */
      XmString                  motif_string;

      motif_string = XmStringCreateLtoR( string,
                              XmSTRING_DEFAULT_CHARSET );

      return( motif_string );

}     /* Str2XmString */

/* end of file */
```

ROUTINES FOR SETTING UP A LABEL WIDGET

The function CreateLabelWidget() creates a Motif label widget and sets the label widget to display a text message. For convenience you pass a C string as the message. CreateLabelWidget() converts that C string to an XmString for you. This method is easier and tends to hide some of the Motif toolkit's messy details.

The first step in CreateLabelWidget() is to convert the char *message to an XmString, using the utility function Str2XmString() described above.

Then you set the labelString resource, identified by XmNlabelString, to be your new XmString. You create the label widget by using XtCreateManagedWidget(), passing a class pointer of xmLabelWidgetClass as defined in the file Xm/Label.h.

Finally you free the XmString, using XmStringFree(), and return your new widget. Here's what the function looks like:

```
Widget CreateLabelWidget( parent, name, message, args, n )

Widget          parent;
char            name[];
char            message[];
Arg             *args;      /* args you can pass */
int             n;          /* number of args passed in */

{       /* CreateLabelWidget */
        Widget          label_widget;
        XmString        Str2XmString(); /* string.c */
        XmString        label_text;

        /*
         * Convert message to XmString
         */
        label_text = Str2XmString( message );

        /*
         * Set label_text as text for a label widget.
         * Note that n already has a value when
         * passed to CreateLabelWidget(), so
         * we don't initialize n to zero here.
         */
        XtSetArg( args[n], XmNlabelString, label_text ); n++;

        label_widget = XtCreateManagedWidget( name,
                        xmLabelWidgetClass,
                        parent,
                        args,
                        n );

        XmStringFree( label_text );

        return( label_widget );

}       /* CreateLabelWidget */
```

CreateLabelWidget() returns a value of type Widget and takes the following parameters:

```
Widget CreateLabelWidget( parent, name, message, args, n )

        Widget          parent;
        char            *name;
        char            *message;
        Arg             *args;      /* args you can pass */
    int         n;              /* number of args passed in */
```

These parameters are defined as follows:

• parent is the widget under which to create the label widget. In other words, the new label widget is a child of another widget—the parent. In the hello program, shown later, you use the top-level shell widget returned by XtInitialize() as the parent widget.

• name is the name for your new widget, i.e. "label" (an inspired name if there ever was one). This name is used in X resource files (described in Section III).

• message is the text string you want the label widget to display—it can be something like "Hello World."

• args are an array of type Arg, which you can pass to CreateLabelWidget(). You do this to allow the label widget to be customized by whatever routine wants to create a new label widget. You will use that feature later on.

• n is the number of args passed in the args array.

You can call CreateLabelWidget() like this:

```
Widget    parent, label_widget, CreateLabelWidget();
Arg       args[20];
int       n;

n = 0;
label_widget = CreateLabelWidget( parent,
                      "label",
                      "Hello World",
                      args, n );
```

This creates a label widget with a name of "label," and a message of "Hello World" with no extra resources set, since n = 0.

Changing the Text of a Created Label

All of this code only allows you to modify the widget defaults before the widget is created. There are many times when you'll want to modify a widget after it has been created.

The function XtSetValues() changes resource values stored in a widget. To use XtSetValues(), you first use the macro XtSetArg() to set up an array of type Arg with the new values you want for the widget.

Call `XtSetValues()` to change the resource values within the widget:

```
Widget      widget;
Arg         Listargs;
Cardinal    number_of_args;

XtSetValues( widget, args, number_of_args );
```

To set the "labelString" resource of a label widget (the "labelString" resource holds the text that the label widget displays), you would use:

```
XmString    motif_string;
Arg         args[20];
intn;

n = 0;
XtSetArg( args[n], XmNlabelString, motif_string ); n++;

XtSetValues( widget, args, n );
```

`XtSetValues()` comes in handy for changing many widgets on the fly, especially list, text, and label widgets.

The function `SetLabel()`, below, changes the text that a label widget displays:

```
SetLabel( widget, string )

Widget          widget;
char            string[];

{               /* SetLabel */
        XmString        Str2XmString(); /* string.c */
        XmString        label_text;
        Arg             args[ 10 ];
        int             n;

        /*
         * Convert string to XmString
         */
        label_text = Str2XmString( string );

        /*
         * Set label_text as text for a label widget
         */
        n = 0;
        XtSetArg( args[n], XmNlabelString, label_text ); n++;

        XtSetValues( widget, args, n );

        XmStringFree( label_text );

}               /* SetLabel */
```

39

SetLabel() uses XtSetValues() to do the dirty work. SetLabel() takes a label widget and a C string as parameters. The C string contains the new text for the label widget.

Source Code for Label.c

The following is the source code for the file label.c.

```
/*
 *         label.c
 *         Motif label widget routines
 *
 *         Written for Power Programming Motif
 *
 */

#include <X11/Intrinsic.h>
#include <X11/StringDefs.h>
#include <Xm/Xm.h>

/*
 *         LabelWidget class include file
 */
#include        <Xm/Label.h>

Widget CreateLabelWidget( parent, name, message, args, n )

Widget          parent;
char            name[];
char            message[];
Arg             *args;
int             n;

/*
 *         CreateLabelWidget() creates a simple Motif
 *         label widget, with the given parent, name
 *         and message.
 */

{               /* CreateLabelWidget */
        Widget  label_widget;
        XmString        Str2XmString(); /* string.c */
        XmString        label_text;

        /*
         * Convert message to XmString
```

continued...

...from previous page
```
            */
        label_text = Str2XmString( message );

        /*
         * Set label_text as text for a label widget.
         * Note that n already has a value when
         * passed to CreateLabelWidget(), so
         * we don't initialize n to zero here.
         */
        XtSetArg( args[n], XmNlabelString, label_text ); n++;

        /*
         * Create label widget
         */
        label_widget = XtCreateManagedWidget( name,
                        xmLabelWidgetClass,
                        parent,
                        args,
                        n );

        /*
         * Free the string when done with
         * it.
         */
        XmStringFree( label_text );

        return( label_widget );

}       /* CreateLabelWidget */

SetLabel( widget, string )

Widget          widget;
char string[];

/*
 *      Sets the given label widget to
 *      have the given string
 */

{       /* SetLabel */
        XmString        Str2XmString(); /* string.c */
        XmString        label_text;
        Arg             args[ 10 ];
        int             n;

        /*
```
continued...

...from previous page
```
             * Convert string to XmString
             */
            label_text = Str2XmString( string );

            /*
             * Set label_text as text for a label widget
             */
            n = 0;
            XtSetArg( args[n], XmNlabelString, label_text ); n++;

            XtSetValues( widget, args, n );

            XmStringFree( label_text );

}           /* SetLabel */

/*end of file */
```

Note that file `label.c` contains two utilities for working with label widgets. These utilities were described above.

Hello World Using the Label Widget

The `hello` program demonstrates the use of the Motif label widget. This program creates a label widget, with the label widget's labelString set to "Hello World." You'll use the label widget in Motif applications that are much more complex than the hello program.

The `hello` program starts out by calling `XtInitialize()`, just like the first program in Chapter 1. After that, though, you use `XtSetValues()`, introduced above, to modify the top-level shell widget returned by `XtInitialize()`:

```
n = 0;
XtSetArg( args[n], XmNallowShellResize, True );n++;

XtSetValues( parent, args, n );
```

The code above makes sure that the top-level shell can be resized. This is the default on many systems, but use the code just in case it's not. After you modify the top-level shell widget, you create a label widget, using the function `CreateLabelWidget()` from `label.c`. Remember that `CreateLabelWidget()` returns a value of type Widget, so you must predeclare this function:

```
Widget  CreateLabelWidget(); /* label.c */
```

Finally, you call `XtRealizeWidget()` and `XtMainLoop()` to realize the widget hierarchy and handle all events:

```
XtRealizeWidget( parent );
XtMainLoop();
```

Note that you haven't set up a way to stop this program. If you're running the Motif window manager (mwm), you can use the close choice from the windows menu. The widget hierarchy you create in the `hello` program looks like:

> * Top-level Shell
>   * Label Widget "Hello World"

Source Code for Hello.c

Here is the source code for the `hello` program:

```
/*
 *      hello.c
 *      Motif label widget test program
 *
 *      Written for Power Programming Motif
 *
 */

#include <X11/Intrinsic.h>
#include <X11/StringDefs.h>
#include <Xm/Xm.h>

main( argc, argv )

int     argc;
char    *argv[];

{       /* main */
        Widget          parent, label_widget;
        Widget          CreateLabelWidget(); /* label.c */
        Arg             args[ 10 ];
        int             n;

        /*
         * Initialize Xt Intrinsics
         */
        parent = XtInitialize( argv[0],
                "Hello",
                NULL,
                0,
                &argc,
                argv );

        /*
         * You normally want to
         * do this in every Motif
```

continued...

43

...from previous page

```
           * program to be sure your
           * top-level shell can be
           * resized.
           */
          n = 0;
          XtSetArg( args[n], XmNallowShellResize, True ); n++;
          XtSetValues( parent, args, n );

          /*
           * Create a label widget called
           * "label" that has a message of
           * "Hello World". The CreateLabelWidget()
           * routine converts "Hello World" to
           * a Motif XmString.
           */
          n = 0;
          label_widget = CreateLabelWidget( parent,
                      "label",
                      "Hello World",
                      args, n );

          XtRealizeWidget( parent );
          XtMainLoop();

}          /* main */

/* end of file */
```

Compiling and Linking the Hello Program

On most UNIX-based systems you can compile and link the `hello` program with:

```
cc -o hello hello.c label.c string.c -lXm -lXt -lX11
```

On SCO's Open Desktop you can use:

```
cc -o hello hello.c label.c string.c -DLAI_TCP -Di386 -DSYSV \
    -lXm -lXt -lX11 -ltlisock -lsocket -lnsl_s
```

or you can use `Makefile` in Appendix C, and type:

```
make hello
```

or

```
make all
```

Running the Hello Program

The `hello` program displays the message, "Hello World," in a small window, as shown in Figure 2-2.

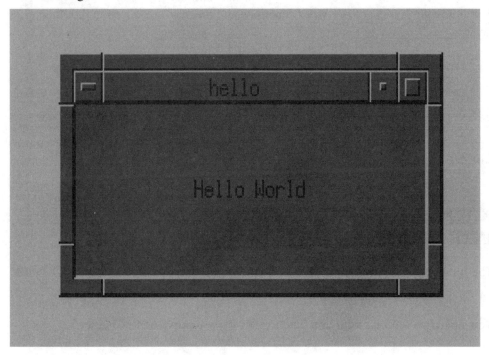

Figure 2-2. The Hello Program.

This program, like the `first` program in Chapter 1, needs no command-line parameters. This program, however, has no normal means to quit operation. If you're running the Motif window manager (mwm) you can use the close choice from the window menu.

MOTIF FUNCTIONS AND MACROS INTRODUCED IN THIS CHAPTER

The following is a list of the Motif functions and macros introduced in this chapter.

```
XmStringCompare()
XmStringConcat()
XmStringCopy()
XmStringCreate()
XmStringCreateLtoR()
XmStringFree()
XmStringGetLtoR()
```

You should be familiar with these functions and macros before you move on to Chapter 3.

X TOOLKIT FUNCTIONS AND MACROS INTRODUCED IN THIS CHAPTER

The following is a list of the Xtookit functions and macros introduced in this chapter.

```
XtSetValues()
```

You should be familiar with this function before you move on to Chapter 3.

SUMMARY

This chapter introduced a new widget class, the label widget class. It also discussed how Motif stores strings: XmStrings are a means to internationalize the handling of text strings in Motif. As you worked through the chapter, you created a utility function in the file string.c to convert C text strings to Motif XmStrings Str2XmString()—that takes a C string (char *) as a parameter and returns an XmString. You now know how to call XmStringFree() after you are done with an XmString to release the storage needed for the XmString.

You have also learned to create a utility function CreateLabelWidget()—in the file label.c—to hide the details of creating and managing a Motif label widget.

# Chapter 3

Using Multiple Widgets

U ntil this point, you've been creating only two widgets: a top-level shell, that all Motif applications need, and a single child widget. These programs haven't been all that interesting because most Motif applications use many widgets tied together, as shown in Figure 3-1.

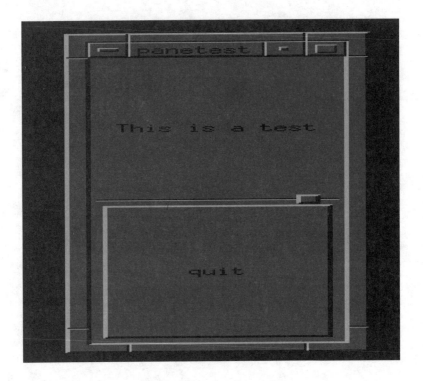

Figure 3-1. A Motif Program with Multiple Widgets.

In Figure 3-1, there are four widgets in use:

      * Top-Level Shell
        * Paned Window
          * Label
          * Pushbutton

The paned window widget (with a formal name of `XmPanedWindow`), is one of many Motif *container widgets*—widgets that hold other widgets (the top-level shell, of course, is also a container widget). Some container widgets are called *constraint widgets*, since they not only contain other widgets, but also constrain the sizes of these widgets. This chapter focuses on constraint widgets.

CONTAINER WIDGETS

Container widgets are used extensively in almost every Motif program. The file browser program, shown in Figure 3-2, will be presented in Chapter 17. It uses a paned window widget, a menubar, and menu widgets to contain other widgets.

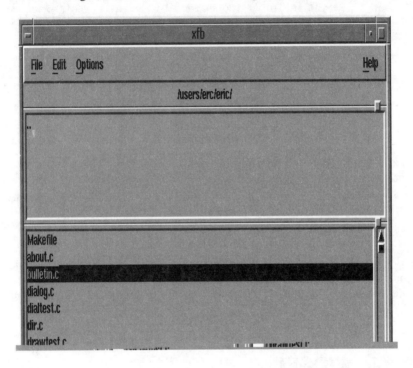

Figure 3-2. The File Browser Program from Chapter 17.

In fact, just about everything you see in Figure 3-2 is a Motif widget—from the scroll bars to the arrows on the scroll bars to the menu choice labeled "File" to the list of file names in the lower window (a scrolled list widget).

The common container widgets are listed in Figure 3-3.

49

Widget Class Name	Class Pointer	Created By
XmDrawingArea	xmDrawingAreaWidgetClass	XmCreateDrawingArea()
XmFrame	xmFrameWidgetClass	XmCreateFrame()
XmForm	xmFormWidgetClass	XmCreateForm()
XmMainWindow	xmMainWindowWidgetClass	XmCreateMainWindow()
XmPanedWindow	xmPanedWindowWidgetClass	XmCreatePanedWindow()
XmRowColumn	xmRowColumnWidgetClass	XmCreateRowColumn()
XmScale	xmScaleWidgetClass	XmCreateScale()
XmScrolledWindow	xmScrolledWindowWidgetClass	XmCreateScrolledWindow()

Figure 3-3. Common Container Widgets.

All the widgets listed in Figure 3-3 are subclasses of the XmManager widget (a meta-class widget that will never be created in your application programs). XmManager is, in turn, a subclass of Core (the parent of all widgets), Composite, and Constraint. XmManager is only important because it defines resources common to most container widgets.

In the rest of this chapter, we're going to concentrate on two container widgets: the paned window widget and the form widget. From these examples, you'll be able to extrapolate the use of the other container widgets, which we'll cover in later chapters.

THE FORM WIDGET

The form widget, XmForm, is actually considered a dialog widget, but it acts as a container. (XmForm descends from XmManager through XmBulletinBoard.) You can create a form widget as a dialog widget with XmCreateFormDialog(), or you can simply create a form widget with XmCreateForm() or XtCreateManagedWidget(). We use the two latter functions in the source code examples that follow.

The form widget include file is Xm/Form.h. Form widgets are very complex, but they allow a host of ways to attach child widgets. For example, you can attach a label widget to the top, left, right, or bottom of the form. You could actually attach it to all sides of a form, but that would be boring.

A form widget holds other widgets as children and allows you to control the placement of these children. What happens to the size of the children when the parent form changes size—does every child grow when a form grows larger, or

50

should only some children grow? With the form widget, you can control these answers. A form widget is only useful, though, with child widgets.

Attaching Child Widgets to Forms

Follow these rules to create a form and its children and then to attach the children to the form:

1) Create the form widget. This will be the parent widget for the child widgets.

2) Create the child widget as a child of a form widget.

3) Set up an `Arg` array with the proper form attachments for the child widget by specifying the proper resources and values.

4) Use `XtSetValues()` to add the proper resources to the child widget.

The source code example program, `formtest.c`, which appears later in this chapter, shows how to create a form. The hardest part is getting the child widgets to appear in the form in the way you want them. Motif allows four basic styles of attaching child widgets to a form: the form, position, self, and widget attachments. These so-called attachments aren't easy to figure out, so expect to spend some time experimenting with the form widget.

Each child in the form can have an attachment specified for the top, bottom, left, and right sides of the child. In each case, you'll use `XtSetArg()` to set up the attachments for the following resources:

* `topAttachment`   (`XmNtopAttachment` in C programs)
* `bottomAttachment`   (`XmNbottomAttachment` in C programs)
* `leftAttachment`   (`XmNleftAttachment` in C programs)
* `rightAttachment`   (`XmNrightAttachment` in C programs)

The XmATTACH_FORM Attachment

`XmATTACH_FORM` attaches a widget to a particular side of the parent form itself. You can also attach a child to a number of sides of the form. For example if you attached a child widget to both the right and left sides of a form, as shown in Figure 3-4, the child widget would maintain contact with both the left and right sides of the form as the form grew or shrunk, causing the child to grow and shrink horizontally as the form did.

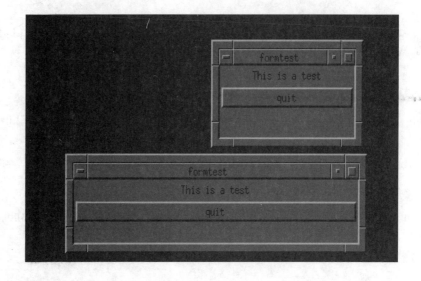

Figure 3-4. Left and Right Attachments.

To set up a child to attach to the left and right sides of a parent form, use the following:

```
Widget          parent_form;
Widget          child;
Arg             args[10];
int             n;

n = 0;
XtSetArg( args[n],      XmNleftAttachment,      XmATTACH_FORM );    n++;
XtSetArg( args[n],      XmNrightAttachment,     XmATTACH_FORM );    n++;

XtSetValues( child, args, n );
```

To attach the child to all the sides of the form (generally not a good idea, since this would obscure other children in the form), you would use:

```
Widget          child;
Arg             args[10];
int             n;

n = 0;
XtSetArg( args[n],      XmNleftAttachment,      XmATTACH_FORM );    n++;
XtSetArg( args[n],      XmNrightAttachment,     XmATTACH_FORM );    n++;
XtSetArg( args[n],      XmNbottomAttachment,    XmATTACH_FORM );    n++;
XtSetArg( args[n],      XmNtopAttachment,       XmATTACH_FORM );    n++;

XtSetValues( child, args, n );
```

XmATTACH_FORM is the easiest method of attachment.

52

The XmATTACH_OPPOSITE_FORM Attachment

The XmATTACH_OPPOSITE_FORM attachment is just like XmATTACH_FORM, only XmATTACH_OPPOSITE_FORM attaches to the opposite side (i.e., the following code attaches a widget's TOP side to the BOTTOM of the form):

```
Widget          child;
Arg             args[10];
int             n;

n = 0;
XtSetArg( args[n], XmNtopAttachment, XmATTACH_OPPOSITE_FORM ); n++;

XtSetValues( child, args, n );
```

If this seems odd to you (and it should), you'll want to experiment with the formtest program below. Try out different types of attachments and see what they really do. Experimenting will make this text a lot clearer.

The XmATTACH_POSITION Attachment

The XmATTACH_POSITION attachment attaches a side of the child to a relative position in the form that is contained in the corresponding position resource—normally a percent:

```
Widget          child;
Arg             args[10];
int             n;

/*
 * Maintain a position in the middle of the form,
 * at about one-half the horizontal width of the
 * form, that is, start on the left at 25% and
 * continue onto 75% of the form.
 */
n = 0;
XtSetArg( args[n], XmNleftAttachment,    XmATTACH_POSITION );   n++;
XtSetArg( args[n], XmNleftPosition,      25 );n++;
XtSetArg( args[n], XmNrightAttachment,   XmATTACH_POSITION );   n++;
XtSetArg( args[n], XmNrightPosition,     75 ); n++;

XtSetValues( child, args, n );
```

Use XmATTACH_POSITION to set up widgets that all maintain their sizes relative to one another (such as four child widgets, each 1/4 the width of the parent form). Each time you use XmATTACH_POSITION, you must indicate a position for the side, using one of the following specifications:

  * topPosition (XmNtopPosition in C programs)
  * bottomPosition (XmNbottomPosition in C programs)

```
* leftPosition (XmNleftPosition in C programs)
* rightPosition (XmNrightPosition in C programs)
```

The XmATTACH_SELF Attachment

XmATTACH_SELF, as shown below, makes the given side attach to its initial position where it remains.

```
Widget          child;
Arg             args[10];
int             n;

n = 0;
XtSetArg( args[n], XmNbottomAttachment, XmATTACH_SELF ); n++;

XtSetValues( child, args, n );
```

Once the initial placement is made, the side (or sides) with XmATTACH_SELF remain where they are. This code makes the bottom side of the child stay put.

The XmATTACH_WIDGET Attachment

In most forms, you'll only use two types of attachment: XmATTACH_FORM and XmATTACH_WIDGET. XmATTACH_WIDGET makes one side of a child widget attach to a side of another widget: you may want the first widget to attach to the top of the form, and the next child widget in line to attach right below the first child and so on. When you use XmATTACH_WIDGET, you must indicate the widget to which you want the other widget to attach using one of the following specifications:

```
* XmNtopWidget
* XmNbottomWidget
* XmNleftWidget
* XmNrightWidget
```

The code for XmATTACH_WIDGET is as follows::

```
Widget          first_child;
Widget          second_child;
Arg             args[10];
int             n;

n = 0;
XtSetArg( args[n],     XmNtopAttachment,  XmATTACH_WIDGET );   n++;
XtSetArg( args[n],     XmNtopWidget,      first_child );       n++;

XtSetValues( second_child, args, n );
```

The code above specifies that the second_child's top side should attach to the BOTTOM side of the first_child.

The code below attaches the `first_child` widget to the top, left, and right of the form. The `second_child` widget attaches to the bottom of the first_child, and also to the left and right sides of the form:

```
Widget              first_child;
Widget              second_child;
Arg                 args[10];
int                 n;

/*
 * Attach first child to the top, left and
 * right of the form.
 */
n = 0;
XtSetArg( args[n],     XmNtopAttachment,   XmATTACH_FORM );   n++;
XtSetArg( args[n],     XmNleftAttachment,  XmATTACH_FORM );   n++;
XtSetArg( args[n],     XmNrightAttachment, XmATTACH_FORM );   n++;

XtSetValues( first_child, args, n );

/*
 * Attach the top of the second_child
 * to the bottom of the first_child.
 */
n = 0;
XtSetArg( args[n],     XmNtopAttachment,   XmATTACH_WIDGET ); n++;
XtSetArg( args[n],     XmNtopWidget,       first_child );     n++;

XtSetArg( args[n],     XmNleftAttachment,  XmATTACH_FORM );   n++;
XtSetArg( args[n],     XmNrightAttachment, XmATTACH_FORM );   n++;

XtSetValues( second_child, args, n );
```

You'll use code like this in the file `formtest.c`, shown later in the chapter.

The XmATTACH_OPPOSITE_WIDGET Attachment

`XmATTACH_OPPOSITE_WIDGET` attaches a side of a child widget to the same side of another child widget:

```
Widget              first_child;
Widget              second_child;
Arg                 args[10];
int                 n;

n = 0;
XtSetArg( args[n], XmNtopAttachment,XmATTACH_OPPOSITE_WIDGET ); n++;
XtSetArg( args[n], XmNtopWidget,      first_child ); n++;

XtSetValues( second_child, args, n );
```

55

The code above attaches the top side of the second_child widget to the top side of the first_child widget. This seems to make even less sense than the XmATTACH_OPPOSITE_FORM, but try it out and it will make more sense.

The XmATTACH_NONE Attachment

The XmATTACH_NONE Attachment—an "un-attachment"—is the default for all sides not attached any other way. In most cases, however, it's a good idea to specify all the proper attachments you want in a form and not use XmATTACH_NONE.

THE FORMTEST PROGRAM

The formtest program, shown in Figure 3-5, creates a form widget and two child widgets (a label and a pushbutton). Clicking on the quit button quits the program.

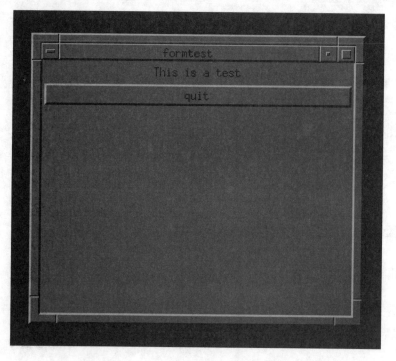

Figure 3-5. The Formtest Program.

If you change the size of the form, you'll see how the form widget controls the attachments. The widget hierarchy for the formtest program looks like:

> * Top-Level Shell
> > * Form Widget
> > > * Label
> > > * Pushbutton (quit)

After creating a top-level shell, the formtest program creates a form widget, which holds two child widgets: a label and a quit button.

The label widget is created with the utility function CreateLabelWidget(), in label.c (see Chapter 2). The quit pushbutton is created with a special utility function, CreatePushButton(), in push.c, shown later in this chapter.

The file formtest.c contains the meat of the formtest program. You create the form widget using the following:

```
Widget    parent;
Widget    form_widget;
Arg       args[10];
int       n;

/*
 * Create a form widget,
 * using an arbitrary size
 */
n = 0;
XtSetArg( args[n], XmNwidth, 300 );      n++;
XtSetArg( args[n], XmNheight, 250 );     n++;

form_widget = XtCreateManagedWidget( "form",
                         xmFormWidgetClass,
                         parent,
                         args,
                         n );
```

Source Code for Formtest.c

In the file formtest.c, shown below, a line is normally commented out:

```
/* XtSetArg( args[n], XmNbottomAttachment, XmATTACH_FORM ); n++; */
```

You should try the formtest program both with this line in and with it commented out. You'll quickly figure out the basics of how the form widget works. Try playing with some of the other attachments listed above, but be warned that the form widget is trickier than you might think. Here is the source code for the file formtest.c:

```
/*
 *        formtest.c
 *        Motif test program using the form widget.
 *
 *        Written for Power Programming Motif
 */

#include       <X11/Intrinsic.h>
#include       <X11/StringDefs.h>
#include       <Xm/Xm.h>
#include       <Xm/Form.h>

void quit_callback( widget, client_data, call_data )

Widget         widget;
caddr_t        client_data;
caddr_t        call_data;

/*
 *        quit_callback() is the callback for the
 *        Motif quit button. This function
 *        terminates the program by calling exit().
 */

{              /* quit_callback */

        XtCloseDisplay( XtDisplay( widget ) );
        exit( 0 );

}              /* quit_callback */

main( argc, argv )

int     argc;
char    *argv[];

{              /* main */
        Widget              parent, form_widget;
        Widget              quit_widget, CreatePushButton();
        Widget              label_widget, CreateLabelWidget();
        Arg                 args[ 10 ];
        int                 n;

        /*
         * Initialize Xt Intrinsics
         */ parent = XtInitialize( argv[0],
                        "Formtest",
                        NULL,
                        0,
                        &argc,
                        argv );
```

continued...

...from previous page

```
n = 0;
XtSetArg( args[n], XmNallowShellResize, True ); n++;
XtSetValues( parent, args, n );

/*
 * Create a form widget,
 * using an arbitrary size
 */
n = 0;
XtSetArg( args[n], XmNwidth, 300 ); n++;
XtSetArg( args[n], XmNheight, 250 ); n++;

form_widget = XtCreateManagedWidget( "form",
                         xmFormWidgetClass,
                         parent,
                         args,
                         n );

/*
 * Create label widget
 */
n = 0;
label_widget = CreateLabelWidget( form_widget,
                           "label",
                           "This is a test",
                           args, n );

/*
 * Attach label widget
 */
n = 0;
XtSetArg( args[n], XmNtopAttachment, XmATTACH_FORM ); n++;
XtSetArg( args[n], XmNleftAttachment, XmATTACH_FORM ); n++;
XtSetArg( args[n], XmNrightAttachment, XmATTACH_FORM ); n++;

XtSetValues( label_widget, args, n );

/*
 * Create a quit pushbutton widget.
 * Note that we could specify the
 * form attachments here or after
 * creating.
 */
n = 0;
 quit_widget = CreatePushButton( form_widget,  /* parent */
                           "quit",          /* widget name */
                           args,            /* arguments */
                           n,               /* number of args */
                           quit_callback ); /* callback func */

/*
```

continued...

...from previous page

```
 * Set up where the quit-button widget
 * fits in the form.
 */
n = 0;
XtSetArg( args[n], XmNtopAttachment,    XmATTACH_WIDGET ); n++;
XtSetArg( args[n], XmNtopWidget,        label_widget ); n++;
XtSetArg( args[n], XmNleftAttachment,   XmATTACH_FORM ); n++;
XtSetArg( args[n], XmNrightAttachment,  XmATTACH_FORM ); n++;

/*
 * Try this next line commented out and then try it
 * again with the line in.
 */
/* XtSetArg( args[n], XmNbottomAttachment, XmATTACH_FORM ); n++;  */

/*
 * Set the new resources into the quit button
 */
XtSetValues( quit_widget, args, n );

XtRealizeWidget( parent );
XtMainLoop();

} /* main */

/* end of file */
```

Compiling and Linking the Formtest Program

The `formtest` program uses the following C files:

```
formtest.c
label.c  (from chapter 2)
push.c
string.c  (from chapter 2)
```

On UNIX systems, you can compile it with something akin to:

```
cc -o formtest formtest.c label.c push.c string.c -lXm -lXt -lX11
```

If you use `Makefile` in Appendix C, you can type:

```
make formtest
```

or

```
make all
```

to compile and link all the programs in this book.

Running the Formtest Program

Simply typing `formtest` should run the `formtest` program. Play around with different sizes for the program's main window (using mwm or your favorite window manager).

CREATING A PUSHBUTTON WIDGET

The function `CreatePushButton()` creates a pushbutton widget and sets up a callback function. The callback is called whenever the user clicks the mouse pointer (usually button 1) in the pushbutton.

`CreatePushButton()` serves as a convenience function for creating pushbuttons. The `first.c` program in Chapter 1, showed how to create a pushbutton widget. Since pushbuttons are used in almost every program in this book, we placed a handy utility function into `push.c`.

Source Code for Push.c

Here is the source code for the file `push.c`:

```
/*
 *    push.c
 *    Motif push-button widget utility function.
 *
 *    Written for Power Programming Motif
 */

#include        <X11/Intrinsic.h>
#include        <X11/StringDefs.h>
#include        <Xm/Xm.h>
#include        <Xm/PushB.h>

Widget CreatePushButton( parent, name, args, n, callback_func )

Widget          parent;
char            name[];
Arg             *args;
int             n;
void            (*callback_func)();

/*
 * CreatePushButton() creates a Motif
 * XmPushButton widget, using whatever
 * args are passed to the function.
 * callback_func() is set up
continued...
```

61

...from previous page
```
 * as the activateCallback function
 * for this push-button widget.
 */

{       /* CreatePushButton */
        Widget  push_widget;
        push_widget = XtCreateManagedWidget( name,
                                 xmPushButtonWidgetClass,
                                 parent,
                                 args,
                                 n );

        /*
         * Set up a callback function
         * to be called whenever
         * the push button is
         * "activated".
         */
        XtAddCallback( push_widget,
                XmNactivateCallback,
                callback_func,
                NULL );

        return( push_widget );

}       /* CreatePushButton */

/* end of file */
```

THE PANED WINDOW WIDGET

The paned window widget places its child widgets from top to bottom in vertical "panes"—hence the name XmPanedWindow. Between each child there is an optional "sash"—a line with a control box. The user can use the mouse pointer to move the sash up and down, thus controlling the size of each individual pane. Sashes are described in more detail in the next section. You can also specify minimum and maximum sizes for panes, which the paned window widget will enforce.

The class pointer is xmPanedWindowWidgetClass and the include file for the paned window class is Xm/PanedW.h.

Using the Paned Window Sash to Resize a Pane

As mentioned above, users can adjust the sizes of the panes in a paned window widget by adjusting the control sash that separates the panes, as shown in Figure 3-6.

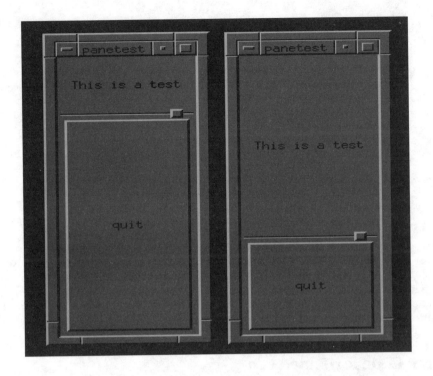

Figure 3-6. Adjusting the Sash on a Paned Window Widget.

The control sash is optional. To use it, you'll need to set two resources for the paned window widget:

```
XtSetArg( args[n], XmNseparatorOn, True ); n++;
XtSetArg( args[n], XmNallowResize, True ); n++;
```

The `separatorOn` resource turns on the separating line between panes. The `allowResize` resource allows the panes to be resized. The paned window widget sizes itself horizontally to the width of its widest child.

The Panetest Program

The `panetest` program, in the next section, looks a lot like the `formtest` program previously shown, except you're dealing with a paned window widget.

You can create a paned window widget with:

```
Widget    parent;
Widget    pane_widget;
Arg       args[10];
int       n;

n = 0;
XtSetArg( args[n], XmNseparatorOn, True ); n++;
XtSetArg( args[n], XmNallowResize, True ); n++;

pane_widget = XtCreateManagedWidget( "pane",
              xmPanedWindowWidgetClass,
              parent,
              args,
              n );
```

The rest of the `panetest` program looks suspiciously like the `formtest` program, but note that you don't have to attach the child widgets; however, you do give each child widget (and the paned window widget itself) an arbitrary width and height. In Chapter 13, you'll learn how to use a resource file to specify the sizes you want at run-time, not at compile-time.

Source Code for Panetest.c

The main part of the panetest program is in the file `panetest.c`. Here is the source code for the file `panetest.c`:

```
/*
 *          panetest.c
 *          Motif test program using the pane widget.
 *
 *          Written for Power Programming Motif
 */

#include               <X11/Intrinsic.h>
#include               <X11/StringDefs.h>
#include               <Xm/Xm.h>
#include               <Xm/PanedW.h>

void quit_callback( widget, client_data, call_data )

Widget        widget;
caddr_t       client_data;
caddr_t       call_data;

/*
 *          quit_callback() is the callback for the
 *          Motif quit button. This function
continued...
```

...from previous page
```
 *         terminates the program by calling exit().
 */

{          /* quit_callback */

           XtCloseDisplay( XtDisplay( widget ) );
           exit( 0 );

}          /* quit_callback */

main( argc, argv )

int        argc;
char       *argv[];

{          /* main */
Widget     parent, pane_widget;
Widget     label_widget, CreateLabelWidget(); /* label.c */
Widget     quit_widget, CreatePushButton(); /* push.c */
Arg        args[ 10 ];
int        n;

           /*
            * Initialize Xt Intrinsics
            */
           parent = XtInitialize( argv[0],
                        "Panetest",
                        NULL,
                        0,
                        &argc,
                        argv );

           n = 0;
           XtSetArg( args[n], XmNallowShellResize, True ); n++;
           XtSetValues( parent, args, n );

           /*
            * Create a pane widget,
            * using an arbitrary size
            */
           n = 0;
           XtSetArg( args[n], XmNwidth, 300 ); n++;
           XtSetArg( args[n], XmNheight, 250 ); n++;
           XtSetArg( args[n], XmNseparatorOn, True ); n++;
           XtSetArg( args[n], XmNallowResize, True ); n++;

           pane_widget = XtCreateManagedWidget( "pane",
                             xmPanedWindowWidgetClass,
                             parent,
                             args,
```
continued...

...from previous page

```
                                 n );

        /*
         * Create label widget
         */
        n = 0;
        XtSetArg( args[n], XmNwidth, 100 ); n++;
        XtSetArg( args[n], XmNheight, 150 ); n++;
        label_widget = CreateLabelWidget( pane_widget,
                        "label",
                        "This is a test",
                        args, n );

        /*
         * Create the quit-button widget
         */
        n = 0;
        XtSetArg( args[n], XmNwidth, 100 ); n++;
        XtSetArg( args[n], XmNheight, 150 ); n++;

        quit_widget = CreatePushButton( pane_widget,
                        "quit",
                        args,
                        n,
                        quit_callback );

        XtRealizeWidget( parent );
        XtMainLoop();

}               /* main */

/* end of file */
```

Compiling and Linking the Panetest Program

The `panetest` program uses the following C files:

```
panetest.c
label.c (from chapter 2)
push.c
string.c (from chapter 2)
```

On UNIX systems, you can compile it with:

```
cc -o panetest panetest.c label.c push.c string.c -lXm -lXt -lX11
```

If you use `Makefile` in Appendix C, you can type:

```
make panetest
```

or

```
make all
```

Running the Panetest Program

As shown in Figure 3-7, the `panetest` program requires no command-line parameters, so you can just type `panetest` to launch it. When the `panetest` program is running, try to adjust the "sashes" and make the label widget or the quit widget grow in size. See what happens if you make the application's main window larger and smaller.

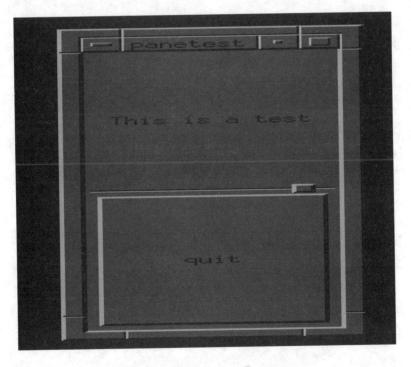

Figure 3-7. The Panetest Program.

Problems with the Paned Window Widget under X11 RELEASE 4

If you are running a Release 4 X server and Motif 1.0, you may need to enable the so-called "bug compatibility" mode when using the paned window widget. In Release 4, the requirements for grabbing the mouse pointer have changed from Release 3, which is what Motif 1.0 was written under. You will try to adjust the sash on a paned window and your program will suddenly exit, printing out an X error something like:

```
XProtocolError: BadValue, integer parameter out of range for operation
    Major opcode of failed request: 26 (X_GrabPointer)
    Minor opcode of failed request: 0
    Resource id in failed request: 0x813c
    Serial number of failed request: 67
    Current serial number in output stream: 67
```

If you experience this problem, try using the xset program to enable the "bug compatibility" mode:

```
xset bc
```

SUMMARY

In this chapter, we've discussed container widgets, which are widgets that have other widgets as children. The form widget allows you to specify how child widgets are placed within the form. The paned window widget allows users to resize the vertical panes to adjust the sizes of the child widgets. In most of the example programs to come, we'll use this concept of container widgets.

# Chapter 4

Dialogs

I f you've ever used MS-DOS on an IBM-compatible personal computer and seen the infamous "Abort, Retry, Ignore?" message, you've experienced a dialog. The DOS dialog is cryptic and unfriendly. In contrast, the Motif toolkit's purpose is to have dialogs that allow the user to interact with a Motif program in a friendly, clear, and intuitive manner. At least, that's the plan.

In Motif, dialogs are used so the user can reply to a question or to a situation. If the user asks for help, for example, you can present a help message in a dialog, such as an information dialog. A help message is shown in Figure 4-1. You'll want the help message to remain on the screen until the user is done with the message, which may be a long time. How do you know when the user is done with the help message?

In Motif, most dialogs remain on the screen until the user clicks a mouse button in a pushbutton widget or presses the Return key.

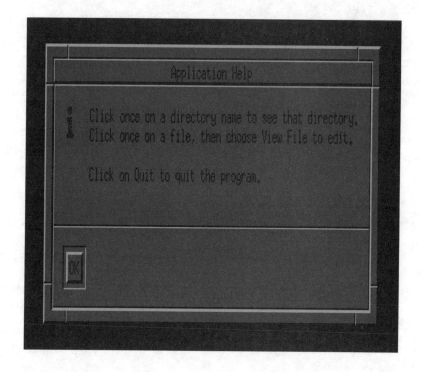

Figure 4-1. A Help Message.

It makes sense to require a user to respond when taking a drastic action like deleting a file; you can use a dialog to warn the user that a deleted file cannot be recovered. Such dialog widgets ask the user whether to go ahead with a task that cannot be undone, as shown in Figure 4-2.

Figure 4-2. An "Are You Really Sure?" Dialog.

Motif dialogs range from simple to the most complex—the file-selection dialog. The file-selection dialog appears in Figure 4-3.

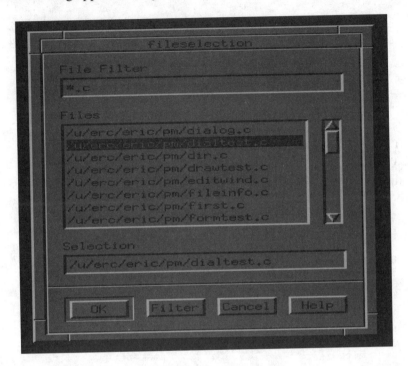

Figure 4-3. The File-Selection Dialog.

The file-selection dialog allows the user to choose a file from a list of file names that match some pattern—the "Filter." This is a complex dialog, but it is easy to create. Since selecting files is so common, it's helpful to have this widget built into the toolkit.

ON-LINE HELP AND OTHER DIALOGS

Motif has a number of primitive dialog widgets, including the form widget discussed in Chapter 3. Figure 4-4 presents a list of Motif's basic dialog widget classes.

Widget Class Name	Class Pointer	Creation Function
XmBulletinBoard	xmBulletinBoardWidgetClass	XmCreateBulletinBoard()
XmCommand	XmCommandWidgetClass	XmCreateCommand()
XmFileSelectionBox	xmFileSelectionBoxWidgetClass	XmCreateFileSelectionBox()
XmForm	xmFormWidgetClass	XmCreateForm()
XmMessageBox	xmMessageBoxWidgetClass	XmCreateMessageBox()
XmSelectionBox	xmSelectionBoxWidgetClass	XmCreateSelectionBox()

Figure 4-4. Motif's Basic Dialog Widget Classes.

You usually won't use the basic dialog widgets. Instead, you'll often use a compound dialog that you build with a convenience function from the base classes listed in Figure 4-4. These compound dialogs are listed in Figure 4-5.

Dialog Type	Creation Function
BulletinBoardDialog	XmCreateBulletinBoardDialog()
ErrorDialog	XmCreateErrorDialog()
FileSelectionDialog	XmCreateFileSelectionDialog()
FormDialog	XmCreateFormDialog()
InformationDialog	XmCreateInformationDialog()
MessageDialog	XmCreateMessageDialog()
PromptDialog	XmCreatePromptDialog()
QuestionDialog	XmCreateQuestionDialog()
SelectionDialog	XmCreateSelectionDialog()
WarningDialog	XmCreateWarningDialog()
WorkingDialog	XmCreateWorkingDialog()

Figure 4-5. Compound Dialogs and Their Convenience Functions.

Compound dialogs have all necessary features built in; the convenience functions that create these dialogs take care of all the messy work.

HOW DIALOGS WORK

A Motif dialog is usually contained within a separate top-level window, at the same level as the top-level application shell widget, as shown in Figure 4-6. A dialog, therefore, often has a window manager title bar (placed by mwm). You can move this title bar around the screen.

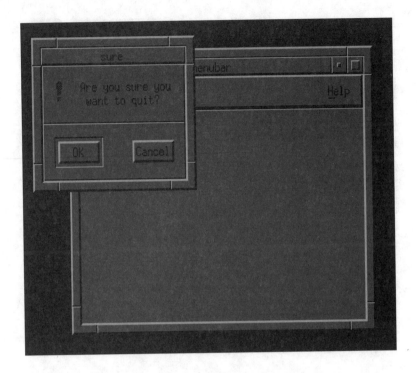

Figure 4-6. An Application Main Window and a Dialog.

Transient Windows

In X Window terminology, pop-up dialog windows are called transient windows since they normally only remain on the screen for a short time. You need some experience with X before you plan on writing commercial Motif applications. For now, if the term transient window is unfamiliar, don't worry about it.

Dialogs are widgets. Most dialogs contain some text and three pushbutton child widgets, as shown in Figure 4-7. The pushbutton child widgets are generally labeled "OK," "Cancel" and "Help," but you can change the labels or remove the pushbuttons entirely. All of the widgets associated with a dialog are created together when you call one of the dialog convenience functions listed in Figure 4-5.

Figure 4-7. Most Dialogs Have OK, Cancel, and Help Pushbuttons.

When the user selects something in the dialog or clicks on a pushbutton, you may have a function called back (if you previously set up a callback). This is how your programs know what the user chose in the dialog.

There are seven basic steps for using dialogs:

1) Include the proper include files for the dialog.

2) Convert your dialog message to an `XmString`.

3) Create the dialog using `XmCreate-what-ever`.

4) Call `XtUnmanageChild()` to get rid of any pushbuttons you don't want.

5) Call `XtAddCallback()` to set up your callback functions for the dialog.

6) Call `XtManageChild()` with the dialog widget to make the dialog pop up.

7) Call `XtUnmanageChild()` with the dialog widget to make the dialog pop down.

Note that steps 6 and 7 are for dialogs you want to repeatedly pop up and down. You may also want to look at using `XtPopup()` and `XtPopdown()` for these steps.

We'll cover the most common Motif dialogs in the sections below. A test program, called `dialtest`, will display five different types of dialogs to show how they work.

THE WARNING DIALOG

One of the simplest forms of compound dialogs has three pushbuttons, a text message (an `XmString`, remember), and an icon that looks like an exclamation mark, a question mark, or an hourglass. The icon shows you what kind of dialog it is and what the text should be relevant to the purpose indicated by the icon.

The first dialog you will learn is a simple dialog to ask the user "Are you sure?" This warning dialog is shown in Figure 4-8.

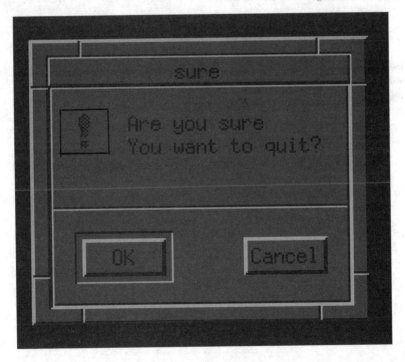

Figure 4-8. The Warning Dialog. - icon is an exclamation mark "!"

75

The warning dialog is a compound dialog made from a base message box (XmMessageBox) and three pushbuttons. You can create a warning dialog with XmCreateWarningDialog(). All of the MessageBox-descended dialogs require the include file Xm/MessageB.h:

```
#include    <Xm/MessageB.h>

Widget      widget;
Widget      parent;
String      name;
ArgList     args;
Cardinal    n;

widget = XmCreateWarningDialog( parent,
                    name,
                    args,
                    n );
```

XmCreate functions have the same order of parameters: parent, name, args, and number of args. This is different than XtCreateManagedWidget(), which you've used up to now to create your widgets. XtCreateManagedWidget() has its parameters in the following order: name, class, parent widget, args, and number of args.

With XmCreateWarningDialog(), the widget returned is the MessageBox widget. This MessageBox widget holds, by default, three pushbutton child widgets, labeled "OK," "Cancel" and "Help." Use the warning dialog to warn the user of the consequences of an action. You can customize any warning dialog by manipulating the dialog's resources, either through an X resource file or in your C code (as you have been doing so far).

DIALOG RESOURCES

The following resources apply to all of the dialogs based on the MessageBox widget. You'll learn more about the resources you're most likely to change in the next few sections.

Set the text message for the dialog by setting the messageString resource:

```
#include    <Xm/MessageB.h>
Arg         args[10];
int         n;
XmString    motif_string;

n = 0;
XtSetArg( args[n], XmNmessageString, motif_string ); n++;
```

Note that in your code, you use the defined symbol XmNmessageString.

CHANGING THE PUSHBUTTON TEXT

The three pushbuttons have default messages: "OK," "Cancel," and "Help." You can change any of these or even get rid of some pushbuttons.

The text of each button's message is an XmString, just like the pushbuttons used in Chapters 1-3. Figure 4-9 lists the resource and defined names for the three pushbuttons.

Button	Resource Name	Defined Name in C Programs
Cancel button	cancelLabelString	XmNCancelLabelString
Help button	helpLabelString	XmNhelpLabelString
OK button	okLabelString	XmNokLabelString

Figure 4-9. Three Pushbuttons.

To set the OK button to display "You Bet!" rather than "OK," you could do the following:

```
#include    <Xm/MessageB.h>

Arg     args[10];
int     n;
XmString motif_string, Str2XmString();   /* string.c */

motif_string = Str2XmString( "You Bet!" );

n = 0;
XtSetArg( args[n], XmNokLabelString, motif_string ); n++;

/*
 * Create your widget...
 */
```

SETTING THE DEFAULT PUSHBUTTON

In Motif toolkit programs, you often press the return key to accept a default choice. With these dialogs, the "OK" button is usually that default choice, but you can change the choice that you want as the default.

The `defaultButtonType` resource specifies the default button; if you press the return key, the default button is "pushed." In C programs, use the defined symbol `XmNdefaultButtonType`. The choices for the default button are: `XmDIALOG_CANCEL_BUTTON` for the button labeled "Cancel," `XmDIALOG_OK_BUTTON` for the button labeled "OK," and `XmDIALOG_HELP_BUTTON` for the button labeled "Help." The default, of course, is `XmDIALOG_OK_BUTTON`.

To set the default button to the "Help" button, use:

```
#include  <Xm/MessageB.h>

Arg    args[10];
int    n;

n = 0;
XtSetArg( args[n], XmNdefaultButtonType, XmDIALOG_HELP_BUTTON ); n++;

/*
 * Create your widget...
 */
```

You usually don't want to change the button defaults.

DIALOG CALLBACKS

Normally, you want to set a callback on the dialog. You may want to set a callback on more than one button, but usually you don't have to, since a cancel choice means don't do the operation. You can set up a callback on the OK button that performs the task you're asking the user to confirm and do nothing with the cancel button. Another option is to set callbacks for the OK and cancel buttons. The next few chapters on menus and menu bars cover help, which is usually handled differently. Figure 4-10 lists the resource and defined names for the two buttons.

Button	Resource Name	Defined Name in C Programs
Cancel button	`cancelCallback`	`XmNcancelCallback`
OK button	`okCallback`	`XmNokCallback`

Figure 4-10. The OK and Cancel Buttons.

When setting up callbacks, like you did in Chapter 1, use `XtAddCallback()`:

```
#include    <Xm/MessageB.h>

Widget      widget;
void        (*callback_func)();

/*
 * Create your widget...
 */

/*
 * Set up callback on OK
 * button.
 */
XtAddCallback( widget,
          XmNokCallback,
          callback_func,
          NULL );
```

Your callback function should look like this:

```
void simple_callback( widget, client_data, call_data )

Widget              widget;
XmAnyCallbackStruct client_data;
caddr_t             call_data;

{       /* simple_callback */

}       /* simple_callback */
```

The `XmAnyCallbackStruct` is defined as:

```
typedef struct
        {
        int     reason;
        XEvent  *event;
        } XmAnyCallbackStruct;
```

If the OK button was pushed, the reason field is `XmCR_OK`. If the cancel button was pushed, the reason field is `XmCR_CANCEL`.

DISABLING PUSHBUTTONS IN A DIALOG

Ridding yourself of a dialog button takes two steps. First, you need to get the widget for the actual button. Then, you call `XtUnmanageChild()` on the pushbutton widget.

XmMessageBoxGetChild() returns the child widget of a MessageBox-based dialog. You need to pass a widget and an ID that specifies which child you want. For example, to get rid of the help button in a warning dialog, you first need to get the help button's widget value:

```
Widget          dialog_widget;          /* parent */
Widget          child_button_widget;    /* RETURN */
unsigned char   which_button;

child_button_widget = XmMessageBoxGetChild( dialog_widget,
                    which_button );
```

The which_button variable can be one of the folowing:

```
XmDIALOG_CANCEL_BUTTON
XmDIALOG_DEFAULT_BUTTON
XmDIALOG_HELP_BUTTON
XmDIALOG_MESSAGE_LABEL
XmDIALOG_OK_BUTTON
XmDIALOG_SEPARATOR
XmDIALOG_SYMBOL_LABEL
```

Once you have the widget, then you can remove it with XtUnmanageChild():

```
Widget   child_button_widget;

XtUnmanageChild( child_button_widget );
```

RemoveDialButton(), below, provides a function that removes the given button from a dialog widget:

```
RemoveDialButton( widget, which_button )

Widget       widget;
int          which_button;

/*           which_button should be one of:
 *                  XmDIALOG_CANCEL_BUTTON
 *                  XmDIALOG_OK_BUTTON
 *                  XmDIALOG_HELP_BUTTON
 */

{            /* RemoveDialButton */
             Widget  dead_widget;

             dead_widget =XmMessageBoxGetChild( widget,
                     which_button );

             XtUnmanageChild( dead_widget );

}            /* RemoveDialButton */
```

CREATING A WARNING DIALOG

`WarningDialog()`, below, creates and pops up a warning dialog widget:

```
Widget      WarningDialog (parent, name, message, callback_func )
Widget      parent;
char        name[];
char        message[];
void        (*callback_func)();

{           /* WarningDialog */
Arg             args[10];
int             n;
Widget          widget, ok_widget;
XmString        motif_string, Str2XmString();

/*
 * Set up the message
 */
motif_string = Str2XmString( message );

n = 0;
XtSetArg(args[n], XmNmessageString, motif_string ); n++;

/*
 * Create widget
 */
widget = XmCreateWarningDialog( parent,
                name,
                args,
                n );

/*
 * Get rid of "Help"
 * push button.
 */
RemoveDialButton( widget,
    XmDIALOG_HELP_BUTTON );

/*
 * Set up callback on OK
 * button.
 */
XtAddCallback( widget,
    XmNokCallback,
    callback_func, NULL );

XtManageChild( widget );

/*
```

continued...

...from previous page
```
                * Free storage for XmString
                */
                XmStringFree( motif_string );

                return( widget );

}               /* WarningDialog */
```

You need to pass a parent widget, a name for the dialog, the message text (as a C string, as the function will convert the message to a Motif XmString), and a callback function.

INFORMATION DIALOGS

You use information dialogs to present information to the user—such as a notice that electronic mail has arrived. Figure 4-11 is a sample information dialog. This book uses information dialogs to present help information.

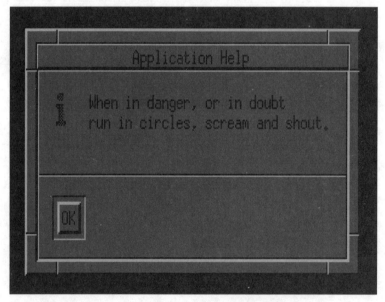

Figure 4-11. An Information Dialog. ~ icon is " i "

You can create a information dialog with the function XmCreateInformationDialog():

```
#include<Xm/MessageB.h>

Widget      widget;
Widget      parent;
String      name;
ArgList     args;
Cardinal    n;

widget = XmCreateInformationDialog( parent,
            name,
            args,
            n );
```

In this book, we've implemented pop-up help messages using this information dialog. The function SetUpHelp(), below, creates and pops up such a dialog:

```
Widget SetUpHelp( parent, name, message )

Widget      parent;
char        name[];
char        message[];

{           /* SetUphelp */
            Arg             args[10];
            int             n;
            Widget          help_widget;
            XmString        motif_string, Str2XmString();

            /*
             * Set up the help message
             */
            motif_string = Str2XmString( message );

            n = 0;
            XtSetArg( args[n], XmNmessageString, motif_string ); n++;

            /*
             * Create help widget
             */
            help_widget = XmCreateInformationDialog( parent,
                        name,
                        args,
                        n );

            /*
             * Normally, an Information dialog
             * has three buttons: OK, Cancel
             * and Help. Since this is the
             * help dialog, we get rid of the
             * Cancel and Help buttons, by
             * making them unmanageable.
```

continued...

...from previous page

```
                      */
            RemoveDialButton( help_widget,
                      XmDIALOG_CANCEL_BUTTON );

            RemoveDialButton( help_widget,
                      XmDIALOG_HELP_BUTTON );

            XtManageChild( help_widget );

            /*
             * Free up storage for XmString
             */
            XmStringFree( motif_string );

            return( help_widget );

    }             /* SetUphelp */
```

You need to pass a parent widget, a name for the dialog, and a help message (a normal text string) such as:

"When in danger or in doubt\nRun in circles, scream and shout\n"

Since obtaining further help is not an option in our help messages, you can call `RemoveDialButton()` to remove both the cancel and the help buttons. `SetUpHelp()`, therefore, creates an information dialog that will go away if you press the return key or click the mouse (button 1) in the OK button. There isn't a callback set up for this widget so it automatically goes away. In your programs, you'll probably want to set up a callback.

ERROR DIALOGS

An error dialog is used to let the user know that something went wrong:

```
#include   <Xm/MessageB.h>

Widget        widget;
Widget        parent;
String        name;
ArgList       args;
Cardinal      n;

widget = XmCreateErrorDialog( parent,
            name,
            args,
            n );
```

A sample error dialog appears in Figure 4-12. The function
XmCreateErrorDialog() creates an error dialog. You're getting the hint that all
the parameters on these XmCreate-what-ever functions are the same, right?

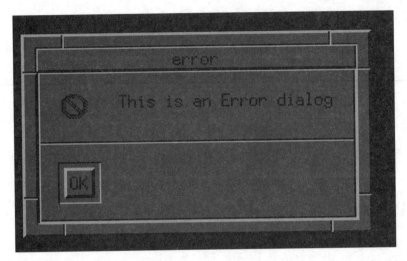

Figure 4-12. An Error Dialog. — ℓ𝒸𝑜𝓇 is "◊"

The function ErrorDialog(), below, acts much the same as SetUpHelp(). The
only difference is that you're creating an error dialog, rather than an information
dialog:

```
Widget ErrorDialog( parent, name, message )

Widget      parent;
char        name[];
char        message[];

{           /* ErrorDialog */
            Arg         args[10];
            int         n;
            Widget      widget;
            XmString    motif_string, Str2XmString();

            motif_string = Str2XmString( message );

            n = 0;
            XtSetArg( args[n], XmNmessageString, motif_string ); n++;

            /*
             * Create widget
             */
```

continued...

85

...from previous page

```
            widget = XmCreateErrorDialog( parent,
                         name,
                         args,
                         n );

            RemoveDialButton( widget, XmDIALOG_HELP_BUTTON );
            RemoveDialButton( widget, XmDIALOG_CANCEL_BUTTON );

            XtManageChild( widget );

            XmStringFree( motif_string );

            return( widget );

}           /* ErrorDialog */
```

A WORKING DIALOG FOR BUSY PROGRAMS

Working or progress dialogs tell you that your program is busy doing some time-consuming operation, such as recalculating a large spreadsheet or printing a document. In Motif toolkit programs, the working dialog allows the user a chance to cancel a lengthy operation. As shown in Figure 4-13, the working dialog displays an hour-glass icon to show that your program is busy.

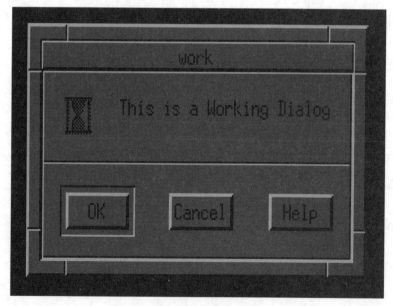

Figure 4-13. A Working Dialog. ~ icon is hour-glass

In the simple example below, the default labels on the pushbuttons are unchanged. Chances are, though, you'll want to replace the "OK" label with "Close." Perhaps you will have other ideas to allow the user to interact regarding a lengthy operation. You may even want to put in a scale widget (see Chapter 10) to show the user how far the operation has gone and how far it is yet to go.

You create the working dialog with XmCreateWorkingDialog():

```
#include   <Xm/MessageB.h>

Widget       widget;
Widget       parent;
String       name;
ArgList      args;
Cardinal     n;

widget = XmCreateWorkingDialog( parent,
           name,
           args,
           n );
```

The function WorkingDialog(), below, creates and pops up a working dialog:

```
Widget WorkingDialog( parent, name, message, callback_func )

Widget       parent;
char         name[];
char         message[];
void         (*callback_func)();

{            /* WorkingDialog */
             Arg         args[10];
             int         n;
             Widget      widget, ok_widget;
             XmString    motif_string, Str2XmString();

             motif_string = Str2XmString( message );

             n = 0;
             XtSetArg( args[n], XmNmessageString, motif_string ); n++;

             /*
              * Create widget
              */
             widget = XmCreateWorkingDialog( parent,
                                        name,
                                        args,
                                        n );

             /*
```

continued...

87

...from previous page

```
                       * Set up callback on
                       * Cancel button.
                       */
                      XtAddCallback( widget,
                                     XmNcancelCallback,
                                     callback_func,
                                     NULL );

                      XtManageChild( widget );

                      XmStringFree( motif_string );

                      return( widget );

}                     /* WorkingDialog */
```

It sets up a callback function to be called when the user clicks the Cancel pushbutton. The callback cancels the lengthy operation. and the OK choice sends the dialog away.

THE PROMPT DIALOG

After learning many dialogs that seem the same, you're probably a bit bored. So, we'll next tackle a different type of dialog: the prompt dialog. As shown in Figure 4-14, the prompt dialog asks the user to fill in a value.

Figure 4-14. The Prompt Dialog.

The prompt dialog is based on the selection box widget and not on the MessageBox widget. XmCreatePromptDialog() creates a prompt dialog:

```
#include <Xm/SelectioB.h>

Widget       widget;
Widget       parent;
String       name;
ArgList      args;
Cardinal     n;

widget =     XmCreatePromptDialog( parent,
             name,
             args,
             n );
```

Note that the extra include file is different; it is now Xm/SelectioB.h.

So far, the prompt dialog is the same as the earlier dialogs. There are, however, two new resources to change: selectionLabelString, which is the text to place above the user's response, and textString, into which you can put a default response.

The selectionLabelString resource, or XmNselectionLabelString in your Motif program, contains a prompting string. It usually defaults to something dumb like "Selection." To make a clear, understandable dialog for your users, you probably want to change this, using:

```
Arg          args[10];
int          n;
XmString     motif_string, Str2XmString(); /* string.c */

/*
 * Set up the message
 */
motif_string = Str2XmString( "Your Prompt Message Here" );

n = 0;
XtSetArg( args[n], XmNselectionLabelString, motif_string ); n++;

/*
 * Create the widget...
 */
```

You can put in a default response by changing the textString resource. These strings are of the Motif type XmString, so convert your normal C program strings to type XmString:

```
      n = 0;
   XtSetArg( args[n], XmNtextString, motif_string ); n++;

   /*
    * Create the widget...
    */
```

The function PromptDialog(), below, creates and pops up a prompt dialog:

```
   Widget PromptDialog( parent, name, message, callback_func )

   Widget       parent;
   char         name[];
   char         message[];
   void         (*callback_func)();

   {            /* PromptDialog */
   Arg          args[10];
   int          n;
   Widget       widget, ok_widget;
   XmString motif_string, Str2XmString();

   motif_string = Str2XmString( message );

   n = 0;
   XtSetArg( args[n], XmNselectionLabelString, motif_string ); n++;

   widget = XmCreatePromptDialog( parent,
                name,
                args,
                n );

   /*
    * Set up callback for activation,
    * Just for OK button.
    */
   XtAddCallback( widget,
           XmNokCallback,
           callback_func,
           NULL );

   XtManageChild( widget );

   XmStringFree( motif_string );

   return( widget );

   }            /* PromptDialog */
```

The Prompt Callback Function

The prompt dialog also differs from other dialogs—it sends different data to its callback function. The call data in your callback receives a pointer to an XmSelectionBoxCallbackStruct structure:

```
typedef struct
    {
    int         reason;
    XEvent      *event;
    XmString    value;
    int         length;
    } XmSelectionBoxCallbackStruct;
```

The key part here is the value field: it contains the string the user entered into the prompt dialog. If you want to prompt the user, you can pop up a prompt dialog and then set up a callback on the OK pushbutton (do nothing on the cancel pushbutton). If the user types something in and clicks the OK pushbutton, your callback will get the string the user typed. This string is, of course, an XmString type.

Here's a sample callback function for a selection box or a prompt dialog:

```
void select_callback( widget, client_data, sel_struct )

Widget                          widget;
caddr_t                         client_data;
XmSelectionBoxCallbackStruct    *sel_struct;

{       /* select_callback */
    char    *string;

    XmStringGetLtoR( sel_struct->value,
        XmSTRING_DEFAULT_CHARSET,
        &string );

    printf( "Selected [%s]\n", string );
    /* free string when done */
}       /* select_callback */
```

THE FILE SELECTION DIALOG

In just about any editor-based application, such as drawing editors, text editors, electronic-publishing packages, and the like, users pick files to load and save, etc. Motif provides the file-selection dialog to help automate this task. With this dialog, users can browse through directories until they find the file they are looking for. The file-selection dialog also has a built in filtering capability to, for example, view only the files that end ".c" (C program files). A sample file-selection dialog appears in Figure 4-15.

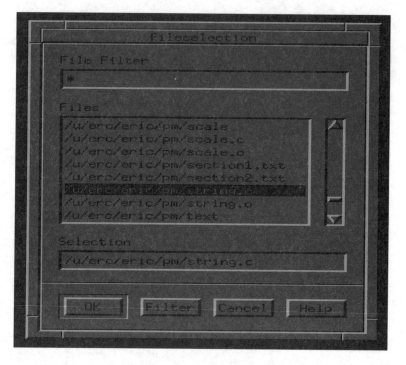

Figure 4-15. The File Selection Dialog.

The file-selection dialog is the most complex of the compound Motif dialogs available. It's handy that the Motif toolkit includes a widget like this, since it handles a very common task. It's also handy that all applications using the file-selection dialog will have a more consistent user interface.

You create a file-selection dialog with XmCreateFileSelectionDialog(). The include file is Xm/FileSB.h:

```
#include <Xm/FileSB.h>

Widget                     widget;
Widget                     parent;
String                     name;
ArgList                    args;
Cardinal                   n;

widget = XmCreateFileSelectionDialog( parent,
                           name,
                           args,
                           n );
```

File Selection Box Resources

Some of the common resources you may want to change in the file selection box include those listed in Figure 4-16.

Resource Name	Defined Name in C	Default
dirMask	XmNdirMask	"*"
dirSpec	XmNdirSpec	NULL
filterLabelString	XmNfilterLabelString	"File Filter"

Figure 4-16. Common Resources.

The dirMask resource is the filtering mask used to choose file names. The default is "*"—that is, display all files in the given directory. You could change that to "*.c" —display only the files ending in ".c". The user can also change this value interactively. The dirMask requires an XmString type, as does the dirSpec resources. (If you're running under SCO Open Desktop 1.0, you'll want to look towards the end of this chapter under the heading, LINKING UNDER SCO'S OPEN DESKTOP.)

The dirSpec resource is the name of the last file chosen by the user. It should contain the complete path and file name for the file. (With a file-selection dialog, users can normally choose more than one file.) By setting this resource, you can specify a default file name.

The filterLabelString resource contains the text string to display as a prompt to the user above the area where the user enters a filter string. The default is the prompt "Filter."

The function FileSelection(), below, creates a file-selection dialog:

```
Widget  FileSelection( parent, name, args, n, callback_func )

Widget        parent;
char          name[];
Arg           args[];
int           n;
void          (*callback_func)();

{             /* FileSelection */
              Widget widget;

              widget = XmCreateFileSelectionDialog( parent,
                            name,
```

continued...

...from previous page

```
                                  args,
                                  n );

        XtAddCallback( widget,
                XmNokCallback,
                callback_func,
                NULL );

        XtManageChild( widget );

        return( widget );

}               /* FileSelection */
```

You can set up any resources in an `Arg` array beforehand to pass to this function. The function also takes a callback function—that is to set up to the OK pushbutton.

The File Selection Callback

The OK pushbutton callback function is called whenever the user clicks in the OK pushbutton. In such a case, the default behavior of the file selection dialog is to remain on the screen. <u>All the other dialogs go away when the default pushbutton is clicked, except for the file-selection dialog.</u> Your callback could unmanage the widget if you want the dialog to go away.

The file selection callback function gets a pointer to an `XmFileSelectionBoxCallbackStruct` structure:

```
    typedef struct
        {
        int         reason;
        XEvent      *event;
        XmString    value;          /* full path name of */
                                    /* selected item */
        int         length;
        XmString    mask;           /* used for filtering */
        int         mask_length;
    } XmFileSelectionBoxCallbackStruct;
```

The most important field of this structure is the `value` field, which contains the full pathname of the selected file.

The following is a sample callback function for the file selection dialog:

```
    void file_callback( widget, client_data, file_struct )

        Widget                              widget;
        caddr_t                                 client_data;
```
continued...

...from previous page

```
    XmFileSelectionBoxCallbackStruct              *file_struct;

{   /* file_callback */
    char    *string;

    XmStringGetLtoR( file_struct->value,
            XmSTRING_DEFAULT_CHARSET,
            &string );

    printf( "File Selection Callback with [%s]\n", string );

}        /* file_callback */
```

Returning the Child Widget

The function XmFileSelectionBoxGetChild() returns the widget of one of the child widgets in a file selection dialog. If you want to find the widget of the OK pushbutton in a file selection dialog, you would use XmFileSelectionBoxGetChild():

```
    Widget          child_widget;
    Widget          dialog_parent;
    unsigned char   which_child;

    child_widget = XmFileSelectionBoxGetChild( dialog_parent,
                                    which_child );
```

The which_child parameter should be one of the following:

```
    XmDIALOG_APPLY_BUTTON (actually the filter button)
    XmDIALOG_CANCEL_BUTTON
    XmDIALOG_DEFAULT_BUTTON
    XmDIALOG_FILTER_LABEL
    XmDIALOG_FILTER_TEXT
    XmDIALOG_HELP_BUTTON
    XmDIALOG_LIST  (we'll cover more on the list widget in Chapter 8)
    XmDIALOG_LIST_LABEL
    XmDIALOG_OK_BUTTON
    XmDIALOG_SELECTION_LABEL
    XmDIALOG_TEXT
```

SOURCE CODE FOR DIALOG.C

The file dialog.c contains a number of convenience routines for creating common dialogs:

```
/*
 *          dialog.c
 *          Functions for Motif dialogs
 *
 *          Written for Power Programming Motif
 *
 */

#include        <X11/Intrinsic.h>
#include        <X11/StringDefs.h>
#include        <Xm/Xm.h>
#include        <Xm/MessageB.h>
#include        <Xm/SelectioB.h>
#include        <Xm/FileSB.h>

Widget ErrorDialog( parent, name, message )

Widget          parent;
char            name[];
char            message[];

/*
 *          ErrorDialog() creates an XmErrorDialog
 *          widget.This widget has no callback set up.
 *          We use this widget to present a simple error
 *          message (with no hope of un-doing the error).
 *
 *          parent = parent widget
 *          name = name of the ErrorDialog widget
 *          message = text string to be displayed.
 */

{               /* ErrorDialog */
    Arg         args[10];
    int         n;
    Widget      widget;
    XmString    motif_string, Str2XmString();

    /*
     * Set up the message
     */
    motif_string = Str2XmString( message );

    n = 0;
    XtSetArg( args[n], XmNmessageString, motif_string ); n++;

    /*
     * Create widget
     */
    widget = XmCreateErrorDialog( parent
            name,
            args,
            n );
```

continued...

...from previous page

```
                    /*
                     * Get rid of "Help"
                     * push button.
                     */
                    RemoveDialButton( widget, XmDIALOG_HELP_BUTTON );
                    RemoveDialButton( widget, XmDIALOG_CANCEL_BUTTON );

                    XtManageChild( widget );

                    /*
                     * Free storage for XmString
                     */
                    XmStringFree( motif_string );

                    return( widget );

}                   /* ErrorDialog */

Widget              FileSelection( parent, name, args, n, callback_func )

Widget              parent;
char                name[];
Arg                 args[];
int                 n;
void                (*callback_func)();

/*
 *                  FileSelection() creates a file selection box
 *                  dialog widget.  This widget normally remains
 *                  on the screen after a file choice is made.
 */

{                   /* FileSelection */
                    Widget    widget;
                    /*
                     * Create widget
                     */
                    widget = XmCreateFileSelectionDialog( parent,
                                    name,
                                    args,
                                    n );

                    /*
                     * Set up callback on OK
                     * button.
                     */
                    XtAddCallback( widget,
                            XmNokCallback,
                            callback_func,
```

continued...

```
...from previous page
                NULL );
        XtManageChild( widget );

        return( widget );

}         /* FileSelection */

void present_help( widget, client_data, call_data )

Widget   widget;
caddr_t  client_data;
caddr_t  call_data;

/*
 *       present_help() creates
 *       an help_widget.
 */

{         /* present_help */
        Widget  help_widget, SetUpHelp();

        help_widget = SetUpHelp( widget,
                        "Application Help", /* name */
                        client_data );      /* message */
}         /* present_help */

Widget SetUpHelp( parent, name, message )

Widget   parent;
char     name[];
char     message[];

/*
 *       SetUpHelp creates a dialog
 *       widget with your help message.
 */

{         /* SetUphelp */
        Arg             args[10];
        int             n;
        Widget          help_widget;
        XmString        motif_string, Str2XmString();

        /*
         * Set up the help message
         */
        motif_string = Str2XmString( message );

        n = 0;
        XtSetArg( args[n], XmNmessageString, motif_string ); n++;
```
continued...

...from previous page

```
/*
            * Create help widget
            */
          help_widget = XmCreateInformationDialog( parent,
                              name,
                              args,
                              n );

          /*
           * Normally, an Information dialog
           * has three buttons: OK, Cancel
           * and Help. Since this is the
           * help dialog, we get rid of the
           * Cancel and Help buttons, by
           * making them unmanageable.
           */
          RemoveDialButton( help_widget,
                      XmDIALOG_CANCEL_BUTTON );

          RemoveDialButton( help_widget,
                      XmDIALOG_HELP_BUTTON );

          XtManageChild( help_widget );

          /*
           * Free up storage for XmString
           */
          XmStringFree( motif_string );

          return( help_widget );

}         /* SetUphelp */

RemoveDialButton( widget, which_button )

Widget    widget;
int       which_button;

/*
 *        Removes (unmanages) the "Help"
 *        push button from a Motif
 *        dialog widget, or other buttons.
 *        which_button should be one of:
 *        XmDIALOG_CANCEL_BUTTON
 *        XmDIALOG_OK_BUTTON
 *        XmDIALOG_HELP_BUTTON
 */

{         /* RemoveDialButton */
          Widget  dead_widget;
```

continued...

...from previous page

```
            /*
             * Normally, an Information dialog
             * has three buttons: OK, Cancel
             * and Help. Here, we get rid of
             * a button.
             */
            dead_widget = XmMessageBoxGetChild( widget,
                            which_button );

            XtUnmanageChild( dead_widget );

}           /* RemoveDialButton */

Widget     PromptDialog( parent, name, message, callback_func )

Widget     parent;
char       name[];
char       message[];
void       (*callback_func)();

/*
 *         PromptDialog() is a convenience routine used to
 *         create a Motif Prompt Dialog.
 */

{          /* PromptDialog */
Arg                args[10];
int                n;
Widget             widget, ok_widget;
XmString           motif_string, Str2XmString();

            /*
             * Set up the message
             */
            motif_string = Str2XmString( message );

            n = 0;
            XtSetArg( args[n], XmNselectionLabelString, motif_string ); n++;

            /*
             * Create widget
             */
            widget = XmCreatePromptDialog( parent,
                            name,
                            args,
                            n );
            /*
             * Set up callback for activation,
             * Just for OK button.
             */
```

continued...

...from previous page

```
            XtAddCallback( widget,
                    XmNokCallback,
                    callback_func,
                    NULL );

            XtManageChild( widget );

            /*
             * Free storage for XmString
             */
            XmStringFree( motif_string );

            return( widget );

}           /* PromptDialog */

Widget  WarningDialog( parent, name, message, callback_func )

Widget     parent;
char       name[];
char       message[];
void       (*callback_func)();

/*
 *      WarningDialog() creates a warning dialog widget.
 *      It has Ok and Cancel buttons. callback_func()
 *      is called if Ok is pressed.
 */

{           /* WarningDialog */
        Arg             args[10];
        int             n;
        Widget          widget, ok_widget;
        XmString        motif_string, Str2XmString();

        /*
         * Set up the message
         */
         motif_string = Str2XmString( message );

        n = 0;
        XtSetArg( args[n], XmNmessageString, motif_string ); n++;

        /*
         * Create widget
         */
        widget = XmCreateWarningDialog( parent,
                        name,
                        args,
                        n );
```

continued...

...from previous page

```
            /*
             * Get rid of "Help"
             * push button.
             */
            RemoveDialButton( widget,
                XmDIALOG_HELP_BUTTON );

            /*
             * Set up callback on OK
             * button.
             */
            XtAddCallback( widget,
                XmNokCallback,
                callback_func,
                NULL );

            XtManageChild( widget );

            /*
             * Free storage for XmString
             */
            XmStringFree( motif_string );

            return( widget );

}           /* WarningDialog */

Widget    WorkingDialog( parent, name, message, callback_func )

Widget    parent;
char      name[];
char      message[];
void      (*callback_func)();

/*
 *        WorkingDialog() creates a working dialog widget,
 *        something to use when your program is off busy
 *        somewhere.
 */

{         /* WorkingDialog */
          Arg               args[10];
          int               n;
          Widget            widget, ok_widget;
          XmString          motif_string, Str2XmString();

          /*
           * Set up the message
           */
          motif_string = Str2XmString( message );
```

continued...

...from previous page

```
            n = 0;
            XtSetArg( args[n], XmNmessageString, motif_string ); n++;
            /*
             * Create widget
             */
            widget = XmCreateWorkingDialog( parent,
                                    name,
                                    args,
                                    n );

            /*
             * Set up callback on
             * Cancel button.
             */
            XtAddCallback( widget,
                    XmNcancelCallback,
                    callback_func,
                    NULL );

            XtManageChild( widget );

            /*
             * Free storage for XmString
             */
            XmStringFree( motif_string );

            return( widget );

}           /* WorkingDialog */

/* end of file */
```

THE DIALTEST PROGRAM

The dialtest program tests out five types of Motif dialogs—probably more types of dialogs than you ever want to use in your programs. The beginning of dialtest.c contains the callback functions. Note the double callback for the quit process—"are you sure" leads to "are you really sure", which then leads to the quit_callback() that terminates the program. The dialtest program shows how to create a number of dialogs and demonstrates what happens when you choose files in the file selection dialog.

Source Code for Dialtest.c

Here is the source code for the dialtest.c program:

```
*       dialtest.c
*       Example Motif dialogs
*
*       Written for Power Programming Motif
*/
#include        <X11/Intrinsic.h>
#include        <X11/StringDefs.h>
#include        <Xm/Xm.h>
#include        <Xm/Command.h>
#include        <Xm/FileSB.h>
#include        <Xm/SelectioB.h>

/*
*       Globals
*/
Widget          quit_widget;

void quit_callback( widget, client_data, call_data )

Widget                          widget;
XmAnyCallbackStruct             client_data;
caddr_t                         call_data;

/*
*       quit_callback() is the callback for the
*       Motif quit button. This function
*       terminates the program by calling exit().
*/

{       /* quit_callback */

XtCloseDisplay( XtDisplay( widget ) );
exit( 0 );

}       /* quit_callback */

void are_you_really_sure( widget, client_data, call_data )

Widget                          widget;
XmAnyCallbackStruct             client_data;
caddr_t                         call_data;

{       /* are_you_really_sure */
        Widget  sure, WarningDialog();

        sure = WarningDialog( quit_widget,
                "ReallySure",
                "Are you REALLY\nREALLY sure\nYou want to quit?\n",
                quit_callback );

}       /* are_you_really_sure */
```

continued...

...from previous page
```
void are_you_sure( widget, client_data, call_data )

Widget          widget;
caddr_t         client_data;
caddr_t         call_data;

{       /* are_you_sure */
        Widget  sure, WarningDialog();

        sure = WarningDialog( widget,
                "sure",
                "Are you sure\nYou want to quit?\n"
                are_you_really_sure );

}       /* are_you_sure */

void generic_callback( widget, client_data, call_data )

Widget          widget;
caddr_t         client_data;
caddr_t         call_data;

{       /* generic_callback */

        printf( "Callback\n" );

}       /* generic_callback */

void file_callback( widget, client_data, file_struct )

Widget                                          widget;
caddr_t                                         client_data;
XmFileSelectionBoxCallbackStruct                *file_struct;

/*
 *      Callback function for a file selection box.
 *      file_struct contains the following:
 *
 *      typedef struct
 *              {
 *              int             reason;
 *              XEvent          *event;
 *              XmString        value;          -- full path name of
 *                                              -- selected item
 *              int             length;
 *              XmString        mask;           -- used for filtering
 *              int             mask_length;
 *              } XmFileSelectionBoxCallbackStruct;
 *
 */
```
continued...

...from previous page

```
{       /* file_callback */
        char    *string;

        XmStringGetLtoR( file_struct->value,
                XmSTRING_DEFAULT_CHARSET,
                &string );

        printf( "File Selection Callback with [%s]\n", string );
        /* free string when done */
}       /* file_callback */

void select_callback( widget, client_data, sel_struct )

Widget                                          widget;
caddr_t                                         client_data;
XmSelectionBoxCallbackStruct                    *sel_struct;

/*
 *      Generic selection box (prompt) callback
 *      function.The sel_struct is defined as:
 *
 *      typedef struct
 *              {
 *              int             reason;
 *              XEvent          *event;
 *              XmString        value;
 *              int             length;
 *              } XmSelectionBoxCallbackStruct;
 *
 */

{       /* select_callback */
        char    *string;

        XmStringGetLtoR( sel_struct->value,
                XmSTRING_DEFAULT_CHARSET,
                &string );

        printf( "Selected [%s]\n", string );
        /* free string when done */
}       /* select_callback */

main( argc, argv )

int     argc;
char    *argv[];

{       /* main */
        Widget  parent, CreatePushButton(); /* push.c */
        Widget  errn, ErrorDialog();                /* dialog.c */
        Widget  filesel, FileSelection();           /* dialog.c */
```
continued...

...from previous page

```
Widget    prompt, PromptDialog();          /* dialog.c */
Widget    work, WorkingDialog();           /* dialog.c */
Arg       args[ 10 ];
int       n;

parent = XtInitialize( argv[0],
                       "DialogTest",
                       NULL,
                       0,
                       &argc,
                       argv );

n = 0;
XtSetArg( args[n], XmNallowShellResize, True ); n++;
XtSetValues( parent, args, n );

/*
 * Set up size for quit button
 */
n = 0;
XtSetArg( args[n], XmNwidth, 180 ); n++;
XtSetArg( args[n], XmNheight, 50 ); n++;

/*
 * Create the quit-button widget
 */
quit_widget = CreatePushButton( parent,
        "quit",                       /* widget name */
        args,
        n,
        are_you_sure );               /* callback_func */

/*
 * Create an Error and Working Dialog
 */
errn = ErrorDialog( parent,
                    "error",
                    "This is an Error dialog" );

work = WorkingDialog( parent,
                      "work",
                      "This is a Working Dialog",
                      generic_callback );

/*
 * The Prompt dialog has a special
 * callback structure, see
 * select_callback(), above.
 */
prompt = PromptDialog( parent,
                       "prompt",
```

continued...

107

...from previous page

```
                                        "This is a Prompt Dialog\nEnter something",
                                        select_callback );
        /*
         * Note that in SCO Open Desktop 1.0,
         * the file selection box is documented
         * to not work.
         */
        n = 0;
        filesel = FileSelection( parent,
                "fileselection",
                args, n,
                file_callback );

        /*
         * Bring the top-level widget
         * (and all its children) to
         * reality, that is map the windows.
         */
        XtRealizeWidget( parent );
        XtMainLoop();

}       /* main */

/* end of file */
```

Compiling and Linking the Dialtest Program

The `dialtest` program needs the following C files:

```
dialog.c
dialtest.c
push.c (from Chapter 3)
string.c (from Chapter 2)
```

It also requires the:

```
PW library                (for the file selection dialog)
```

You can compile the `dialtest` program with a command something like:

```
cc -o dialtest dialtest.c dialog.c push.c string.c -lXm -lXt -lX11 -lPW
```

If you use `Makefile` in Appendix C, you can simply type:

```
make dialtest
```

or

```
make all
```

Note that the file selection dialog usually needs the PW library for its file-searching routines. You can usually link this in with -lPW. On other systems, like SCO's Open Desktop, you'll probably have an easier time using Makefile in Appendix C.

Linking Under SCO Open Desktop

The release notes for Open Desktop 1.0 state that the file selection box doesn't work under Open Desktop. We've found that under SCO you do not want to link in the PW Library. In addition, the filter string of "*" (the dirMask resource) doesn't work—you will see "<NoMatch>" instead of a list of files. If you're using Open Desktop, you probably want to set the dirMask resource to something different than the default "*". We found that a filter string of "*?" works.

Running the Dialtest Program

The dialtest program, like all the sample programs in this book, requires no command-line parameters. When you run the dialtest program, you'll see five top-level windows: the dialtest application's window (which contains only a quit pushbutton), a file selection dialog, a prompt dialog, a work dialog, and an error dialog, as shown in Figure 4-17.

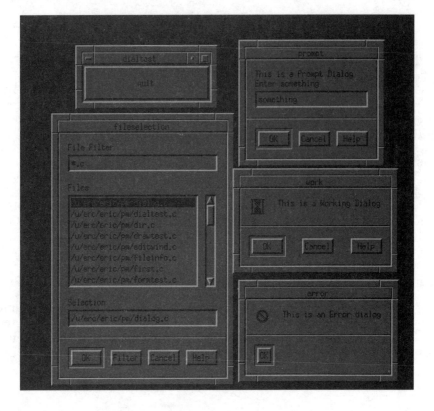

Figure 4-17. The Dialtest Program in Action.

You shouldn't have much of a problem trying to interact with the dialogs. Test them out and see what happens when you type a value into the prompt dialog, for example. You'll use a number of these dialogs in programs later in this book.

To quit the `dialtest` program, click on the quit pushbutton. When you see the "Are you sure?" warning dialog, click on the OK pushbutton. That dialog will go away and will be replaced by one that asks "are you really, really sure." Click on the OK pushbutton again, and the `dialtest` program will quit.

WHICH DIALOG TO USE?

We've presented a host of different types of Motif dialogs and their convenience functions. In your applications, you're going to have to figure out which dialogs are appropriate for what you want to display. A good source of help is the *OSF/Motif Style Guide* that should be part of your Motif developer's package. See Appendix D for more information.

MOTIF FUNCTIONS AND MACROS INTRODUCED IN THIS CHAPTER

The following is a list of Motif functions and macros introduced in this chapter.

```
XmCreateErrorDialog()
XmCreateFileSelectionDialog()
XmCreateInformationDialog()
XmCreatePromptDialog()
XmCreateWarningDialog()
XmCreateWorkingDialog()
XmFileSelectionBoxGetChild()
XmMessageBoxGetChild()
```

You should be familiar with these functions and macros before you move on to Chapter 5.

X TOOLKIT FUNCTIONS AND MACROS INTRODUCED IN THIS CHAPTER

The following is a list of X Toolkit functions and macros that were introduced in this chapter.

```
XtUnmanageChild()
```

You should be familiar with this function before you move on to Chapter 5.

SUMMARY

This chapter introduced Motif's dialog widgets and showed how to create some of the more common dialogs, including the prompt dialog and the file-selection box. These dialogs are created using Motif's convenience routines. Later on in this book, you'll create a dialog from scratch the hard way.

# Chapter 5

Creating Menu Bars

M ost Motif-based applications have a menu bar at the top of the application's main window. Menus are pulled down from this bar—they offer the user an easy-to-learn method of entering commands into an application. Using a menu bar at the top of the main window makes your applications consistent, so the user has an easier time learning your program. The menu bar also allows the user to browse the available menu choices to see what commands are available.

This chapter focuses on creating the actual menu bar—you'll create a menu bar similar to the one shown in Figure 5-1. Chapter 6 documents how to create pulldown menus from the menu bar.

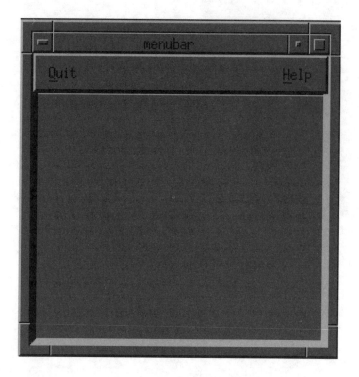

Figure 5-1. A Motif Menu Bar.

As you've probably guessed, there are a number of Motif widgets that when connected together, form the menu bar. The widget hierarchy looks like this:

        * Top-level Shell
            * Main Window Widget
                * Menubar widget
                        * Cascade Widget (quit)
                        * Cascade Widget (help)

THE MAIN WINDOW WIDGET

The main window widget exists as a handy convenience, serving to manage the main window of an application. This widget manages up to five specialized child widgets: the menu bar, a work area (an area where your application performs its functions), a command area (an area for the user to enter single-line commands), and vertical and horizontal scroll bars.

114

You don't have to set up all five children in order to use a main window widget. In fact many applications only use a few children. The scroll bars, in particular, are often not needed since you place the scroll bars on text or list widgets as needed, rather than on the whole work area. (We'll cover scroll bars starting in Chapter 7.)

The primary reason to create a main window widget here is that in order to create a menu bar, you need a parent widget to manage the menu bar. The main window widget serves this purpose quite nicely and encourages your applications to use more of the standard features of Motif. So, after calling XtInitialize(), the first thing you need to do is to create a main window widget:

```
#include <Xm/MainW.h>

Widget        widget;
Widget        parent;
String        name;
ArgList       args;
Cardinal n;

widget = XmCreateMainWindow( parent,
      name,
      args,
      n );
```

Call XtManageChild() after creating the widget:

```
XtManageChild( widget );
```

Figure 5-2 illustrates the XmMainWindow widget class.

Widget Class Name	Class Pointer	Created By
XmMainWindow	xmMainWindowWidgetClass	XmCreateMainWindow()

Figure 5-2. The XmMainWindow Widget Class.

Before you create the main window widget, you may want to customize it. One way to do this is to hard-code a width and height, using the width and height resources (XmNwidth and XmNheight) in your C programs:

```
Arg    args[10];
int    n;
int    width, height;
```

continued...

...from previous page
```
n = 0;
XtSetArg( args[n], XmNwidth, width ); n++;
XtSetArg( args[n], XmNheight, height ); n++;

/* create the widget... */
```

You can also customize the main window widget by specfiying a width and height in a resource file. This approach is discussed in Chapter 13. You can also add a 3D shadowing effect, using the shadowThickness resource (XmNshadowThickness in your C programs):

```
Arg    args[10];
int    n;

n = 0;
XtSetArg( args[n], XmNshadowThickness, 4 ); n++;
/* XtSetArg( args[n], XmNshadowThickness, 0 ); n++; */

/* create the widget... */
```

The number 4 represents a shadow that is four pixels wide.

Figure 5-3 shows a main window with a shadow thickness of 4. Note the 3D effect of the shadow at the bottom of the window.

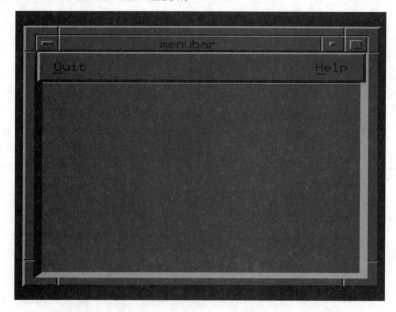

Figure 5-3. A Main Window with a Shadow Thickness of 4.

Use the file `mainwind.c` (given in a later section) to experiment with the shadowing effect, using various pixel sizes for the `shadowThickness` resource. Figure 5-4 shows a main window with a shadow thickness of 0.

Figure 5-4. A Main Window with a Shadow Thickness of 0.

Separators

You can use the `showSeparator` resource (`XmNshowSeparator` in your C programs) to create separators:

```
Arg    args[10];

int    n;

n = 0;
XtSetArg( args[n], XmNshowSeparator, True ); n++;  /*
XtSetArg( args[n], XmNshowSeparator, False ); n++; */

/* create the widget... */
```

The `showSeparator` resource is a boolean value that specifies whether or not separator lines are to be created between the various children of the main window. The default is `False`—meaning that no separators will be used. Try setting the value to `True` and `False` to see which you prefer.

Separators are widgets, and you can use two main window functions—`XmMainWindowSep1()` and `XmMainWindowSep2()`—to retrieve their widget values:

117

```
#include <Xm/MainW.h>

Widget    main_widget; /* main window */
Widget    sep1_widget; /* child separator 1 */
Widget    sep2_widget; /* child separator 2 */

sep1_widget = XmMainWindowSep1( main_widget );

sep2_widget = XmMainWindowSep2( main_widget );
```

What the Main Window Manages

In addition to the optional separators, the main window widget manages five specialized (and optional) child widgets, identified in resources, as shown in Figure 5-5.

Resource Name	Name in C Programs
commandWindow	XmNcommandWindow
horizontalScrollBar	XmNhorizontalScrollBar
menuBar	XmNmenuBar
verticalScrollBar	XmNverticalScrollBar
workWindow	XmNworkWindow

Figure 5-5. Specialized Child Widgets Managed by the Main Window Widget.

There's a trick to these resources, however—you cannot get or set resources until the child widgets are created, but the main window widget is the parent of these children. To work around this trick you first create the main window widget, and then you create the children you want—all with a parent of the main window widget. Then you tell the main window about the children you already created. It's weird, but it works. The function that tells the main window to take care of its children is XmMainWindowSetAreas().

```
#include      <Xm/MainW.h>

Widget        main_window;
Widget        menu_bar;
Widget        command_widget;
Widget        horiz_scrollbar;
Widget        vert_scrollbar;
Widget        work_widget;

XmMainWindowSetAreas( main_window,
      menu_bar,
```
continued...

...from previous page
```
        command_widget,
        horiz_scrollbar,
        vert_scrollbar,
        work_widget );
```

You cannot call `XmMainWindowSetAreas()` until you've created all of the five child widgets you plan to use. In the `menubar` program (in the file `mtest.c`), we created a menu-bar child only. Here's how you'd call `XmMainWindowSetAreas()` with only one child:

```
XmMainWindowSetAreas( main_window,      /* main window */
        menu_bar,                       /* menu bar */
        (Widget) NULL,                  /* command area */
        (Widget) NULL,                  /* horiz scroll */
        (Widget) NULL,                  /* vert scroll */
        (Widget) NULL );                /* work area */
```

The CreateMainWindow() Function

We've put together a convenient routine to create main window widgets. `CreateMainWindow()` takes care of the separators and shadow thickness. `CreateMainWindow()`, takes a parent widget (assumed to be a top-level shell), a name, and a hard-coded width and height, as shown in the next section.

Source Code for Mainwind.c

The following is the source code for the file `mainwind.c`.

```
/*
 *      mainwind.c
 *      Create an XmMainWindow for basic Motif applications
 *
 *      Written for Power Programming Motif
 *
 */

#include     <X11/Intrinsic.h>
#include     <X11/StringDefs.h>
#include     <Xm/Xm.h>
#include     <Xm/MainW.h>

Widget CreateMainWindow( parent, name, width, height )

Widget    parent;            /* a top-level application shell */
char      name[];            /* name of main window */
continued...
```

...from previous page

```
int      width, height;      /* size of main window */

/*
 *    CreateMainWindow() takes a parent widget
 *    (assumed to be a top-level shell), a name
 *    and hard-coded width and height values,
 *    then creates a main window widget, which
 *    will hold an application's menu bar and
 *    main area.
 */

{      /* CreateMainWindow */
       Widget         main_window;
       Arg        args[10];
       int        n;

       /*
        * Set up MainWindow options
        */
       n = 0;
       XtSetArg( args[n], XmNwidth, width ); n++;
       XtSetArg( args[n], XmNheight, height ); n++;

       /*
        * Try different amounts of shadow
        * thicknesses on the main window.
        */
       XtSetArg( args[n], XmNshadowThickness, 4 ); n++;
       /* XtSetArg( args[n], XmNshadowThickness, 0 ); n++; */

       /*
        * Try with the separators on and off.
        * The default is False.
        */
       XtSetArg( args[n], XmNshowSeparator, True ); n++;
       /* XtSetArg( args[n], XmNshowSeparator, False ); n++; */

       /*
        * Create a Main window, on which
        * we'll later hang our menu bar
        */
       main_window = XmCreateMainWindow( parent,
              "main",
              args,
              n );

       XtManageChild( main_window );

       return( main_window );
```

continued...

...from previous page
```
}      /* CreateMainWindow */

/* end of file */
```

THE MENUBAR WIDGET

Now that you've created a main window widget to manage the application's widgets, you need to create a menubar widget to manage a menu bar.

A menubar is really a `RowColumn` widget—one of the set of container widgets. A convenient function, `XmCreateMenuBar()` takes care of all the work involved in creating a `RowColumn` widget and configuring that widget as a menu bar. This widget manages a bar across the application's main window. The bar contains the names of pulldown menus.

If you resize the window to be too small for a single line, the menubar will try to make two or more lines to hold the menu names. Figure 5-6 shows a double-line menubar.

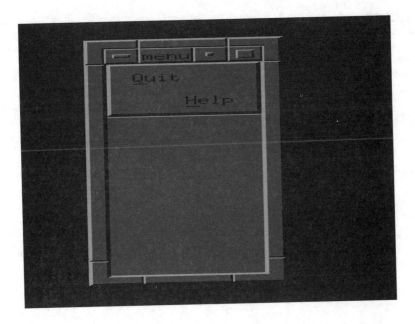

Figure 5-6. A Double-line Menubar.

The function XmCreateMenuBar() creates a menu bar:

```
#include         <Xm/RowColumn.h>

Widget   widget;
Widget   parent;
String   name;
ArgList args; Cardinal n;

widget = XmCreateMenuBar( parent,
         name,
         args,
         n );
```

Call XtManageChild() after creating the widget:

```
XtManageChild( widget );
```

The menubar widget (which we know is really a RowColumn widget) holds only one type of child widget: a cascade button widget.

Cascade Button Widgets

Cascade button widgets hold the names of any pulldown menus on a menu bar. The cascade button widget is a lot like the pushbutton widget, only the cascade button is used to link a menu bar and a menu (or a menu and a submenu). Even so, a cascade button has an activateCallback function, just like a pushbutton, and you can really do what you want in the activateCallback. Chapter 6 covers how to link a cascade button to a menu and how to create pulldown menus. For now, though, we'll treat the cascade button like a pushbutton, and pop-up dialog boxes when the user clicks in the menu bar. Figure 5-7 illustrates the Cascade Button Widget Class.

Widget Class	Name Class Pointer	Created By
XmCascadeButton	xmCascadeButtoWidgetClass	XmCreateCascadeButton

Figure 5-7. The Cascade Button Widget Class.

To create a cascade button, use XmCreateCascadeButton():

```
#include         <Xm/CascadeB.h>

Widget         widget;
```
continued...

122

...from previous page
```
Widget          parent;
String          name;
ArgList         args;
Cardinal        n;

widget = XmCreateCascadeButton( parent,
                name,
                args,
                n );
```

Call XtManageChild() after creating the widget:

```
XtManageChild( widget );
```

You should assume the parent is a menu bar or menu pane (see Chapter 6 for more information on menu panes). In the following sections, you'll create cascade buttons in the menu bar to pop up a help message and to quit the application.

The Help Button

Not only is it a good idea to provide online help in an application, the Motif style guide essentially demands it. In the Motif style, most menu bars have a "Help" choice as the last choice (on the far right) of the menu bar. Figure 5-8 shows a menu bar with a help choice on the far right.

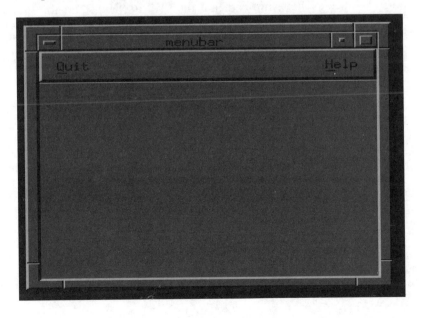

Figure 5-8. A Menu Bar with a Help Choice on the Far Right.

123

The help cascade button normally calls up a help menu. For now, though, you'll use a pop-up help message—an information dialog similar to the one we introduced in Chapter 4. The only thing special about this cascade button is that you want the button to be on the far right, as the Motif Help choice is supposed to be. To do this, you have to set up the resource menuHelpWidget (XmNmenuHelpWidget in your C programs):

```
Widget    menu_bar;

Widget    help_widget;
Arg       args[10];
int    n;

n = 0;
XtSetArg( args[n], XmNmenuHelpWidget, help_widget ); n++;

XtSetValues( menu_bar, args, n );
```

The menuHelpWidget resource needs to be set on the parent menu bar (not on the help cascade button) and needs to specify a widget, in this case, the help cascade button widget. After you've created and managed the help cascade button, use XtSetValues() to set the value of this resource into the menubar widget.

Mnemonics in Menu Bars

In Figure 5-8 you may have noticed that the "H" in "Help" on the menu bar is underlined. This shows that H is a Motif mnemonic. What this means is that you can press Meta-H on the keyboard, and the program will act the same as if you clicked in the Help cascade button. A better term for mnemonic could be keyboard shortcut.

Note

(The Meta key has a different symbol on just about every keyboard. this is why we use the generic term "Meta." On the Data General Aviion, for example, the Meta key is labeled "Alt." "Alt" is also used on any PC keyboard when running SCO's Open Desktop or Interactive's 386 UNIX. On a Sun SPARCStation with a Type 4 keyboard, the Meta key is not the key labeled "Alt," but instead the key with the diamond-shaped label that sits right next to the "Alt" key. On an Hewlett-Packard 300 or 800, the Meta key is labeled "Extend Char." You'll have to experiment to find your Meta key, if you don't know it where it is already.)

Set the mnemonic resource (XmNmnemonic in your C programs) with the value of the letter you want to use as a mnemonic:

```
Arg   arg[10];
continued...
```

124

...from previous page
```
int    n;

n = 0;
XtSetArg( args[n], XmNmnemonic, 'H' ); n++;

/* create the widget... */
```

In this example (as is the Motif style), we use the letter "H." This allows you to type Meta-H rather than using the mouse to click in the help cascade button. The mnemonics help expert users and people who are touch-typists. A lot of folks would rather keep their hands on the keyboard than interrupt their work to track down the mouse on their desk. You'll find that the designers of Motif invested a lot of effort in providing keyboard shortcuts to common functions. You'll use a mnemonic of "Q" when you create a quit button.

Creating a Help Button

CreateHelpWidget () creates a cascade button with the label "Help":

```
Widget CreateHelpWidget( parent, message )

Widget        parent;
char          message[];

{   /* CreateHelpWidget */
    Widget          help_widget;
    Arg             args[ 10 ];
    int             n;
    void            present_help(); /* dialog.c */

    /*
     *      Set Meta-H as a short-cut for calling
     *      up help.
     */
    n = 0;
    XtSetArg( args[n], XmNmnemonic, 'H' ); n++;

    /*
     * Create help menu bar item
     */
    help_widget = XmCreateCascadeButton( parent,
            "Help",
            args,
            n );

    XtManageChild( help_widget );

    /*
     * Add a help call-back,
```
continued...

125

...from previous page
```
          * to pop up help on cue.
          */
         XtAddCallback( help_widget,
                 XmNactivateCallback,
                 present_help,
                 message );

         /*
          * Set our help widget as the
          * default Motif help widget
          */
         n = 0;
         XtSetArg( args[n], XmNmenuHelpWidget, help_widget ); n++;

         XtSetValues( parent, args, n );

         return( help_widget );

    }     /* CreateHelpWidget */
```

CreateHelpWidget() makes Meta-H the mnemonic for help and sets up the cascade button as the menu bar's help button (which is normally placed on the far right of the menu bar). It uses the present_help() function in dialog.c (see Chapter 4) as the help cascade button's callback function. The present_help() function creates a pop-up information dialog that displays the help message. This help message is passed to the CreateHelpWidget() function. The parent widget is assumed to be a menu bar widget.

A Quit Item in a Menu Bar

You're now going to create a very simple menu, with only two choices: quit and help. The quit choice is a lot like the help choice, in that you create a cascade button and set the activateCallback to call a function. This callback function creates and pops up a warning dialog box that asks you, "Are you sure you want to quit?"

The function CreateQuitButton(), in the file menubar.c, shown in the source code in the next section, creates the quit cascade button and sets up the letter "Q" as the mnemonic. The way the quit operation works is essentially the same as the dialtest program in Chapter 4.

Source Code for Menubar.c

The file menubar.c contains a set of utility functions for creating a menu bar with at least two choices: a quit choice that quits your program and a help choice that displays a help message. In your fancier applications, you'll also want to create a help menu, but for purposes of this book, you'll be using just one pop-up help message.

Virtually all of your Motif applications will have a menu bar across the top and pulldown menus. We've covered the menu bar here; the pulldown menus are discussed in Chapter 6. The following is the source code for menubar.c.

```
/*
 *      menubar.c
 *      Motif routines to create a menu bar,
 *      with a quit button and pop-up help.
 *
 *      Written for Programming Motif
 *
 */


#include        <X11/Intrinsic.h>
#include        <X11/StringDefs.h>
#include        <Xm/Xm.h>
#include        <Xm/RowColumn.h>
#include        <Xm/CascadeB.h>

Widget CreateMenubar( parent, help_message )

Widget          parent;
char            help_message[];

/*
 *      CreateMenubar() creates a menu bar in
 *      the parent widget, assumed to be a
 *      main window widget.
 */

{       /* CreateMenubar */
        Widget  menu_bar;
        Widget  help, CreateHelpWidget();
        Widget  quit_widget, CreateQuitButton();
        Arg     args[ 10 ];
        int     n;

        /*
        * Create menu bar. Note: we assume the
        * menu bar is created with a main
        * window widget as a parent.
        */ n = 0;
        menu_bar = XmCreateMenuBar( parent,
                "menu_bar",
                args,
                n );

        XtManageChild( menu_bar );
```

continued...

127

...from previous page

```
        /*
         * Create a help widget, with one
         * help message. This isn't
         * context-sensitive help, but
         * it's better than nothing.
         */
        help = CreateHelpWidget( menu_bar, help_message );

        /*
         * Create a quit button
         */
        quit_widget = CreateQuitButton( menu_bar );

        return( menu_bar );

}       /* CreateMenubar */

Widget CreateHelpWidget( parent, message )

Widget parent;
char    message[];

 /*
  *      CreateHelpWidget() takes a parent (menu bar)
  *      widget and a help message (C text string) and
  *      then creates a help widget and button in the
  *      given menu bar.
  */

{       /* CreateHelpWidget */
        Widget          help_widget;
        Arg             args[ 10 ];
        int             n;
        void            present_help(); /* dialog.c */

        /*
         * Set Meta-H as a short-cut for calling
         * up help.
         */
        n = 0;
        XtSetArg( args[n], XmNmnemonic, 'H' ); n++;

        /*
         * Create help menu bar item
         */
        help_widget = XmCreateCascadeButton( parent,
                        "Help",
                        args,
                        n );

        XtManageChild( help_widget );
```

continued...

...from previous page

```
        /*
         * Add a help call-back,
         * to pop up help on cue.
         */
        XtAddCallback( help_widget,
                       XmNactivateCallback,
                       present_help,
                       message );

        /*
         * Set our help widget as the
         * default Motif help widget
         */
        n = 0;
        XtSetArg( args[n], XmNmenuHelpWidget, help_widget ); n++;

        XtSetValues( parent, args, n );

        return( help_widget );

}       /* CreateHelpWidget */

static void quit_callback( widget, client_data, call_data )

Widget widget;
caddr_t client_data;
caddr_t call_data;

/*
 *      quit_callback() is called when the user
 *      chooses a quit choice. It creates
 *      and pops up a Dialog widget to
 *      ask the user "Are you sure?"
 */

{       /* quit_callback */
        Widget  quit_dialog, WarningDialog(); /* dialog.c */
        void    really_quit();

        /*
         * Create an "Are you sure?" question dialog.
         */
        quit_dialog = WarningDialog( widget,
                        "sure",
                        "Are you sure you\n want to quit?",
                        really_quit ); /* callback function */

}       /* quit_callback */

static void really_quit( widget, client_data, call_data )
```

continued...

...from previous page

```
Widget widget;
caddr_t          client_data;
caddr_t          call_data;

/*
 *       really_quit() quits a Motif program.
 */

{       /* really_quit */

        XtCloseDisplay( XtDisplay( widget ) );

        exit( 0 );

}       /* really_quit */

Widget  CreateQuitButton( parent )

Widget  parent;

/*
 *       CreateQuitButton() creates a quit button
 *       as a menu choice on a Motif menu bar.
 */

{       /* -- CreateQuitButton */
        Widget                          quit_widget;
        Arg             args[ 10 ];
        int             n;
        /*
        * Create a quit button. Meta-Q
        * will also call the quit button.
        */
        n = 0;
        XtSetArg( args[n], XmNmnemonic, 'Q' ); n++;

        quit_widget = XmCreateCascadeButton( parent,
                        "Quit",
                        args,
                        n );

        XtManageChild( quit_widget );

        XtAddCallback( quit_widget,
                XmNactivateCallback,
                quit_callback, /* callback function */
                NULL );

        return( quit_widget );

}       /* -- CreateQuitButton */

/* end of file */
```

THE MENUBAR PROGRAM

The `menubar` program tests the concept of creating a Motif menu bar. The file `mtest.c` contains the `main()` function that launches this procedure. The source code for `mtest.c` appears in the next section.

The widget hierarchy for the `menubar` program looks like:

```
* Top-level Shell
        * Main Window Widget
                * Menubar widget
                * Cascade Widget (quit)
                        * Warning Dialog
                        (pop-up are you sure message)
                * Cascade Widget (help)
                        * Information Dialog
                        (pop-up help message)
```

Almost every program throughout the rest of the book will have the same beginning widget hierarchy, from the top-level shell to the menu bar with the quit and help choices. In Chapter 6, we'll flesh out the menu bar a bit.

As shown in the source code for the next section, the `main()` function calls `XtInitialize()` to set up the Xt intrinsics and then creates a main window widget (see the file `mainwind.c`). After that, you create a menu bar (see `menubar.c`) and call `XmMainWindowSetAreas()` to tell the menubar widget about its children. Note that you really only have one child here. Finally, you realize the widget hierarchy and call `XtMainLoop()`.

Source Code for Mtest.c

The following is the source code for the file `Mtest.c`.

```
/*
 *      mtest.c
 *      Program to test the creation of
 *      a Motif menu bar.
 *
 *      Written for Power Programming Motif
 *
 */

#include     <X11/Intrinsic.h>
#include     <X11/StringDefs.h>
#include     <Xm/Xm.h>
```

continued...

...from previous page

```
main( argc, argv )

int     argc;
char    *argv[];

{       /* main */
        Widget      main_window, CreateMainWindow(); /* mainwind.c */
        Widget parent, menu_bar;
        Widget CreateMenubar();   /* menubar.c */
        char        help_message[ 400 ];
        Arg         args[10];
        int         n;

        parent = XtInitialize( argv[0],
                    "MenuTest",
                    NULL,
                    0,
                    &argc,
                    argv );

        n = 0;
        XtSetArg( args[n], XmNallowShellResize, True ); n++;
XtSetValues( parent, args, n );


        /*
         * Create a main window
         */
        main_window = CreateMainWindow( parent,
                                "main",
                                300, 200 );


        /*
         * Set up a help message.
         */
        strcpy( help_message, "When in danger, or in doubt\n" );
        strcat( help_message, "run in circles, scream and shout.\n" );

        menu_bar    = CreateMenubar( main_window, help_message ) ;
        / *
         *The the main window widget
         * about the various subareas.
         */
        XmMainWindowSetAreas( main_window, /* main window */
            menu_bar,              /* menu bar */
            (Widget) NULL,         /* command area */
            (Widget) NULL,         /* horiz scroll */
            (Widget) NULL,         /* vert scroll */
```

continued...

...from previous page
```
                (Widget) NULL );      /* work area */

        XtRealizeWidget( parent );

        XtMainLoop();

}       /* main */

/* end of file */
```

Compiling and Linking the Menubar Program

The `menubar` program needs the following source files:

```
dialog.c (from Chapter 4)
mainwind.c
menubar.c
mtest.c
string.c (from Chapter 2)
```

You can compile and link this program using:

```
cc -o menubar mtest.c dialog.c mainwind.c \
   menubar.c string.c -lXm -lXt -lX11 -lPW
```

If you use `Makefile` in Appendix C, you can type:

```
make menubar
```
or
```
make all
```

Note that the file `dialog.c` needs the PW library in addition to the normal Motif and X libraries. (On SCO's Open Desktop, you may not want to link in the PW library.)

Running the Menubar Program

As is the case with all the other programs in this book, `menubar` doesn't need any command-line parameters. You click in the Quit cascade button (or press Meta-Q on the keyboard) to call up the quit dialog and then click in the OK button to quit the program. Figure 5-9 shows the `menubar` program in action.

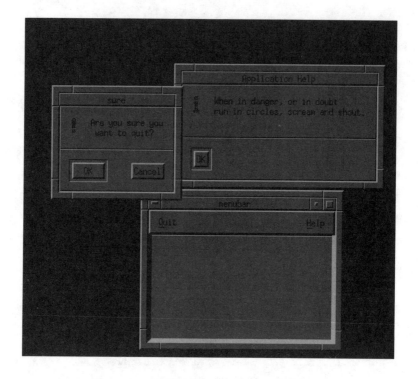

Figure 5-9. The Menubar Program in Action.

MOTIF FUNCTIONS AND MACROS INTRODUCED IN THIS CHAPTER

The following is a list of Motif functions and macros that were introduced in this chapter.

```
XmCreateCascadeButton()
XmCreateMainWindow()
XmCreateMenuBar()
XmMainWindowSep1()
XmMainWindowSep2()
XmMainWindowSetAreas()
```

You should be familiar with these functions and macros before you move on to Chapter 6.

SUMMARY

This chapter introduced an important concept—the Motif menu bar. Menu bars are `RowColumn` widgets that hold only cascade buttons. Almost every application you create with the Motif toolkit will have a menu bar across the top.

The cascade buttons on a Motif menu bar represent the menus available in your program. Just about every application you create will also have online help, using a help cascade button.

This chapter has also covered the Motif main window widget and keyboard shortcuts called mnemonics. Chapter 6 discusses how to create pulldown menus and how to link these menus to a menu bar.

Chapter **6**

Extending Menu Bars

C hapter 5 covered how to create a Motif menu bar. You learned that a menu bar is a `RowColumn` widget that manages a set of cascade button widgets. This chapter extends that discussion by describing how to add pulldown menus to a menu bar. We'll show how to create a pulldown menu and how to tie a cascade button on a menu bar to a pulldown menu.

PULLDOWN MENUS

A pulldown menu is also based on a `RowColumn` widget, which manages all the child widgets (in this case, menu choices). There's more to a pulldown menu than that, but you can use a handy Motif convenience function, `XmCreatePulldownMenu()`, to create a pulldown menu.

137

```
#include    <Xm/RowColumn.h>

Widget      parent;
Widget      menu_widget;
String      name;
ArgList     args;
Cardinal    n;

menu_widget = XmCreatePulldownMenu( parent,
                        name,
                        args,
                        n );
```

You should not call `XtManageChild()` after creating the widget, since the cascade button will do that for you.

The parent should be the menu bar widget, not the cascade button widget on the menu bar. That's all there is for creating a menu. Simple, isn't it? The only problem is now you probably want to add items to the menu—menu choices and perhaps separator lines to fill out your menu.

Filling in Menu Items

Filling in a pulldown menu (or Motif menus in general) is also easy. Each choice is a pushbutton widget (or a pushbutton gadget). That is, each choice needs a widget on the menu. This pushbutton widget then has its own callback function, a callback which is called if the user chooses that menu choice.

So, to create a menu now, we have two steps so far:

* Create a pulldown menu with `XmCreatePulldownMenu()`. Don't call `XtManageChild()`.

* Fill in each menu choice with a pushbutton widget. The widget callback is the function that will be called when the user chooses that item in the menu.

Add the menu items in the order, from top to bottom, as you want them to appear.

Adding Pushbutton Widgets

Creating a pushbutton widget should be old hat by now, as we've used pushbuttons since Chapter 1. The function `Fillmenu()` adds a pushbutton widget—a menu choice—to a menu widget. The `callback_func()` is set up as the pushbutton's callback.

We've added a twist. We pass the name of the menu choice to XtAddCallback(), so our callback function will get the widget's name as client data. What this really means is that your callback function will know the name of the menu choice you picked. With that information, you could share a callback function among all the choices in the menu. Or you could specify a different callback for each menu choice. You'll want to call FillMenu() in the order, from top to bottom, of the menu choices you want:

```
    Widget FillMenu( menu_widget, name, callback_func )

    Widget      menu_widget;
    char        name[];
    void        (*callback_func)();

{       /* FillMenu */
        Widget  menu_item;

        menu_item = XtCreateManagedWidget( name,
            xmPushButtonWidgetClass,
            menu_widget,
            NULL,
            0 );

        XtAddCallback( menu_item,
            XmNactivateCallback,
            callback_func,
            name );

        return( menu_item );

}       /* FillMenu */
```

The Menu Callback Function

The function generic_callback(), is the function we'll use in the menu program, below, to handle menu choices. Note that we're passing the menu choice's name (really the pushbutton widget's name) as the client data.

The call data contains a pointer to an XmAnyCallbackStruct, which looks like this:

```
    typedef struct
        {
        int     reason;
        XEvent  *event;
        } XmAnyCallbackStruct;
```

This structure is on limited use to a menu-choice callback. It's easier to pass the menu choice's name as the client data:

139

```
void generic_callback( widget, name, call_data )

Widget      widget;
char        *name;
caddr_t     call_data;

{       /* generic_callback */

        printf( "Menu choice was [%s]\n", name );

}       /* generic_callback */
```

Since a Motif pulldown menu (and a pop-up menu) is really a RowColumn widget, you can add all sorts of child widgets to a menu. In the sections below, we'll show how to add a menu title at the top of a menu, as well as separator lines between menu choices.

Menu Titles

A menu title—a text label on a menu that is not a menu choice—is really a label widget or a label gadget. To create a title for a menu, we need to get the title at the top of the menu. To get the title at the top, we need to create it first, before any of the menu-choice pushbutton widgets are created. (Note that we're not referring to the name on the menu bar, but a title on the actual pulldown menu itself.) We can use the CreateLabelWidget() utility function introduced in Chapter 2 for this:

```
Widget    menu_widget; /* RowColumn menu */
Arg       args[10];
int       n;
char      *title;

n = 0;
CreateLabelWidget( menu_widget, title, title,
        args, n );
```

You'll see this in the CreatePulldownMenu() utility function.

Menu Separators

A separator, or a line between menu choices, is a Motif separator widget. Figure 6-1 shows the separator widget class.

Widget Class Name	Class Pointer	Created By
XmSeparator	xmSeparatorWidgetClass	XmCreateSeparator()

Figure 6-1. The Separator Widget Class.

You'd be surprised at how many separator resources you can set to change the behavior of a simple line. We really don't need to change any of the defaults, so we can use `XtCreateManagedWidget()` to create and manage a separator widget:

```
#include        <Xm/Separator.h>

Widget   menu_widget;
char     *name;

XtCreateManagedWidget( name,
        xmSeparatorWidgetClass,
        menu_widget,
        NULL,
        0 );
```

We want to create the separator widget right after we create the label widget, so that we have a 3D line separating the menu title from the menu choices.

There are three main separator resources that you may want to change (you may want to experiment with this): the margin resource, the orientation resource, and the `separatorType` resource.

The margin resource specifies how many pixels sit between the edge of the menu and the start of the separator line, on both the right and left hand sides. The default for the margin resource (`XmNmargin` in your C programs) is 0 pixels.

The orientation resource (`XmNorientation` in your C programs) determines whether the separator line is horizontal or vertical. A value of `XmHORIZONTAL` means—you guessed it—a horizontal line. `XmVERTICAL` specifies a vertical line.

The `separatorType` resource (`XmNseparatorType` in your C programs) can be one of the following:

* `XmSINGLE_LINE`
* `XmSINGLE_DASHED_LINE`
* `XmDOUBLE_LINE`
* `XmDOUBLE_DASHED_LINE`
* `XmNO_LINE`
* `XmSHADOW_ETCHED_IN` (the default 3D effect)
* `XmSHADOW_ETCHED_OUT`

141

In addition, there are at least 32 other resources inherited by the separator widget that affect its behavior. Yow! All this for a line. The *OSF/Motif Programmer's Reference Manual* covers this in detail under XmSeparator (see Appendix D for a list of Motif-related books).

Connecting a Pulldown Menu to a Menu Bar

Once we've created our menu, we still need to make it a pulldown menu. We need to connect the menu to the cascade button on the menu bar. To do this, we set the subMenuId resource (XmNsubMenuId in your C programs) on the cascade button widget. The subMenuId resource needs a widget ID, which is the widget ID of the menu we created. We set this resource, using XtSetValues(), on the cascade button widget. That is, we're telling the cascade button to call up our menu as needed:

```
Widget    cascade_widget; /* on menu bar */
Widget    menu_widget;    /* pull-down menu */
Arg       args[10];
int       n;

/*
 * Set up button on menu bar to
 * pull down our menu.
 */
n = 0;
XtSetArg( args[n], XmNsubMenuId, menu_widget ); n++;

XtSetValues( cascade_widget, args, n );

/* create the widget...*/
```

Menu Mnemonics

One final step and then we're ready to create a full-fledged pulldown menu. The quit and help menubar items have mnemonics associated with them. It's probably a good idea to associate a mnemonic with each pulldown menu, especially if we want a consistent interface—a consistent interface is one of the advantages of using a toolkit like Motif.

If we pass a letter to our menu-creation function, then we can set up that letter as a mnemonic. It's up to the application developer (that's you) to use a unique mnemonic. You don't want Meta-Q to call down every menu, do you?

```
Arg        args[10];
int        n;
int        mnemonic;

n = 0;
XtSetArg( args[n], XmNmnemonic, mnemonic ); n++;

/* create the widget...*/
```

Creating a Pulldown Menu

The function, CreatePulldownMenu(), below, creates a Motif pulldown menu, using these steps:

* Create and manage a cascade button on the parent menu bar, using XmCreateCascadeButton() and XtManageChild().

* Create a pulldown menu, using XmCreatePulldownMenu().

* Create and manage a label widget for a title in the pulldown menu, using the utility function CreateLabelWidget() from Chapter 2.

* Create and manage a separator widget, to separate the menu title from the menu choices that follow, using XtCreateManagedWidget().

* Set the subMenuId resource on the cascade button widget, using XtSetValues(), to tie the cascade button to the pulldown menu.

Use the following code:

```
Widget CreatePulldownMenu( parent, name_on_bar, title, mnemonic )

Widget     parent;
char          name_on_bar[];
char          title[];
int           mnemonic;

{          /* CreatePulldownMenu */
           Widget cascade_widget, menu_widget;
           Widget CreateLabelWidget();  /* label.c */
           Arg           args[ 10 ];
           int           n;
           char          new_name[ 256 ];

           /*
continued...
```

...from previous page

```
            * Create a menu button
            */
            n = 0;
            XtSetArg( args[n], XmNmnemonic, mnemonic ); n++;

            cascade_widget = XmCreateCascadeButton( parent,
                        name_on_bar,
                        args,
                        n );

            XtManageChild( cascade_widget );

            /*
             * Create the menu
             */
            strcpy( new_name, title );
            strcat( new_name, "-menu" );

            menu_widget = XmCreatePulldownMenu( parent,
                            new_name,
                            NULL,
                            0 );

            /*
             * Fill in a title in the menu
             */
            n = 0;
            CreateLabelWidget( menu_widget, title, title,
                    args, n );

            /*
             * Add in a separator
             */
            XtCreateManagedWidget( "sep",
                    xmSeparatorWidgetClass,
                    menu_widget,
                    NULL,
                    0 );

            /*
             * Set up button on menu bar to
             * pull down our menu.
             */
            n = 0;
            XtSetArg( args[n], XmNsubMenuId, menu_widget ); n++;
            XtSetValues( cascade_widget, args, n );

            return( menu_widget );

}           /* CreatePulldownMenu */
```

Source Code for Menu.c

The file menu.c, below, contains two utility functions for creating a pulldown menu and populating the menu:

```
/*
 *   menu.c
 *   Motif functions for pull-down menus
 *
 *   Written for Power Programming Motif
 *
 */

#include            <X11/Intrinsic.h>
#include            <X11/StringDefs.h>
#include            <Xm/Xm.h>
#include            <Xm/RowColumn.h>
#include            <Xm/CascadeB.h>
#include            <Xm/PushB.h>
#include            <Xm/Separator.h>

Widget  CreatePulldownMenu( parent, name_on_bar, title,
mnemonic )

Widget          parent;
char            name_on_bar[];
char            title[];
int             mnemonic;

{       /* CreatePulldownMenu */
        Widget  cascade_widget, menu_widget;
        Widget  CreateLabelWidget(); /* label.c */
        Arg     args[ 10 ];
        int     n;
        char    new_name[ 256 ];

/*
 * Create a menu button
 */
n = 0;
XtSetArg( args[n], XmNmnemonic, mnemonic ); n++;

cascade_widget = XmCreateCascadeButton( parent,
                        name_on_bar,
                        args,
                        n );

XtManageChild( cascade_widget );

/*
 * Create the menu
```
continued...

...from previous page
```
 */
strcpy( new_name, title );
strcat( new_name, "-menu" );

menu_widget = XmCreatePulldownMenu( parent,
                         new_name,
                         NULL,
                         0 );

/*
 * Fill in a title in the menu
 */
n = 0;
CreateLabelWidget( menu_widget, title, title,
           args, n );

/*
 * Add in a separator
 */
XtCreateManagedWidget( "sep",
           xmSeparatorWidgetClass,
           menu_widget,
           NULL,
           0 );

/*
 * Set up button on menu bar to
 * pull down our menu.
 */
n = 0;
XtSetArg( args[n], XmNsubMenuId, menu_widget ); n++;
XtSetValues( cascade_widget, args, n );

return( menu_widget );

}               /* CreatePulldownMenu */


Widget FillMenu( menu_widget, name, callback_func )

Widget          menu_widget;
char            name[];
void            (*callback_func)();

{     /* FillMenu */
      Widget menu_item;

      menu_item = XtCreateManagedWidget( name,
                  xmPushButtonWidgetClass,
                  menu_widget,
                  NULL,
```
continued...

...from previous page

```
                        0 );
      XtAddCallback( menu_item,
      XmNactivateCallback, callback_func, name );

      return( menu_item );

}                 /* FillMenu */

/* end of file */
```

POP-UP MENUS

Pop-up menus are a lot like the pulldown menus we've used here, except that you use a different mechanism to trigger a pop-up menu. Typically, you use a mouse-button press event or something like that. Pop-up menus use the function `XmCreatePopupMenu()` for creation, instead of `XmCreatePulldownMenu()`:

```
#include <Xm/RowColumn.h>

Widget          parent;
Widget          menu_widget;
String          name;
ArgList         args;
Cardinal        n;

menu_widget = XmCreatePopupMenu( parent,
                      name,
                      args,
                      n );
```

To pop up a pop-up menu, call `XtManageChild()` on the widget returned by `XmCreatePopupMenu()`. Note that this means you shouldn't call `XtManageChild()` until you're ready to pop up the menu. Just call `XmCreatePopupMenu()` to create the menu. Don't call `XtManageChild()` until later, when you're ready to pop up the menu.

We've concentrated the most on pulldown menus since just about every Motif application you write will have pulldown menus. Only a few will need pop-up menus.

CASCADED MENUS

Cascaded menus are really just like the pulldown menus we've been using so far. So, to make a menu choice that cascades to another submenu, you can call

CreatePulldownMenu() to create the choice that cascades to a new menu. Using the widget returned by CreatePulldownMenu(), you can then call FillMenu() to add menu choices to your new cascaded menu. It's sort of like creating a menu choice just like we created a menu in the first place (and treating the original menu as a menu bar).

When we do this in the menu program, you'll notice that the "Font" choice (our cascaded submenu) had a right-pointing arrow after its name. This signifies a Motif cascaded submenu.

THE MENU PROGRAM

The menu program is a simple program that demonstrates the use of Motif pulldown menus. The widget hierarchy for the menu program looks like this:

    * Top-level Shell
    * Main Window Widget
        * Menubar widget
            * Cascade Widget (quit)
                * Warning Dialog
                (pop-up are you sure message)
            * Cascade Widget (help)
                * Information Dialog (pop-up help message)
            * Cascade widget (file menu)
            * Pulldown menu (file menu)
                * Label widget (menu title)
                * Separator widget
                * Pushbutton widget (New)
                * Pushbutton widget (Open...)
                * Pushbutton widget (Save)
                * Pushbutton widget (Save As...)
                * Pushbutton widget (Print...)
                * Cascade button widget (Print...)
                * Pulldown Menu (Font Submenu)
                    * Pushbutton widget (Times)
                    * Pus button widget (Helvetica)
                    * Pushbutton widget (Garamond)

Up until the file menu's cascade widget, the hierarchy is exactly like the hierarchy used in the menubar program in Chapter 5.

The menu program simply adds a File menu (a common menu in Motif applications). When you choose a menu, the generic_callback() functions prints out the name of the menu choice. The file mtest2.c contains the menu program's main() function. Notice how easy it is to add a pulldown menu using CreatePulldownMenu() and FillMenu().

Source Code for Mtest2.c

The following is the source code for mtest2.c.

```
/*
 * mtest2.c
 * Program to test the creation of
 * a Motif menu bar, with pull-down menus.
 *
 * Written for Power Programming Motif *
 */

#include        <X11/Intrinsic.h>
#include        <X11/StringDefs.h>
#include        <Xm/Xm.h>

void generic_callback( widget, name, call_data )

Widget  widget;
char    *name;
caddr_t call_data;

{       /* generic_callback */

        printf( "Menu choice was [%s]\n", name );

}       /* generic_callback */

main( argc, argv )

int     argc;
char    *argv[];

{ /* main */
    Widget  parent, menu_widget;
    Widget  main_window, CreateMainWindow(); /* mainwind.c */
    Widget  menu_bar, CreateMenubar(); /* menubar.c */
    Widget  CreatePulldownMenu(), FillMenu();
    Widget  sub_menu;
    char    help_message[ 400 ];
    Arg     args[10];
    int     n;

    parent = XtInitialize( argv[0],
            "MenuTest2",
            NULL,
            0,
            &argc,
            argv );

    n = 0;
continued...
```

...from previous page

```
    XtSetArg( args[n], XmNallowShellResize, True ); n++;
    XtSetValues( parent, args, n );

    main_window = CreateMainWindow( parent, "main", 300, 200 );

    strcpy( help_message, "When in danger, or in doubt\n" );
strcat( help_message, "run in circles, scream and shout.\n" );

    menu_bar    = CreateMenubar( main_window, help_message );

    menu_widget = CreatePulldownMenu( menu_bar, "File",
                                "File Menu", 'F' );

    FillMenu( menu_widget, "New", generic_callback );
    FillMenu( menu_widget, "Open...", generic_callback );
    FillMenu( menu_widget, "Save", generic_callback );
    FillMenu( menu_widget, "Save As...", generic_callback );
FillMenu( menu_widget, "Print...", generic_callback );

    /*
     * Create a submenu
     */
    sub_menu = CreatePulldownMenu( menu_widget, "Font",
                    "Font Menu", '\0' );

    /*
     * Fill the submenu with
     * some menu choices.
     */
    FillMenu( sub_menu, "Times", generic_callback );
    FillMenu( sub_menu, "Helvetica", generic_callback );
    FillMenu( sub_menu, "Garamond", generic_callback );

    XmMainWindowSetAreas( main_window,
                menu_bar,
                (Widget) NULL,
                (Widget) NULL,
                (Widget) NULL,
                (Widget) NULL );

XtRealizeWidget( parent );
XtMainLoop();

}       /* main */

/* end of file */
```

Compiling and Linking the Menu Program

The menu program uses the following source files:

```
dialog.c (from chapter 4)
label.c (from chapter 2)
mainwind.c (from chapter 5)
menu.c
menubar.c (from chapter 5)
mtest2.c
string.c (from chapter 2)
```

You can compile and link the menu program with a command like:

```
cc -o menu  dialog.o label.o mainwind.o menu.o menubar.o \
    mtest2.o string.o -lXm -lXt -lX11 -lPW
```

Or, using Makefile in Appendix C:

```
make menu
```

or

```
make all
```

Note that the file dialog.c needs the PW library (for the file selection box dialog). and that you many not want to link in this library under SCO's Open Desktop.

Running The Menu Program

Figure 6-2 shows the menu program.

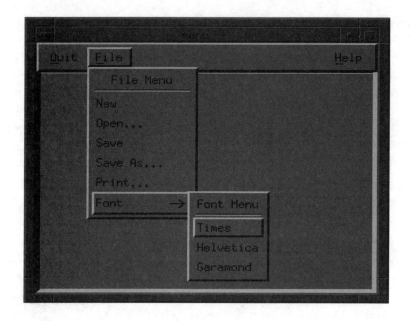

Figure 6-2. The Menu Program.

When you run the menu program, try picking menu choices and see the program print out your choice. As you can tell, it's fairly easy in Motif to have a menu choice call a function in your application.

MOTIF FUNCTIONS AND MACROS INTRODUCED IN THIS CHAPTER

The following is a list of motif fuctions and macros indroduced in this chapter.

```
XmCreatePopupMenu()
XmCreatePulldownMenu()
```

You should be familiar with these functions and macros before you move on to Chapter 7.

SUMMARY

The Motif style encourages having a menu bar and pulldown menus. Motif also allows for cascading or submenus, and pop-up menus.

Create a pulldown menu with `XmCreatePulldownMenu()`, but don't call `XtManageChild()`, since a cascade button will do that for you. Create a pop-up menu with `XmCreatePopupMenu()`. We've covered the pulldown menus is far more depth than the pop-up menus, since virtually every Motif application will have a set of pulldown menus. Few will have pop-up menus.

Submenus—also called cascading menus—are really pulldown menus created as a child of an existing parent menu. Instead of a pushbutton menu choice, the triggering button on the parent menu should be a cascade button widget.

So far, we've covered the top part of most Motif application main windows: the menu bar and pulldown menus. In Chapter 7, we begin the task of fleshing out the area underneath the menu bar, where the meat of most applications reside.

# Chapter 7

Text Entry in Motif

T hus far, we've covered how to create the top part of an application—its menu bars and menus. Now we'll start concentrating on what is below the menu bar, where the meat of most applications lie—text entry. This chapter concentrates on a common need. Most applications need some form of text entry: a single-line prompt, or a full-fledged text editor. In Motif, the handy text widget covers this need.

TEXT WIDGETS

The text widget covers most text entry in Motif. Because of that, the text widget's options become rather complex. The text widget can be an all-purpose text editor or a single-line prompt. The best part about the text widget though, is that it abstracts a very common application task into one widget, saving you, the application writer, a lot of work. Figure 7-1 shows the text widget.

Widget Class	NameClass Pointer	Created By
XmTextxm	TextWidgetClass	XmCreateText()
		XmCreateScrolledText()

Figure 7-1. The Text Widget.

The text widget needs the Xm/Text.h include file and can be created by the function XmCreateText() or XmCreateScrolledText():

```
#include         <Xm/Text.h>

Widget      parent;
Widget      text_widget;
String      name;
ArgList     args;
Cardinal    n;

text_widget = XmCreateText( parent,
                           name,
                           args,
                           n );

text_widget = XmCreateScrolledText( parent,
                           name,
                           args,
                           n );
```

Call XtManageChild() after creating the widget:

```
XtManageChild( text_widget );
```

XmCreateScrolledText() creates a text widget as a child of a scrolled window widget, while XmCreateText() creates just a text widget. We'll cover more on scroll bars below. For now, though, we'll show some of the text widget resources common to both functions.

Single and Multiline Text Widgets

You can have a text widget as a single-line prompt, or you can make the text widget span a number of lines (and even add scroll bars). The editMode resource controls this. Figure 7-2 shows the resource name, the program definition, and the default value.

Resource Name	C Program Definition	Default Value
editMode	XmNeditMode	XmSINGLE_LINE_EDIT

Figure 7-2. The Edit Mode Resource.

The editMode resource can be one of the following:

```
* XmSINGLE_LINE_EDIT
* XmMULTI_LINE_EDIT
```

XmSINGLE_LINE_EDIT means that only one line of text is allowed in the widget. This is basically a prompt. XmMULTI_LINE_EDIT means that the text in the text widget can span many lines, providing you with a built-in Motif text editor.

To set the editMode resource, use:

```
#include <Xm/Text.h>

Arg    args[10];
int    n;

n = 0;
XtSetArg( args[n], XmNeditMode, XmMULTI_LINE_EDIT ); n++;

/* create widget ... */
```

The prompt dialog shown in Chapter 3 uses a single-line text widget under the hood as the place where the user enters data. In the example program in the next section, we'll use a multiple-line text widget to show more about scroll bars and the like.

SCROLL BARS

Scroll bars are used in most graphical interfaces as a means of showing only a part of something too large to fit into a window. The scroll bars are controls that allow the user to browse through the larger text (or graphics), while only using a much smaller portion of the screen's real estate. The concept of scroll bars is simple and intuitive—and scroll bars are used in just about every graphical interface. Figure 7-3 shows Motif scroll bars.

Figure 7-3. Motif Scroll Bars.

Motif's scroll bars have a nice 3D shadowed effect. We'll use scroll bars with the text widget below and the list widget in Chapter 8.

The Text Widget with Scroll Bars

When you create a text widget with the XmCreateScrolledText() function, a scrolled window widget is first created and then a text widget is created as a child of the scrolled window. Normally, if you don't have enough data to need a scroll bar, either horizontally or vertically, then the scroll bar won't be visible. If, however, you always want a scroll bar visible, you can set the values of the scrollVertical (XmNscrollVertical in C programs) and scrollHorizontal (XmNscrollHorizontal in C programs) resources.

If you set the resource to True, you'll always have a scroll bar. If you set the resource to False, you will not have the scroll bar in the particular direction. Figure 7-4 shows a scrolled text widget.

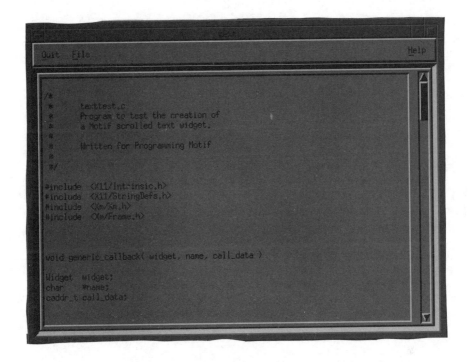

Figure 7-4. A Scrolled Text Widget with scrollHorizontal set to False.

The following code will turn on both horizontal and vertical scroll bars permanently:

```
#include <Xm/Text.h>

Arg   args[10];
int   n;

n = 0;
XtSetArg( args[n], XmNscrollVertical, True ); n++; XtSetArg(
args[n], XmNscrollHorizontal, True ); n++;

/* create widget ... */
```

Usually, a vertical scroll bar will appear on the right side of the widget. You can change that however, with the `scrollLeftSide` resource (`XmNscrollLeftSide` in C programs). The default value for this resource is `False`. If you set it to `True`, then the scroll bar, if there is a scroll bar, will appear on the left side of the window. Now, this really doesn't seem to fit in with the Motif Style Guide's requirements, so most applications won't set this resource.

The `scrollTopSide` resource (`XmNscrollTopSide` in C programs) functions the same way as for the horizontal scroll bar. If set to `True`, the scroll bar will appear at the top of the widget. If set to the default `False`, the scroll bar will appear at the bottom of the widget.

Again, this isn't in the spirit of the Motif style, so you're advised to stay away from this resource, unless you just want to experiment.

CHANGING THE TEXT IN A TEXT WIDGET

The most important operation you'll want to perform on a text widget is to set the text inside the widget. `XmTextSetString()` sets the text inside a text widget to a C string. Note that this is not a Motif `XmString`, but an everyday, normal C string.

You pass the text widget you want to set and a character pointer to `XmTextSetString()`:

```
Widget   widget;
char     *new_text; /* your text to put in the widget */

XmTextSetString( widget, new_text );
```

To replace portions of the text within a text widget, use `XmTextReplace()`:

```
Widget                    widget;
XmTextPosition            start_position;
XmTextPosition            end_position;
char                      *new_text;

XmTextReplace( widget,
               start_position,
               end_position,
               new_text );
```

`XmTextReplace()` replaces the text starting at a given position and going to an end position with the new text you pass as a parameter to `XmTextReplace()`.

Normally, `XmTextPosition` is defined as a long integer in the file `Xm/Text.h`:

```
typedef long XmTextPosition;
```

The position counting is in bytes and starts with the first position as zero (0). If both the `start_position` and `end_position` are the same, the `new_text` is inserted after the `start_position`. We'll use `XmTextSetString()` in the function `FillWidgetWithFile()`.

LOADING ASCII TEXT FILES INTO MULTILINE TEXT WIDGETS

The function `FillWidgetWithFile()` fills a text widget with the text of an ASCII text file. The function opens the given text file for reading, checks how large the file is, allocates a buffer for the file's bytes, reads in the file's bytes, and then calls `XmTextSetString()` to place the text into the text widget.

We use `XtMalloc()` to allocate the memory and `XtFree()` to free it if the `fread()` operation fails:

```
char      *data;
Cardinal number_of_bytes;

data = XtMalloc( number_of_bytes );

XtFree( data );
```

Note that we use the UNIX `stat()` function to determine how large the file is. If you are using another operating system, like VMS or AmigaDOS, you may have to convert `FillWidgetWithFile()` to your system:

```
#include <stdio.h>
#include <sys/types.h>
#include <sys/stat.h>

Boolean FillWidgetWithFile( widget, filename )
Widget   widget;
char filename[];

{    /* FillWidgetWithFile */
     FILE                *fp;
     struct stat         file_info;
     char                *buffer;
     long                bytes_read;

     fp = fopen( filename, "r" );

     if ( fp == NULL )
          {
          return( False );
          }

     /*
      * Get file size
      */
     if ( stat( filename, &file_info )  != 0 )
               {
               fclose( fp );
               return( False );
```

continued...

161

...from previous page

```
                }
    buffer = (char *) XtMalloc( file_info.st_size + 5 );

    if ( buffer == (char *) NULL )
                {
                fclose( fp );
                return( False );
                }

    bytes_read = fread( buffer, 1, file_info.st_size, fp );
    fclose( fp );

    buffer[ file_info.st_size -1 ] = '\0'; /* truncate */

    if ( bytes_read <  file_info.st_size )
                {
                XtFree( buffer );
                return( False );
                }

    XmTextSetString( widget, buffer );
    XtFree (buffer);
    return( True );

}    /* FillWidgetWithFile */
```

Now that you know how to put text into a text widget, the next task is to learn how to retrieve text from a text widget.

RETRIEVING THE TEXT IN A TEXT WIDGET

You can retrieve text from a text widget with XmTextGetString():

```
char      *text;
Widget    widget;

text = XmTextGetString( widget );
```

When you're done with the returned text, free the memory it uses with XtFree():

```
XtFree( text );
```

Note that for a multiline text widget, you could be dealing with megabytes of text data. Just think how much text a text widget used in a CD-ROM-based application could hold.

MORE TEXT WIDGET RESOURCES

The editable resource (XmNeditable in C programs) determines whether you can modify the text in the text widget. The default is True, so that you can edit the text. If you set this resource to False, you can only view the text in the widget, not modify the text:

```
#include <Xm/Text.h>

Arg    args[10];
int    n;

n = 0;
XtSetArg( args[n], XmNeditable, False ); n++;

/* create the widget ... */
```

There are two Motif functions you can also use with the text widget to get and set the editable resource.

XmTextGetEditable() returns the value of the editable resource: True or False. False means you cannot modify the text. True means you can modify the text:

```
Boolean status;
Widget text_widget;

status = XmTextGetEditable( text_widget );
```

XmTextSetEditable() sets the value of the editable resource:

```
status = True;
XmTextSetEditable( text_widget, status );
```

The wordWrap resource (XmNwordWrap in C programs) controls whether the text widget should break lines at word boundaries. When set to True, a multiline text widget will wrap words onto the next line if they would extend beyond the current number of visible columns. The default value for this resource is False.

The column (XmNcolumns in C programs) and row (XmNrows in C programs) resources control the number of visible columns and rows of text. The default number of columns is twenty and the default number of rows is one (for the default single-line text widget). In the function CreateScrolledText(), below, we'll set the number of rows to twenty-four and the number of columns to eighty:

```
#include <Xm/Text.h>

Arg    args[10];
int    n;
```
continued...

...from previous page

```
n = 0;
XtSetArg( args[n], XmNrows, 24 ); n++;
XtSetArg( args[n], XmNcolumns, 80 ); n++;

/* create the widget... */
```

Note that since the text widget will be the child of another widget, any requests to change the size of the text widget may be ignored or modified by the text widget's parent widget.

TEXT WIDGET CALLBACK

An `activateCallback` resource (XmNactivateCallback in C programs) can be set up to specify a C function you want to be called back when the user presses the return key or activates the text widget in some other manner. Unless you're using a single-line text widget, you probably won't need to set up a callback.

If you do though, your callback's `call_data` will be in the form of a pointer to an XmAnyCallbackStruct (covered in Chapter 4):

```
typedef struct
    {
    int       reason;
    XEvent    *event;
    } XmAnyCallbackStruct;
```

The reason field will be set XmCR_ACTIVATE.

CREATING A TEXT WIDGET

The function `CreateScrolledText()` creates a read-only multiline scrolled text widget:

```
Widget CreateScrolledText( parent, name )

Widget              parent;
char                name[];

{       /* CreateScrolledText */
        Widget  text_widget;
        Arg     args[10];
        int     n;
```

continued...

...from previous page
```
        n = 0;
        XtSetArg( args[n], XmNrows, 24 ); n++;
        XtSetArg( args[n], XmNcolumns, 80 ); n++;
        XtSetArg( args[n], XmNscrollHorizontal, True ); n++;
        XtSetArg( args[n], XmNscrollVertical, True ); n++;
        XtSetArg( args[n], XmNeditable, False ); n++;
        XtSetArg( args[n], XmNeditMode, XmMULTI_LINE_EDIT ); n++;

        text_widget = XmCreateScrolledText( parent,
                    name,
                    args,
                    n );

        XtManageChild( text_widget );

        return( text_widget );

}       /* CreateScrolledText */
```

It takes a parent widget and a name for the widget. No text is placed in the text widget, as we leave this task to the function `FillWidgetWithFile()`. While we've just covered the most text widget common options, there are a host of other options available. You should look in the `XmText` section in the *OSF/Motif Programmer's Reference* for more information on these options.

Source Code for Text.c

The file `text.c` has two functions, `CreateScrolledText()` and `FillWidgetWithFile()`, both introduced previously in this chapter. Note again that `FillWidgetWithFile()` is somewhat UNIX-specific and you may have to port this to your particular operating system:

```
/*
 *      text.c
 *      Motif functions for text widgets
 *
 *      Written for Programming Motif
 *
 */

#include     <stdio.h>
#include     <sys/types.h>
#include     <sys/stat.h>
#include     <X11/Intrinsic.h>
#include     <X11/StringDefs.h>
#include     <Xm/Xm.h>
#include     <Xm/Text.h>
```

continued...

...*from previous page*

```
Widget      CreateScrolledText( parent, name )
Widget      parent;
char        name[];

/*
 *      CreateScrolledText() creates a scrolled
 *      multiline text widget as a child of the
 *      parent widget. The default size is 80 columns
 *      by 24 lines.
 */

{       /* CreateScrolledText */
        Widget      text_widget;
        Arg         args[10];
        int         n;

        n = 0;
        XtSetArg( args[n], XmNrows, 24 ); n++;
        XtSetArg( args[n], XmNcolumns, 80 ); n++;
        XtSetArg( args[n], XmNscrollHorizontal, True ); n++;
        XtSetArg( args[n], XmNscrollVertical, True ); n++;
        XtSetArg( args[n], XmNeditable, False ); n++;
        XtSetArg( args[n], XmNeditMode, XmMULTI_LINE_EDIT ); n++;

        text_widget = XmCreateScrolledText( parent,
                        name,
                        args,
                        n );

        XtManageChild( text_widget );

        return( text_widget );

}       /* CreateScrolledText */

Boolean FillWidgetWithFile( widget, filename )

Widget      widget;
char        filename[];

/*
 *      FillWidgetWithFile() fills a multiline
 *      text widget with the contents of an
 *      ASCII file.
 */

{       /* FillWidgetWithFile */
        FILE          *fp;
        struct stat   file_info;
        char          *buffer;
        long          bytes_read;
```

continued...

...from previous page

```
      fp = fopen( filename, "r" );

      if ( fp == NULL )
          {
          return( False );
          }
      /*
       * Get file size
       */
      if ( stat( filename, &file_info )  != 0 )
          {
          fclose( fp );
          return( False );
          }

      buffer = (char *) XtMalloc( file_info.st_size + 5 );

      if ( buffer == (char *) NULL )
          {
          fclose( fp );
          return( False );
          }

      bytes_read = fread( buffer, 1, file_info.st_size, fp );
      fclose( fp );

      buffer[ file_info.st_size -1 ] = '\0'; /* truncate */

      if ( bytes_read <  file_info.st_size )
          {
          XtFree( buffer );
          return( False );
          }

      XmTextSetString( widget, buffer );
      XtFree (buffer);
      return( True );

}      /* FillWidgetWithFile */

/* end of file */
```

FRAME WIDGETS

In our example program, text, we'll use a Motif frame widget to create a 3D border around our text widget. The frame widget doesn't have anything to do with a text widget, but it does enhance a user interface, so we decided to use one here. Figure 7-5 shows the frame widget class.

Widget Class Name	Class Pointer	Created By
XmFrame	xmFrameWidgetClass	XmCreateFrame()

Figure 7-5. The Frame Widget Class.

The frame widget's include file is Xm/Frame.h, and you can create a frame widget with the function XmCreateFrame():

```
#include <Xm/Frame.h>

Widget      parent, frame_widget;
String      name;
ArgList     args;
Cardinal    n;

frame_widget = XmCreateFrame( parent,
                name,
                args,
                n );

XtManageChild( frame_widget );
```

You'll want to set only a few resources with the frame widget. The shadowThickness resource (XmNshadowThickness in C programs) controls the width (in pixels) of the 3D shadow. In the following code, we'll set the shadowThickness width to four (4) pixels:

```
# include <Xm/Frame.h>

Arg   args[10];
int   n;

n = 0;
XtSetArg( args[n], XmNshadowThickness, 4 ); n++;

/* create the widget... */
```

The other resource you may want to set is the shadowType resource (XmNshadowType in C programs). The available types of shadowing include:

* XmSHADOW_IN
* XmSHADOW_OUT
* XmSHADOW_ETCHED_IN
* XmSHADOW_ETCHED_OUT

`XmSHADOW ETCHED IN` is the default, which makes an inward-looking 3D line (by drawing a double line with the proper colors to make it look 3D going inward). `XmSHADOW ETCHED OUT` makes a 3D double line that is outward-looking. `XmSHADOW IN` and `XmSHADOW OUT` operate much the same, only these options don't create the 3D double line.

The best way to understand these options is to try out each one. You can easily modify the following `text` program to try out all four shadow types.

THE TEXT PROGRAM

To show how the text widget works, we're going to create a program that loads in a ASCII text file (one of the source files to the program itself) and presents this ASCII file in a read-only scrolled text widget. To build this `text` program, we take the menu program from Chapter 6 and just add the 3D frame and text widgets introduced in this chapter. So, we finally flesh out a simple application by using the work area of the main window widget. The widget hierarchy of the `text` program shown below, looks the same as the `menu` program, but adds to widgets at the end.

```
    * Top-level Shell
        * Main Window Widget
            * Menubar widget
                * Cascade Widget (quit)
                    * Warning Dialog
                      (pop-up are you sure message)
                * Cascade Widget (help)
                    * Information Dialog
                  (pop-up help message)
                * Cascade widget (file menu)
                * Pulldown menu (file menu)
                        * Label widget (menu title)
                        * Separator widget
                        * Pushbutton widget (New)
                        * Pushbutton widget (Open...)
                        * Pushbutton widget (Save)
                        * Pushbutton widget (Save As...)
                        * Pushbutton widget (Print...)
                        * Cascade button widget (Print...)
                            * Pulldown Menu (Font Submenu)
                                * Pushbutton widget (Times)
                                * Pushbutton widget (Helvetica)
                    * Pushbutton widget (Garamond)
            * Frame Widget
                * Scrolled text Widget
```

Source Code for Texttest.c

The text program, in the file texttest.c, below, acts much like the menu program from Chapter 6. In fact, we borrowed the file mtest2.c and then added in two new widgets.

```
/*
 *   texttest.c
 *   Program to test the creation of
 *   a Motif scrolled text widget.
 *
 *   Written for Power Programming Motif
 *
 */

#include <X11/Intrinsic.h>
#include <X11/StringDefs.h>
#include <Xm/Xm.h>
#include <Xm/Frame.h>

void generic_callback( widget, name, call_data )

Widget    widget;
char*name;
caddr_t   call_data;

{   /* generic_callback */

        printf( "Menu choice was [%s]\n", name );

}   /* generic_callback */

main( argc, argv )

int       argc;
char*argv[];

{   /* main */
    Widget   parent, menu_bar, menu_widget;
    Widget   main_window, CreateMainWindow(); /* mainwind.c */
    Widget   CreateMenubar(); /* menubar.c */
    Widget   CreatePulldownMenu(), FillMenu(); /* menu.c */
    Widget   sub_menu;
    Widget   text_widget, CreateScrolledText(); /* text.c */
    Widget   frame_widget;
    char     help_message[ 400 ];
    Arg      args[10];
    int      n;

    parent = XtInitialize( argv[0],
            "TextTest",
```
continued...

...from previous page

```
            NULL,
            0,
            &argc,
            argv );

    n = 0;
    XtSetArg( args[n], XmNallowShellResize, True ); n++;
    XtSetValues( parent, args, n );

    main_window = CreateMainWindow( parent, "main", 400, 300 );

    strcpy( help_message, "When in danger, or in doubt\n" );
    strcat( help_message, "run in circles, scream and shout.\n" );

    menu_bar   = CreateMenubar( main_window, help_message );

    menu_widget = CreatePulldownMenu( menu_bar, "File",
                                "File Menu", 'F' );

    FillMenu( menu_widget, "New", generic_callback );
    FillMenu( menu_widget, "Open...", generic_callback );
    FillMenu( menu_widget, "Save", generic_callback );
    FillMenu( menu_widget, "Save As...", generic_callback );
    FillMenu( menu_widget, "Print...", generic_callback );

    /*
     * Create a sub menu
     */
    sub_menu = CreatePulldownMenu( menu_widget, "Font",
                                "Font Menu", '\0' );

    /*
     * Fill the submenu with
     * some menu choices.
     */
    FillMenu( sub_menu, "Times", generic_callback );
    FillMenu( sub_menu, "Helvetica", generic_callback );
    FillMenu( sub_menu, "Garamond", generic_callback );

    /*
     * Create a frame widget around the
     * main command area. This adds a
     * 3D effect.
     */
    n = 0;
    XtSetArg( args[n], XmNshadowThickness, 4 ); n++;

    frame_widget = XmCreateFrame( main_window,
                                "frame",
                                args,
```

continued...

...from previous page

```
                                        n );
        XtManageChild( frame_widget );

        /*
         * Create a scrolled text widget
         * as a child of the frame widget.
         */
        text_widget = CreateScrolledText( frame_widget,
                                  "mytext");

        /*
         * Load up an arbitrary text
         * file into this widget.
         * In this case, we're loading
         * this file.
         */
        FillWidgetWithFile( text_widget, "texttest.c" );

        /*
         * Set up the main window
         * areas.
         */
        XmMainWindowSetAreas( main_window,
                        menu_bar,
                        (Widget) NULL,
                        (Widget) NULL,
                        (Widget) NULL,
                        frame_widget ); /* work area */

        XtRealizeWidget( parent );
        XtMainLoop();

}    /* main */

/* end of file */
```

If you're typing this in by hand, make a copy of the file `mtest2.c` and then start from there.

Note that the call to `XmMainWindowSetAreas()` is different this time, as we set the work area widget to be the 3D frame widget.

Compiling and Linking the Text Program

The text program needs the following source files:

```
dialog.c (from Chapter 4)
label.c (from Chapter 2)
mainwind.c (from Chapter 5)
menubar.c (from Chapter 5)
menu.c (from Chapter 6)
string.c (from Chapter 2)
texttest.c
text.c
```

You can compile and link this program using:

```
cc -o text dialog.c label.c mainwind.c menubar.c menu.c \
      string.c texttest.c text.c -lXm -lXt -lX11 -lPW
```

Or, using Makefile in Appendix C:

```
make text
```

or

```
make all
```

Note that the file dialog.c needs the PW library (for the file selection box dialog). Note also that you may not want to link in this library under SCO's Open Desktop.

Running the Text Program

The text program creates the menu bar and menus from the last program, as well as a frame widget with a scrolled text widget as its child. The source file texttest.c is loaded into the text widget, so you'll want to be in the same directory as the file texttest.c is when you run the text program. (Of course, you could modify this simple program to take any file name as a command-line parameter or to load a different hard-coded file name, if you prefer.) Figure 7-6 shows the text program.

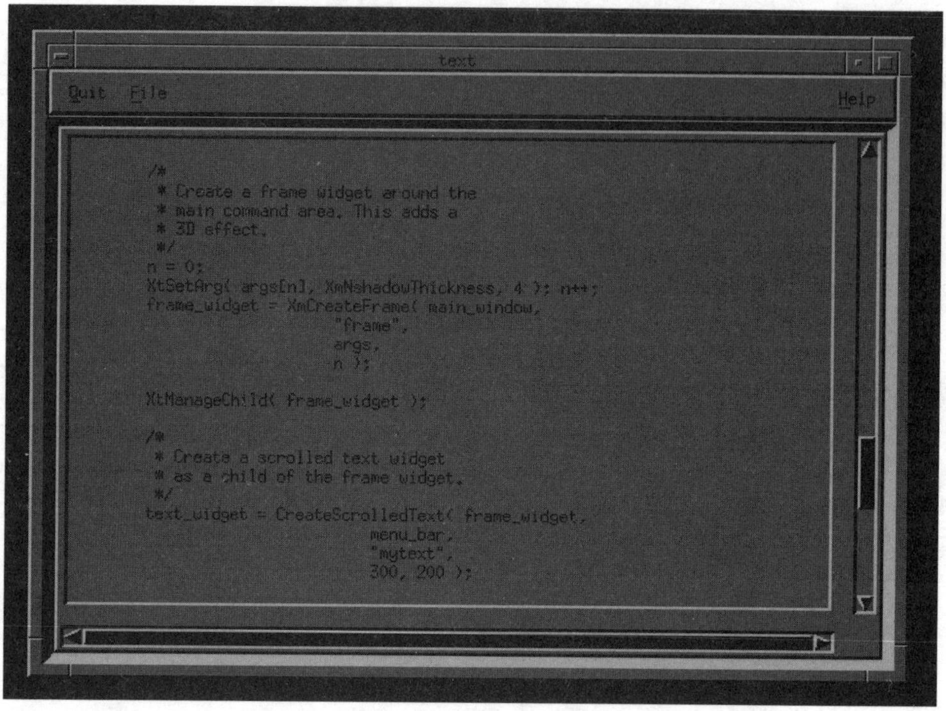

Figure 7-6. The Text Program.

MOTIF FUNCTIONS AND MACROS INTRODUCED IN THIS CHAPTER

The following is a list of Motif functions and macros that were introduced in this chapter.

```
XmCreateFrame()
XmCreateScrolledText()
XmCreateText()
XmTextGetEditable()
XmTextGetString()
XmTextReplace()
XmTextSetEditable()
XmTextSetString()
```

You should be familiar with these functions and macros before you go on to Chapter 8.

X TOOLKIT FUNCTIONS AND MACROS INTRODUCED IN THIS CHAPTER

The following is a list of X toolkit functions and macros introduced in this chapter.

```
XtFree()
XtMalloc()
```

You should be familiar with these functions and macros before you go on to Chapter 8.

SUMMARY

This chapter introduced the text widget—a widget you will use over and over again in your applications. The complex text widget handles most text entry in Motif. It can be either a single-line prompt or a multiline text editor. You can add scroll bars to a multiline text widget, especially if you want to edit a large amount of text, such as a text file. The function XmCreateText() creates a text widget. XmCreateScrolledText() creates a text widget as a child of a scrolled window widget—making a text widget with scroll bars.

We also introduced the Motif 3D frame widget, a widget that does nothing but enhance the look of your user interface. XmCreateFrame() creates a frame widget.

In each chapter we've enhanced a basic Motif program to keep adding things that you will need in your applications, from dialogs to menu bars to menus. This step-by-step progression was intentional; we wanted to provide a firm foundation in the Motif toolkit. In addition, we wanted to focus on the basic tasks of creating Motif applications rather than the abstract concept of the Motif toolkit. Our aim is always to concentrate on real problems faced by real application designers rather than explore the Motif toolkit in depth.

In Section II, we'll jump around and enhance our knowledge of the essentials in the Motif toolkit. The following chapters will cover subjects such as: the list widget; the scale widget; and using raw Xlib function calls in a Motif application.

More Motif Widgets

S ection I built an application shell for Motif programs. Section II, is going to enhance the coverage of essential features in the Motif toolkit. Section II features more Motif widgets, including:

* The list widget, which allows you to choose an item from a list or a scrolled list (Chapter 8).
* Creating two or more top-level windows, by creating top-level shell widgets. Many applications need to have a number of top-level windows visible at the same time (Chapter 9).
* The scale widget, which is used to let the user select an analog value between a program-set minimum and maximum value (Chapter 10).
* The drawing area widget, a raw window widget that lets you call raw Xlib functions when the basic widgets of the Motif toolkit don't prove to be adequate (Chapter 11).
* Background processing—using timers and work procedures from the Xt Intrinsics to perform work while an application is idle (Chapter 12).

# Chapter 8

List Widgets

C hapter 7 covered text entry, a very common application task. This chapter, is going to cover another very common task: presenting items in a list and letting the user choose items from the list.

Motif has a number of functions to aid this task, and aligns these functions under the Motif list widget. This widget manages a number of items and allows you to scroll through those items (with optional scroll bars). The user can then choose items from the list, after which, a user function is called back by the list widget (the callbacks are optional, too). Figure 8-1 shows the list widget in action.

Figure 8-1. The List Widget in Action.

We've already seen a list widget in the file-selection box in Chapter 4. In this chapter, we're going to delve deeper into the list widget. Figure 8-2 shows the list widget class.

Widget Class Name	Class Pointer	Created By
XmList	xmListWidgetClass	XmCreateList()

Figure 8-2. The List Widget Class.

The include file for the list widget is Xm/List.h. There are two main functions to create a list widget, XmCreateList() and XmCreateScrolledList().

CREATING A LIST

You can create a list by using the following program:

```
#include <Xm/List.h>

Widget          parent, list_widget;
String          name;
continued...
```

180

...from previous page
```
ArgList          args;
Cardinal         n;
list_widget = XmCreateList( parent,
             name,
             args,
             n );

list_widget = XmCreateScrolledList( parent,
             name,
             args,
             n );
```

Call `XtManageChild()` after creating the widget:

```
XtManageChild( list_widget );
```

`XmCreateList()` creates a list widget, while `XmCreateScrolledList()` creates a scrolled window widget and then a list widget as a child of the scrolled window widget. (The scrolled window widget was covered in depth in the last chapter on the text widget). You can view `XmCreateList()` as an analog to `XmCreateText()` and `XmCreateScrolledList()` as an analog to `XmCreateScrolledText()`.

Use the X toolkit function `XtParent()` to get the widget ID of the parent scrolled window widget or to get the widget ID of the parent of any widget:

```
Widget   child_widget, parent_widget;

parent_widget = XtParent( child_widget );
```

The two most common list operations are adding items into a list and selecting items from a list. The latter is an incredibly complex operation and is described in the following section.

SELECTING ITEMS IN A LIST

There are four selection polices that govern how you can select items in a list:

```
*  XmBROWSE_SELECT
*  XmEXTENDED_SELECT
*  XmMULTIPLE_SELECT
*  XmSINGLE_SELECT
```

If you intend to use any selection policy other than single select, we strongly advise you to read and re-read the *OSF/Motif Programmer's Reference Manual* entry on `XmList`. Each of these policies acts differently and has its own callback type. You will probably want to try out all four of the selection types described below by

181

modifying the listtest program, so that you can gain a better understanding of how they function.

Single Selection

The single-selection policy is the easiest to use and understand. When the user clicks (using mouse button 1 in the default case) on an item, that item becomes selected. Any previously selected item becomes unselected, which means that only one single item may be selected at a time—hence the term "single selection." To set the selection policy, you place a value in the selectionPolicy resource (XmNselectionPolicy in C programs). To set the selection policy to single selection, set the selectionPolicy resource to XmSINGLE_SELECT as shown below:

```
Arg        args[10];
int        n;

n = 0;
XtSetArg( args[n], XmNselectionPolicy,XmSINGLE_SELECT ); n++;

/* create list widget... */
```

Since the single selection mechanism is the easiest to use and understand, this is the selection policy we'll use in the listtest program.

Multiple Selection

With multiple selection, you click on an item and it becomes selected. If other items were already selected, then those other items remain selected (thus, multiple items can be selected). Note that if you click on an item that is already selected, then that item becomes unselected. The listtest program for multiple section is as follows:

```
Arg        args[10];
int        n;

n = 0;
XtSetArg( args[n], XmNselectionPolicy, XmMULTIPLE_SELECT ); n++;

/* create list widget... */
```

Browse Selection

With browse selection, while the mouse button is pressed, you can move the mouse pointer over a number of items. Each item is selected when the mouse pointer moves on top of the item, and unselected when the mouse pointer moves away from the item. When the mouse button is released, the item underneath the mouse pointer, if there is one, is selected. XmBROWSE_SELECT is shown below:

```
Arg       args[10];
int       n;

n = 0;
XtSetArg( args[n], XmNselectionPolicy, XmBROWSE_SELECT ); n++;

/* create list widget... */
```

Extended Selection

With extended selection, you can press and hold down mouse button 1, and while continuing to hold the mouse button down, drag the mouse over a number of items. All these items are then selected. This selection policy is as follows:

```
Arg       args[10];
int       n;

n = 0;
XtSetArg( args[n], XmNselectionPolicy, XmEXTENDED_SELECT ); n++;

/* create list widget... */
```

THE LIST CALLBACKS

Each of the four selection policies has its own callback. These are shown in Figure 8-3.

Resource Name	Name in C Programs
browseSelectionCallback	XmNbrowseSelectionCallback
extendedSelectionCallback	XmNextendedSelectionCallback
multipleSelectionCallback	XmNmultipleSelectionCallback
singleSelectionCallback	XmNsingleSelectionCallback

Figure 8-3. List Widget Callback Types.

Here's how to set up the different callbacks (you'll only use one of these selection policies at a time):

```
Widget   list_widget;
void list_callback();

XtAddCallback( list_widget,
        XmNbrowseSelectionCallback,
        list_callback,
        NULL );

XtAddCallback( list_widget,
        XmNextendedSelectionCallback,
        list_callback,
        NULL );

XtAddCallback( list_widget,
        XmNmultipleSelectionCallback,
        list_callback,
        NULL );

XtAddCallback( list_widget,
        XmNsingleSelectionCallback,
        list_callback,
        NULL );
```

All the different list callbacks send the data structure as the callbacks' `call_data`, an `XmListCallbackStruct` structure:

```
typedef struct
        {
        int          reason;
        XEvent       *event;
        XmString     item;
        int          item_length;
        int          item_position;
        XmString     *selected_items;
        int          selected_item_count;
        int          selection_type;
        } XmListCallbackStruct;
```

The item field is the most important field in the `XmListCallbackStruct` structure as this field contains the actual item selected (as a Motif `XmString`).

Here's a sample callback function, used in the file `listtest.c`, below, for a single-selection policy list widget:

```
void list_callback( widget, client_data, list_data )

Widget                       widget;
caddr_t                      client_data;
XmListCallbackStruct         *list_data;
```
continued...

184

...from previous page

```
{            /* list_callback */
             char    *string;
             XmStringGetLtoR( list_data->item,
                  XmSTRING_DEFAULT_CHARSET,
                  &string );

             printf( "Item chosen was %s, item # %d\n",
                  string, list_data->item_position );
              * XtFree (string);
}            /* list_callback */
```

SPECIFYING THE HEIGHT OF THE LIST WIDGET

You can set the height of the list widget by setting the number of visible items. This list widget will then try to size itself to be tall enough to hold that many items. The visibleItemCount resource (XmNvisibleItemCount in C programs) holds this value.

To set the number of visible lines to ten, use the following:

```
Arg       args[10];
int       n;

n = 0;
XtSetArg( args[n], XmNvisibleItemCount, 10 ); n++;

/* create the list widget... */
```

Note that this is a request. The list widget or the list's parent are all free to refuse the resize request.

CONTROLLING LIST SCROLL BARS

The scrollBarDisplayPolicy resource (XmNscrollBarDisplayPolicy in C programs) specifies the policy used for displaying scroll bar as one of the following:

* XmAS_NEEDED
* XmSTATIC

The default is XmAS_NEEDED. With this value, the vertical scroll bar will only be displayed if there are more items in the list than there are visible items. With a scrollBarDisplayPolicy of XmSTATIC, then the vertical scroll bar will always be visible.

185

The horizontal scroll bar depends on the value of another resource, the listSizePolicy resource (XmNlistSizePolicy in C programs). The listSizePolicy resource can have one of the following values:

```
* XmCONSTANT
* XmRESIZE_IF_POSSIBLE
* XmVARIABLE
```

The default is XmVARIABLE. XmVARIABLE means that the list widget will try to grow to the width of the widest item. Thus, no horizontal scroll bar will be visible. With a value of XmCONSTANT, a horizontal scroll bar is added when necessary, and the list is not made wider. With a value of XmRESIZE_IF_POSSIBLE, the list will first try to resize itself so that it fits the widest item within the list. If the list cannot grow that wide, then a horizontal scroll bar is added.

SETTING THE NUMBER OF ITEMS IN A LIST

The itemCount resource (XmNitemCount in C programs) keeps a count of the number of items in the list.and is automatically updated when you add or delete items in the list. The number of items should be set to zero (0) in the Arg array before a list widget is created to make sure that an item can be appended to the list. This is shown below:

```
Arg        args[10];
int        n;

n = 0;
XtSetArg( args[n], XmNitemCount, 0 ); n++;

/* create the list widget... */
```

Note that the number of items should reflect the actual number of items in the list. You may encounter problems if you set the number of items to reflect a value that is not accurate.

The items resource (XmNitems in C programs) is the current list. This resource is an array of XmStrings. We've found it easier to use the function XmListAddItem() or XmListAddItemUnselected() to add an item to the list.

A FUNCTION TO CREATE A LIST WIDGET

The function CreateScrolledList() creates a scrolled list as a child of the given parent widget. It requires a name, a callback function and an Arg array (with a number of items already used in the Arg array). CreateScrolledList() sets up the scrolled list widget to use a single-selection policy, with zero (0) initial items. This is shown below:

```
Widget CreateScrolledList( parent, name, args, n, list_callback )

Widget parent;
char    name[];
Arg     *args;
int     n;
void    (*list_callback)(); /* call back function */

{       /* CreateScrolledList */
        Widget  list_widget;

        /*
         * Set up size. Note that
         * n is passed as a parameter to
         * CreateScrolledList().
         */
        XtSetArg( args[n], XmNitemCount, 0 ); n++;
        XtSetArg( args[n], XmNselectionPolicy, XmSINGLE_SELECT ); n++;

        list_widget = XmCreateScrolledList( parent,
                                    name,
                                    args,
                                    n );

        XtManageChild( list_widget );

        XtAddCallback( list_widget,
                       XmNsingleSelectionCallback,
                       list_callback,
                       NULL );

        return( list_widget );

}       /* CreateScrolledList */
```

Adding Items to a List

To add an item to a list, you can use `XmListAddItem()` or `XmListAddItemUnselected()`. Both functions take the same parameters:

```
#include <Xm/List.h>

Widget      list_widget;
XmString    motif_string;
```
continued...

187

...from previous page

```
int          position;

XmListAddItem( widget,
               motif_string,
               position );

XmListAddItemUnselected( widget,
               motif_string,
               position );
```

The difference between `XmListAddItem()` and `XmListAddItemUnselected()` is that `XmListAddItemUnselected()` makes sure the new item is not added to the list being already selected. That is, if you add an item to a list between two selected items, your new item may become selected (depending on the selection policy in use). To avoid any problems in this area, we always use `XmListAddItemUnselected()`.

The position parameter specifies where in the list you want to add the new item. The first position in the list is position 1 in Motif programming as compared to C programming, which assumes you start counting at 0. Position zero (0) is used to specify the last position in the list, especially for appending items.

The function `AddToList()` adds an item in a regular C string to the given position in a list. This is as follows:

```
AddToList( widget, string, position )

Widget       widget;
char         string[];
int          position;

{            /* AddToList */
      XmString      motif_string, Str2XmString(); /* string.c */

      motif_string = Str2XmString( string );

      XmListAddItemUnselected( widget,
            motif_string,
            position );

      XmStringFree( motif_string );

}            /* AddToList */
```

`AddToList()` first converts the new item to an `XmString` type and then calls `XmListAddItemUnselected()`.

Determining How Many Items are in a List

Since the `itemCount` resource is automatically updated when you add an item to the list using `XmListAddItem()` or `XmListAddItemUnselected()`, we can read the value of this resource to determine how many items are presently in the list.

The `function ListSize()` does just that. To read the value of a resource though, we use the Xtoolkit function `XtGetValues()`:

```
Widget      widget;
ArgList     args;
Cardinal    n;

XtGetValues( widget, args, n );
```

Using `XtGetValues()` is tricky. The basic concept follows these steps. First, use `XtSetArg()` to set up the `Arg` array for the values you want. For each resource you place in the `Arg` array, the value part should be a pointer to a variable. Second, call `XtGetValues()`. After this call, the variables now hold the proper values.

There are a few caveats, however. You must always provide a variable of the proper type. If you provide too little storage, your program may corrupt memory and will probably lead to a core dump. This creates a tough problem for debugging. If you're trying to access the value of a string resource, you pass the string, which is a char pointer, not a pointer to a pointer to char. The resulting string should be treated as a read-only value. If you want to change this string, copy the string into local storage.

Here's how to use `XtGetValues()` to get the number of items in a list:

```
int     size;        /* local storage for the number of items */
Arg     args[10];

XtSetArg( args[0], /* Arg array */
    XmNitemCount,           /* which resource to retrieve */
    &size );                /* pointer to local storage for result */

XtGetValues( widget,        /* widget to get the value for */
    args,                   /* Arg array from above  */
    1 );                    /* how many items are used in Arg array */

/*
 * Now, size contains the number of
 * items in the list
 */
```

`XtGetValues()` is kind of tricky, especially since older versions of the X Toolkit Intrinsics allow for some tricks that Release 4 of the X Window System no longer allow. Be very careful when using `XtGetValues()`. If your Motif programs crash and create a core dump, any call to `XtGetValues()` should be checked out, as this may very well be the problem.

The function ListSize(), below, uses the above techniques to retrieve the number of items in a list:

```
ListSize( widget )

Widget      widget;

{      /* ListSize */
       int   size;
       Arg   args[10];

       /*
        * Get the number of items
        * in the list widget
        */
       XtSetArg( args[0], XmNitemCount, &size );

       XtGetValues( widget, args, 1 );

       return( size );

}      /* ListSize */
```

Removing Items from a List

There are a number of functions to delete an item or a number of items from a list. The hardest part here is that only two are available in Motif 1.0. Motif 1.1 adds a number of very useful list item deletion functions.

In Motif 1.1, you can delete all items in a list with a call to XmListDeleteAllItems():

```
Widget  list_widget;

XmListDeleteAllItems( list_widget );
```

This function is really useful when you have a list widget that you want to clear out and then fill with a new set of items. This is a very common task.

XmListDeleteItem() deletes an item from a list. Unfortunately, it is only useful when you know exactly what you want to delete. To use XmListDeleteItem(), first create a Motif XmString and fill it with the item you want removed from the list. Then call XmListDeleteItem():

```
Widget    list_widget;
XmString  motif_string;

XmListDeleteItem( list_widget,
          motif_string;
```

190

Unless you know exactly what you want to delete, XmListDeleteItem() won't help. More often than not, you'll know the position of what you want to delete, but not the actual contents of the list at that position. In that case, use XmListDeletePos():

```
Widget      list_widget;
int         position;

XmListDeletePos( list_widget,
          position );
```

Note that position 1 is the first item in the list. If you use a position of zero (0), then calling XmListDeletePos() means to delete the last item in the list. We'll use XmListDeletePos() in the function ClearList().

Clearing out a List

The function ClearList() clears out all the items in a list widget. This function takes a very simple-minded approach to this task and you should be able to write a more efficient version yourself. First, get the number of items in the list be calling the function ListSize() as shown in the previous section. Then, call XmListDeletePos() in a loop to keep deleting the last list item—using a position of 0. Finally, we delete the very first list item with a call to XmListDeletePos() with a position of 1.

Using XmListDeleteAllItems() would be much more efficient, but as of this writing not all Motif systems have upgraded to Motif 1.1 yet. It will probably take about a year to get the majority of installations upgraded, and some installations will probably never upgrade. So, we've taken the least common denominator approach. If you can guarantee that all your installations will be using Motif 1.1 or higher, then go ahead and use XmListDeleteAllItems():

```
ClearList( widget )

Widget  widget;

{       /* ClearList */
        int  max, i;

        max = ListSize( widget );

        for( i = 2; i <= max; i++ )
            {
            XmListDeletePos( widget,
                    0 ); /* delete last list item */
            }
```

continued...

191

...from previous page

```
        XmListDeletePos( widget, 1 ); /* first item */

}        /* ClearList */
```

Moving to a Given Position in the List

In your applications, you may have a particular item in a list that you want the user to see. For example, you may want to start out at the last choice a user made. Or maybe the list is the result of some query and you want a particular item to be at the top of the list display as shown below.

```
Widget      list_widget;
XmString    motif_string;

XmListSetItem( list_widget,
        motif_string );
```

Before using `XmListSetItem()`, you must create and fill a Motif `XmString` with the item you are looking for.

`XmListSetPos()` works like `XmListSetItem()`, but `XmListSetPos()` sets the top of the visible list display to a given item number. That is, if you know you want to show position 45 in the list, but you're not sure what is at position 45, then use `XmListSetPos()`:

```
Widget    list_widget;
int       position;

XmListSetPos( list_widget,
        position );
```

Note once again, that position 1 is the first item in the list, position 2 is the second item in the list and position zero (0) is the last item in the list.

Source Code for List.c

The file `list.c` contains a number of utility functions for working with list widgets. This is shown below:

```
/*
 *      list.c
 *      Motif Scrolled List Widget Functions
 *
 *      Written for Power Programming Motif
 *
```

continued...

...from previous page
```
 */

#include        <X11/Intrinsic.h>
#include        <X11/StringDefs.h>
#include        <Xm/Xm.h>
#include        <Xm/List.h>

AddToList( widget, string, position )

Widget          widget;
char            string[];
int             position;

/*
 *      AddToList() adds a text string to a list
 *      widget at a given position in the list.
 */

{       /* AddToList */
        XmString                motif_string, Str2XmString();

        motif_string = Str2XmString( string );

        XmListAddItemUnselected( widget,
                motif_string,
                position );

        XmStringFree( motif_string );

}       /* AddToList */

ClearList( widget )

Widget          widget;

/*
 * Clears out all items in
 * a list widget. In Motif 1.1,
 * we could use XmListDeleteAllItems(),
 * but that's missing in 1.0.
 */

{       /* ClearList */
        int     max, i;

        max = ListSize( widget );

        for( i = 2; i <= max; i++ )
                {
                XmListDeletePos( widget,
```
continued...

...from previous page

```
                              0 ); /* delete last list item */
              }

      XmListDeletePos( widget, 1 ); /* first item */

}       /* ClearList */

Widget CreateScrolledList( parent, name, args, n, list_callback )

Widget        parent;
char          name[];
Arg           *args;
int           n;
void          (*list_callback)(); /* call back function */

/*
 * Creates a scrolled list widget.
 */

{       /* CreateScrolledList */
        Widget  list_widget;

        /*
         * Set up size. Note that
         * n is passed as a parameter to
         * CreateScrolledList().
         */
        XtSetArg( args[n], XmNitemCount, 0 ); n++;
        XtSetArg( args[n], XmNselectionPolicy, XmSINGLE_SELECT ); n++;

        list_widget = XmCreateScrolledList( parent,
                        name,
                        args,
                        n );

        XtManageChild( list_widget );

        XtAddCallback( list_widget,
               XmNsingleSelectionCallback,
               list_callback,
               NULL );

        return( list_widget );

}       /* CreateScrolledList */

ListSize( widget )
```

continued...

...from previous page

```
Widget          widget;

/*
 * Returns the number of elements in a list
 */

{       /* ListSize */
        int     size;
        Arg     args[10];

        /*
         * Get the number of items
         * in the list widget
         */
        XtSetArg( args[0], XmNitemCount, &size );

        XtGetValues( widget, args, 1 );

}       /* ListSize */

/* end of file */
```

A PROGRAM TO SHOW HOW THE LIST WIDGET WORKS

The listtest program creates a simple scrolled list widget and fills it with eight items. When you click on an item, the function list_callback() will print out the item you clicked on. This program is as simple as possible so as to concentrate just on the list widget, since you'll no doubt use lists in just about every application you write. You'll learn the most if you experiment around with all the list resources described above. So, while this program uses the single-selection policy, you may want to try the other three selection policies, as well.

Source Code for Listtest.c

The file listtest.c contains the main() function for the listtest program, as shown in the source code below:

```
/*
 *      listtest.c
 *      Program to test the creation of
 *      a Motif scrolled list widget.
 *
 *      Written for Power Programming Motif
 *
```

continued...

...from previous page
```
 */

#include        <X11/Intrinsic.h>
#include        <X11/StringDefs.h>
#include        <Xm/Xm.h>
#include        <Xm/List.h>

void list_callback( widget, client_data, list_data )

Widget                                  widget;
caddr_t                                 client_data;
XmListCallbackStruct                    *list_data;

{       /* list_callback */
        char    *string;

        XmStringGetLtoR( list_data->item,
                XmSTRING_DEFAULT_CHARSET,
                &string );

        printf( "Item chosen was %s, item # %d\n",
                string, list_data->item_position );
        XtFree (string);
}       /* list_callback */

main( argc, argv )

int     argc;
char    *argv[];

{       /* main */
        Widget    parent;
        Widget    list_widget, CreateScrolledList();
        Arg       args[10];
        int       n;

        parent = XtInitialize( argv[0],
                "Listtest",
                NULL,
                0,
                &argc,
                argv );

        n = 0;
        XtSetArg( args[n], XmNallowShellResize, True ); n++;
        XtSetValues( parent, args, n );


        n = 0;
        XtSetArg(args[n], XmNvisibleItemCount, 10); n++;
        list_widget = CreateScrolledList( parent,
                        "list",
```
continued...

196

...from previous page

```
                        args, n,
                        list_callback );

        AddToList( list_widget, "Jo is not here 1", 1 );
        AddToList( list_widget, "Jo is not here 2", 0 );
        AddToList( list_widget, "Jo is not here 3", 0 );
        AddToList( list_widget, "Jo is not here 4", 0 );
        AddToList( list_widget, "Jo is not here 5", 0 );
        AddToList( list_widget, "Jo is not here 6", 0 );
        AddToList( list_widget, "Jo is not here 7", 0 );
        AddToList( list_widget, "Jo is not here 8", 0 );

        XtRealizeWidget( parent );
        XtMainLoop();

}       /* main */

/* end of file */
```

Compiling and Linking the Listtest Program

The `listtest` program needs the following C source files:

```
list.c
listtest.c
string.c (from Chapter 2)
```

You can compile and link the `listtest` program with:

```
cc -o listtest list.c listtest.c string.c -lXm -lXt -lX11
```

If you use `Makefile` in Appendix C, you can type:

```
make listtest
```

or

```
make all
```

Running the Listtest Program

As with all the programs in this book, you can run the `listtest` program without any command-line parameters. It will present a simple list. When you click on a list item, the `list_callback()` function will be called back and will print out the text of the item that you selected. Quit the program by using the close choice in the Motif window menu. Figure 8-4 shows the `listtest` program.

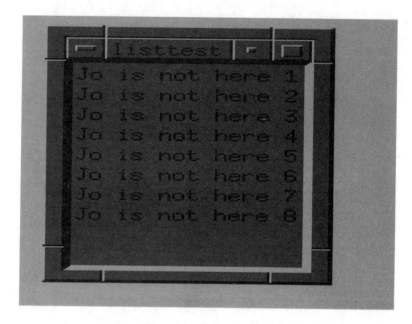

Figure 8-4. The Listtest Program.

When it starts up, the listtest program will size itself so that the whole list is visible. If you make the window shorter vertically, then a scroll bar should appear. Figure 8-5 shows the listtest program with a scroll bar.

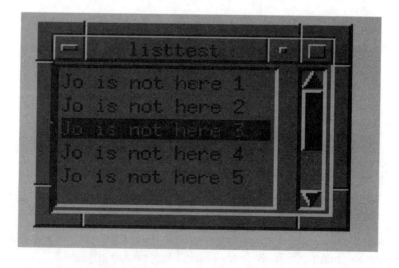

Figure 8-5. The Listtest Program with a Scroll Bar.

MOTIF FUNCTIONS AND MACROS INTRODUCED IN THIS CHAPTER

The following is a list of the Motif functions and macros introduced in this chapter.

```
XmCreateList()
XmCreateScrolledList()
XmListAddItem()
XmListAddItemUnselected()
XmListDeleteAllItems()
XmListDeleteItem()
XmListDeletePos()
XmListSetItem()
```

You should be familiar with these functions and macros before you move on to Chapter 9.

X TOOLKIT FUNCTIONS AND MACROS INTRODUCED IN THIS CHAPTER

The following is a list of Xtoolkit functions and macros introduced in this chapter.

```
XtGetValues()
XtParent()
```

You should be familiar with these functions and macros before you move on to Chapter 9.

SUMMARY

This chapter introduced the list widget which is commonly used to present a list of items. The list widget is used in the file selection box widget discussed in Chapter 4. `XmCreateList()` is used to create a list widget. If you have a large number of items and want to present those items in a scrolled window use `XmCreateScrolledList()`.

`XmListAddItem()` is used to add an item to a list, and `XmListDeleteItem()` is used to remove an item from the list.

The next chapter diverges a bit—it presents a technique to allow your applications to have two top-level windows (and widgets), rather than the more common one top-level window that we've used in every program so far.

# Chapter 9

Creating Two Top-Level Windows

E very Motif program we've created throughout this book thus far, has used only one top-level window (i.e., only one window was set up as an application main window under a top-level shell). In this chapter, we'll show how to add another top-level shell widget which will create another top-level window. Many sophisticated applications, such as electronic-publishing systems, need to have a number of top-level shell windows on the screen at the same time. Some of these windows could be dialogs, but many will be top-level shells.

SHELL WIDGETS

Shell widgets exist to provide a layer between your program and the X Window System. A window manager in X, such as the Motif window manager mwm, requires that all top-level windows register certain information. This process of registering the proper information is rather complex, and the necessary information is defined in the *Inter-Client Communications Conventions Manual—* the ICCCM.

Thus far, we've been spared these messy details as we've used the top-level application shell widget created by XtInitialize(), and the pop-up shell widgets created by all menu and dialog pop-ups. Now, if we want to create more top-level windows, we need to create new top-level shell widgets.

Each top-level shell widget has its own widget hierarchy, and this hierarchy must be realized with XtRealizeWidget(), just like we've always done with the parent widget returned by XtInitialize(). Remember that when you realize a widget, all of its managed children are realized too.

Each of these top-level shells, when realized, can have only one child widget (usually a main window or a form or some widget that manages its own child widgets)—just like the top-level application shell widget created by XtInitialize().

Top-level shells are used for all permanent (or semi-permanent) top-level windows. Pop-up shells are used for windows that won't be up for a long period of time, such as dialogs and menus. (Menus actually use an override shell while dialogs use a transient shell, but for our purposes now, both of these are not intended to remain on the screen for a long time.) So, the task before us now is to create another top-level shell widget.

CREATING ANOTHER TOP-LEVEL SHELL

With another top-level shell, we have two application windows on the screen. XtCreateApplicationShell(), an X Toolkit Intrinsics function, will create another top-level shell, of a particular widget class:

```
Widget          parent2;
String          name;
WidgetClass     widget_class;
ArgList         args;
Cardinal        n;

parent2 = XtCreateApplicationShell( name,
            widget_class,
            args,
            n );
```

You'll want to eventually call XtRealizeWidget() after you create the descendents of the new top-level shell.

THE TOP-LEVEL SHELL WIDGET CLASS

For our purposes, we want to create our widget top-Level Shell Widget Class, as shown in Figure 9-1.

Widget Class Name	Class Pointer	Created By
TopLevelShell	topLevelShellWidgetClass	XtCreateApplicationShell()

Figure 9-1. The Top-Level Shell Widget Class.

When using a top-level shell, be sure to include both Xm/Xm.h and X11/Shell.h. This last file is part of the Xt Intrinsics.

Here's how we create our second top-level shell in the file toptest.c:

```
#include <Xm/Xm.h>
#include <X11/Shell.h>

Widget    parent2;
Arg       args[10];
int       n;

n = 0;
parent2 = XtCreateApplicationShell( "parent2",
                topLevelShellWidgetClass,
                args,
                n );
```

Use XtAppCreateShell() in Release 4 Systems

If you are using Release 4 of the X Window System, XtCreateApplicationShell() is considered obsolete. Instead, a new function, XtAppCreateShell(), has been added to act as XtCreateApplicationShell(). XtAppCreateShell() takes the following parameters:

```
Widget       parent2;
String       application_name;
String       application_class;
WidgetClass  widget_class = topLevelShellWidgetClass;
Display      *display;
ArgList      args;
Cardinal     n;

parent2 = XtAppCreateShell( application_name,
        application_class,
        widget_class,
        display,
        args,
        n );
```

The display parameter specifies which X display connection you want to use. The Xt Intrinsics keeps some resource values indexed by the display connection and allows you to have multiple display connections in one application. (See *Advanced X Window Applications Programming* for more information on the low-level details of multiple display connections and the issues you will have to face.)

Remember, you can use XtDisplay() to get the display connection (a pointer to a Display structure) that was set up for the first top-level shell widget (the application's shell).

```
Widget  parent1;
Display *display;

display = XtDisplay( parent1 );
```

When you are creating a second (or third and so on) top-level shell widget, the widget_class should be topLevelShellWidgetClass.

THE TOPTEST PROGRAM

The `toptest` program tests the use of `XtCreateApplicationShell()` by creating a second top-level shell widget. When running this program, you'll see two top-level windows that you can resize and move around independently of one another. These top-level windows don't do much, but they do demonstrate the use of top-level shells. If you're writing complex applications, chances are you'll need an extra top-level shell or two. The `toptest` program is shown in Figure 9-2.

Figure 9-2. The Toptest Program in Action.

Source Code for Toptest.c

The file `toptest.c` contains the meat of the `toptest` program, its `main()` function. Notice how the program calls `XtInitialize()` and returns one top-level shell widget. This widget is used as a parent to create a main window, using `CreateMainWindow()` from `mainwind.c`.

We then create a menu bar with `quit` and `help` choices. This should be old hat by now, as we've done this in every program since Chapter 5.

The new wrinkle is that we call `XtCreateApplicationShell()` to create another top-level shell. Then we create another main window and menu bar. You end up with two top-level windows, two menu bars and two chances to quit the application (with two chances to ask for a not-so-helpful help message):

```
/*
 *      toptest.c
 *      Test Motif Top-Level Shells
 *
 *      Written for Power Programming Motif
 *
 */

#include   <X11/Intrinsic.h>
#include   <X11/StringDefs.h>

#include   <Xm/Xm.h>
#include   <X11/Shell.h>

main( argc, argv )

int        argc;
char       *argv[];

{       /* main */
        Widget   main_window;
        Widget   CreateMainWindow(); /* mainwind.c */
        Widget   parent, main_widget, menu_bar;
        Widget   CreateMenubar(); /* menubar.c */
        Widget   parent2, main_window2, main_widget2, menu_bar2;
        char     help_message[ 400 ];
        Arg      args[10];
        int      n;


        /*
         * Set up Xt Intrinsics and
         * create first top-level shell.
         */
        parent = XtInitialize( argv[0],
            "TopLevelShell",
            NULL,
            0,
            &argc,
            argv );

        n = 0;
```
continued...

...from previous page

```
     XtSetArg( args[n], XmNallowShellResize, True ); n++;
     XtSetValues( parent, args, n );

     /*
      * Create a menu bar for the first
      * top-level shell.
      */
     main_widget = CreateMainWindow( parent,
                     "main",
                     300, 200 );

     strcpy( help_message, "When in danger, or in doubt\n" );
     strcat( help_message, "run in circles, scream and shout.\n" );

     menu_bar  = CreateMenubar( main_widget, help_message );

     XmMainWindowSetAreas( main_widget,        /* main window */
         menu_bar,               /* menu bar */
         (Widget) NULL,          /* command area */
         (Widget) NULL,          /* horiz scroll */
         (Widget) NULL,          /* vert scroll */
         (Widget) NULL )         /* work area */

     /*
      * Realize the widget
      * Hierarchy for the first
      * top-level shell.
      */
     XtRealizeWidget( parent );

     /*
      * Create second top-level shell
      */
     n = 0;
     parent2 = XtCreateApplicationShell( "parent2",
             topLevelShellWidgetClass,
             args,
             n );

     main_widget2 = CreateMainWindow( parent2,
                     "main2",
                     300, 200 );

     menu_bar2    = CreateMenubar( main_widget2, help_message );

     XmMainWindowSetAreas( main_widget2,       /* main window */
         menu_bar2,              /* menu bar */
         (Widget) NULL,          /* command area */
         (Widget) NULL,          /* horiz scroll */
```

continued...

...from previous page

```
            (Widget) NULL,         /* vert scroll */
            (Widget) NULL );       /* work area */

        XtRealizeWidget( parent2 );

        /*
         * After BOTH top-level
         * shells are realized, then
         * we enter the XtMainLoop().
         */
        XtMainLoop();

}       /* main */

/* end of file */
```

Compiling and Linking the Toptest Program

The `toptest` program requires the following C source files:

> `dialog.c` (from Chapter 4)
> `mainwind.c` (from Chapter 5)
> `menubar.c` (from Chapter 5)
> `string.c` (from Chapter 2)
> `toptest.c`

You can compile and link the `toptest` program with the following command on most UNIX-based systems:

```
cc -o toptest dialog.o mainwind.o menubar.o string.o \
    toptest.o -lXm -lXt -lX11 -lPW
```

The PW library is needed for `dialog.c`. If you're running under SCO's Open Desktop 1.0 though, you may not want to link in this library.

If you're using `Makefile` in Appendix C, you can type:

```
make toptest
```

or

```
make all
```

Running the Toptest Program

The `toptest` program looks a lot like the `menubar` program in Chapter 5, only you get two menu bars—one each in two main windows). Click on the Quit choice (and click again on OK in the pop-up dialog) to quit the program. Figure 9-3 shows the `toptest` program.

Figure 9-3. The Toptest Program.

X TOOLKIT FUNCTIONS AND MACROS INTRODUCED IN THIS CHAPTER

The following is a list of Xtoolkit functions and macros introduced in this chapter.

```
XtCreateApplicationShell()
XtAppCreateShell()
```

You should be familiar with these functions and macros before moving on to Chapter 10.

SUMMARY

This chapter introduced a concept that is simple in practice, but difficult to figure out. The use of multiple top-level shell widgets will be fairly common in your applications, especially if you tend to write very complex applications such as electronic-publishing systems.

The basic concept is to create a second (or third, or whatever) top-level shell widget, using `XtCreateApplicationShell()` or `XtAppCreateShell()`—the latter for those who have Release 4 of the X Window System. You can use this second top-level shell as a parent to create a child widget, and then create many more child widgets of that child, and so on, just like we've done in every application so far (only now we have two top-level parents to choose from).

Now that you have `XtCreateApplicationShell()` figured out, add it to your bag of tricks in case you ever need to have multiple top-level windows.

The next chapter introduces another candidate for your bag of tricks—the scale widget.

# Chapter 10

The Scale Widget

T he scale widget allows values to be adjusted using an analog scale or slide. Often called a valuator or slider, the scale widget provides you with the ability to select a value within a prespecified range.

This chapter is going to introduce the scale widget and show how you can use this widget in your programs. The scale widget, like other Motif widgets, provides you with a host of options.

The scale widget is shown in Figure 10-1. The scale widget class is shown in Figure 10-2.

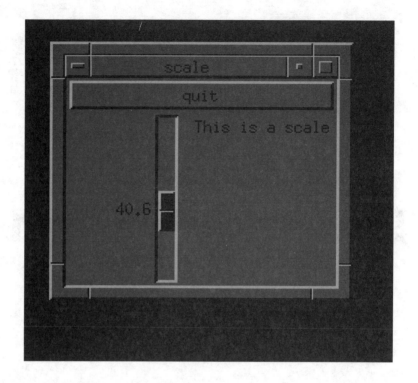

Figure 10-1. The Scale Widget.

Widget Class Name	Class Pointer	Creation Function
XmScale	xmScaleWidgetClass	XmCreateScale()

Figure 10-2. The Scale Widget Class.

The scale widget include file is Xm/Scale.h. Use XmCreateScale() to create
a scale widget:

```
#include <Xm/Scale.h>

Widget      parent;
Widget      scale_widget;
String      name;
ArgList     args;
Cardinal    n;
```

continued...

...from previous page
```
scale_widget = XmCreateScale( parent,
                    name,
                    args,
                    n );

XtManageChild( scale_widget );
```
Scale widgets can go up, down, left or right, all by setting resource values.

HORIZONTAL SCALES

Horizontal scales are created by setting the orientation resource (XmNorientation in C programs). This value can be set to either XmHORIZONTAL or XmVERTICAL:

```
Arg         args[20];
int         n;

n = 0;
XtSetArg( args[n], XmNorientation, XmHORIZONTAL ); n++;

/* create widget... */
```

With a horizontal scale, the high value on the scale (the maximum) can be on the right side or the left side. The processingDirection resource (XmNprocessingDirection in C programs) controls this. For horizontal scales, the choices are XmMAX_ON_RIGHT or XmMAX_ON_LEFT.

```
Arg         args[20];
int         n;

n = 0;
XtSetArg( args[n], XmNprocessingDirection, XmMAX_ON_RIGHT ); n++;

/* create widget... */
```

Figure 10-3 shows a horizontal, max on right scale widget.

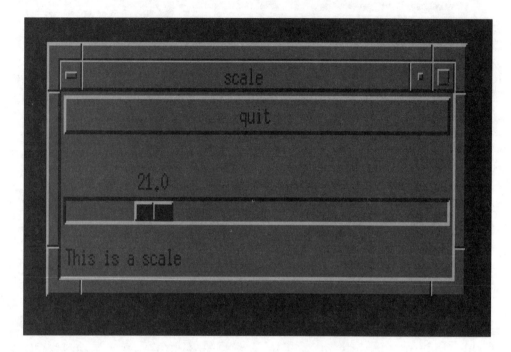

Figure 10-3. A Horizontal, Max on Right Scale Widget.

VERTICAL SCALES

Vertical scales are also created by setting the orientation resource
(XmNorientation in C programs). This value should be set to XmVERTICAL
for a vertical scale:

```
Arg      args[20];
int      n;

n = 0;
XtSetArg( args[n], XmNorientation, XmVERTICAL ); n++;

/* create widget... */
```

Once the scale is set to go up and down, you need to decide the maximum value.
Again, the processingDirection resource (XmNprocessingDirection in
C programs) controls this. For vertical scales, the choices are XmMAX_ON_TOP or
XmMAX_ON_BOTTOM.

214

```
Arg       args[20];
int       n;

n = 0;
XtSetArg( args[n], XmNprocessingDirection, XmMAX_ON_TOP ); n++;

/* create widget... */
```

Figure 10-4 shows a vertical, max on top scale widget.

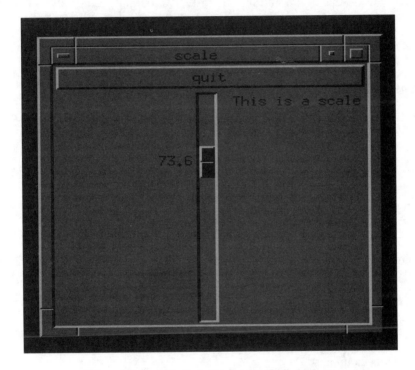

Figure 10-4. A Vertical, Max on Top Scale Widget.

SCALE VALUES

Thus far, we've mentioned maximum (and by assumption) minimum values. The scale widget allows you to select a value between the maximum and minimum. You can, of course, set both of these (the defaults and 100 and 0, respectively). The `maximum` (XmNmaximum in C programs) and `minimum` (XmNminimum in C programs) resources are both `int` types. In the following code we set the maximum to 1,000 and the minimum to 10:

```
Arg        args[20];
int        n;

n = 0;
XtSetArg( args[n], XmNmaximum, 1000 ); n++;
XtSetArg( args[n], XmNminimum, 10 ); n++;

/* create widget... */
```

Note that with the maximum and minimum (as well as the value), the scale widget just deals in integers, yet you've seen the scale widget display fixed-point decimal values in all the screen dumps in this chapter so far. The explanation for this is that the scale widget allows you to specify how many decimal points to shift over the value—for display purposes only. The real value under the hood remains an integer. This is very important when you set up a value-changed callback function—you'll get an integer, not a float.

The decimalPoints resource (XmNdecimalPoints in C programs) controls how many decimal points to shift the number over. The default is zero (0).

```
Arg        args[20];
int        n;

n = 0;
XtSetArg( args[n], XmNdecimalPoints, 1 ); n++;

/* create widget... */
```

Using the example provided, with decimalPoints set to one, a value of 100 will be displayed as 10.0. If decimalPoints was set to two, the value displayed would be 1.00. The value under the hood would be 100 in both cases. Just the value displayed in the scale is different.

You can get or set the value of the scale widget using the value resource (XmNvalue in C programs). The following code sets up a value of 100, as we used in the previous examples:

```
Arg        args[20];
int        n;

n = 0;
XtSetArg( args[n], XmNvalue, 100 ); n++;

/* create widget... */
```

In addition to using the value resource directly, Motif has two functions for getting and setting the scale widget's value. XmScaleGetValue() returns the value resource:

```
Widget    scale_widget;
int       value;

XmScaleGetValue( scale_widget, &value );
```

Of course, the scale widget must already be created before calling XmScaleGetValue().

XmScaleSetValue() does the opposite of XmScaleGetValue() (evident from the function name):

```
Widget    scale_widget;
int       value;

XmScaleSetValue( scale_widget, value );
```

Remember, the value parameter is an integer—the integer before the decimalPoints are applied.

Setting the showValue Resource

In all the screen dumps so far, the scale widget, an analog selector, had a digital value right next to the scale (i.e., similar to digital and analog watches side by side). This value represents the value of the scale (as modified by the decimalPoints resource). This digital value follows the scale's slider around (play with this a bit—it's kind of fun). You can elect to display the digital value or not, by setting the showValue resource (XmNshowValue in C programs) to True or False. This is shown below:

```
Arg       args[20];
int       n;

n = 0;
XtSetArg( args[n], XmNshowValue, True ); n++;

/* create widget... */
```

A value of True means that the digital value will be shown. A value of False (the default) means that the digital value will not be shown.

SCALE TITLES

Each scale widget can also have a title associated with the scale. This title, like most strings in Motif, is of the XmString type, so you must convert your C strings (as we've been doing since Chapter 2). If you set the titleString resource (XmNtitleString in C programs) it will hold the title for the scale widget. This title will be displayed alongside the scale. This is shown as follows:

```
Arg          args[20];
int          n;
XmString     motif_string;

n = 0;
XtSetArg( args[n], XmNtitleString, motif_string ); n++;

/* create widget... */
```

CREATING A SCALE WIDGET

In the code below, we set up several scale widget options, using `XtSetArg()`, and then created a scale widget using `XmCreateScale( )`:

```
Widget       scale_widget;
Widget       parent;
Arg          args[20];
int          n;
XmString     motif_string;

motif_string = Str2XmString( "This is a scale" );

n = 0;
XtSetArg( args[n], XmNtitleString, motif_string ); n++;

XtSetArg( args[n], XmNwidth, 300 ); n++;
XtSetArg( args[n], XmNheight, 80 ); n++;

XtSetArg( args[n], XmNmaximum, 1000 ); n++;
XtSetArg( args[n], XmNminimum, 10 ); n++;
XtSetArg( args[n], XmNdecimalPoints, 1 ); n++;

XtSetArg( args[n], XmNvalue, 100 ); n++;

XtSetArg( args[n], XmNshowValue, True ); n++;

XtSetArg( args[n], XmNorientation, XmHORIZONTAL ); n++;
XtSetArg( args[n], XmNprocessingDirection, XmMAX_ON_RIGHT ); n++;

/* XtSetArg( args[n], XmNprocessingDirection, XmMAX_ON_TOP ); n++; */
/* XtSetArg( args[n], XmNorientation, XmVERTICAL ); n++; */

scale_widget = XmCreateScale( parent,
                   "scale",
                   args,
                   n );

XtManageChild( scale_widget );
```

continued...

...from previous page
```
XtAddCallback( scale_widget,
          XmNvalueChangedCallback,
          scale_callback,
          NULL );
```

We call `XtManageChild()` to manage the scale widget. You probably want to play with all the different options to see how they fit together. (That's a not-so-subtle hint. You'll find Motif is a lot easier to learn when you try out the different options to see what they do. This process can get a little frustrating at times, but it's the best way to learn Motif.)

Finally, `XtAddCallback()` sets up the scale widget's `valueChangedCallback`.

THE SCALE CALLBACK

You can have the scale widget call a function whenever the value in the scale changes. The `valueChangedCallback` resource (`XmNvalueChangedCallback` in C programs) holds the callback function:

```
Widget        scale_widget;
void          scale_callback();

XtAddCallback( scale_widget,
          XmNvalueChangedCallback,
          scale_callback,
          NULL );
```

In your callback function, the `call_data` will be in the form of a pointer to an `XmScaleCallbackStruct` structure. The `XmScaleCallbackStruct` looks like this:

```
typedef struct
      {
      int       reason;
      XEvent    *event;
      int       value;
      } XmScaleCallbackStruct;
```

With the `valueChangedCallback`, the reason field should be `XmCR_VALUE_CHANGED`.

The value field is the new value of the scale. Note that this is an integer, even if the `decimalPoints` resource is greater than zero(0). If so, you'll have to divide the value by 10 raised to the `decimalPoints` power. That is, if the `decimalPoints` resource is set to three, you'll have to divide the returned value by 10 raised to the third power (1000) to get the proper value. So, with a value field of 12345 and a `decimalPoints` of 3, the real value (the value displayed on the scale widget) would be 12.345. The value field is the only important element of this callback. The following code shows a very simple callback function for the scale widget:

```
void scale_callback( widget, client_data, scale_struct )

Widget                  widget;
caddr_t                 client_data;
XmScaleCallbackStruct   *scale_struct;

{       /* scale_callback */

        /*
         * scale_struct->value is the value.
         */
        if ( scale_struct != (XmScaleCallbackStruct *) NULL )
            {
                printf( "New value %d\n", scale_struct->value );
            }

}       /* scale_callback */
```

READ-ONLY SCALE WIDGETS

If you want a read-only scale widget, set the sensitive resource (XmNsensitive in C programs)—inherited from the Core widget—to False. The default value is True, so you normally don't have to mess with it—if you want a read-write scale, that is:

```
Arg     args[20];
int     n;

n = 0;
XtSetArg( args[n], XmNsensitive, False ); n++;

/* create the widget... */
```

THE SCALE PROGRAM

We've created a very simple program, called scale, to demonstrate how the scale widget works. The program is comprised of the file scale.c.

Source Code for Scale.c

The file `scale.c` contains the `main()` function and the meat of the scale test program. We create a form widget, a quit pushbutton and a scale widget. You should be familiar with everything but the scale widget at this point.

Try `scale.c` with the scale set to XmVERTICAL and XmHORIZONTAL, with the `processingDirection` set to XmMAX_ON_TOP, XmMAX_ON_RIGHT and so on. The following is the source code for `scale.c`.

```
/*
 *    scale.c
 *    Test program using the Motif Scale Widget
 *
 *    Written for Power Programming Motif
 *
 */

#include        <X11/Intrinsic.h>
#include        <X11/StringDefs.h>
#include        <Xm/Xm.h>
#include        <Xm/Form.h>
#include        <Xm/Scale.h>

void quit_callback( widget, client_data, call_data )

Widget   widget;
caddr_t  client_data;
caddr_t  call_data;

/*
 *    quit_callback() is the callback for the
 *    Motif quit button. This function
 *    terminates the program by calling exit().
 */

{    /* quit_callback */

    XtCloseDisplay( XtDisplay( widget ) );
    exit( 0 );

}    /* quit_callback */

void scale_callback( widget, client_data, scale_struct )

Widget                    widget;
caddr_t                   client_data;
XmScaleCallbackStruct     *scale_struct;

/*
 *    The XmScaleCallbackStruct looks like:
```
continued...

...from previous page

```
 *            typedef struct
 *            {
 *            int       reason; -- XmCR_VALUE_CHANGED
 *            XEvent    *event;
 *            int       value;
 *            } XmScaleCallbackStruct;
 */

{    /* scale_callback */

    /*
     * scale_struct->reason should be
     * XmCR_VALUE_CHANGED.
     */

    /*
     * scale_struct->value is the value.
     */
    if ( scale_struct != (XmScaleCallbackStruct *) NULL )
        {
        printf( "New value %d\n", scale_struct->value );
        }

}    /* scale_callback */

main( argc, argv )

int  argc;
char *argv[];

{    /* main */
    Widget      parent;
    Widget      form_widget;
    Widget      quit_widget;
    Widget      CreatePushButton(); /* push.c */
    Widget      scale_widget;
    Arg         args[ 10 ];
    int         n;
    XmString    motif_string, Str2XmString(); /* string.c */

    /*
     * Initialize Xt Intrinsics
     */
    parent = XtInitialize( argv[0],
            "Scale",
            NULL,
            0,
            &argc,
            argv );
```

continued...

...from previous page

```
    n = 0;
    XtSetArg( args[n], XmNallowShellResize, True ); n++;
    XtSetValues( parent, args, n );

    /*
     * Create a form widget,
     * using an arbitrary size
     */
    n = 0;
    XtSetArg( args[n], XmNwidth, 300 ); n++;
    XtSetArg( args[n], XmNheight, 100 ); n++;

    form_widget = XtCreateManagedWidget( "form",
        xmFormWidgetClass,
        parent,
        args,
        n );

    /*
     * Create the quit-button widget
     */
    n = 0;
    XtSetArg( args[n], XmNtopAttachment, XmATTACH_FORM ); n++;
    XtSetArg( args[n], XmNleftAttachment, XmATTACH_FORM ); n++;
    XtSetArg( args[n], XmNrightAttachment, XmATTACH_FORM ); n++;

    quit_widget = CreatePushButton( form_widget,
                "quit",
                args,
                n,
                quit_callback );

    /*
     * Convert string to XmString
     */
    motif_string = Str2XmString( "This is a scale" );

    n = 0;
    XtSetArg( args[n], XmNwidth, 300 ); n++;
    XtSetArg( args[n], XmNheight, 80 ); n++;

    XtSetArg( args[n], XmNtitleString, motif_string ); n++;
    XtSetArg( args[n], XmNmaximum, 1000 ); n++;
    XtSetArg( args[n], XmNminimum, 10 ); n++;
    XtSetArg( args[n], XmNdecimalPoints, 1 ); n++;
    XtSetArg( args[n], XmNvalue, 100 ); n++;
    XtSetArg( args[n], XmNshowValue, True ); n++;
    XtSetArg( args[n], XmNorientation, XmHORIZONTAL ); n++;
    XtSetArg( args[n], XmNprocessingDirection, XmMAX_ON_RIGHT ); n++;
    /* XtSetArg( args[n], XmNprocessingDirection, XmMAX_ON_TOP ); n++; */
    /* XtSetArg( args[n], XmNorientation, XmVERTICAL ); n++; */
```

continued...

...from previous page

```
        scale_widget = XmCreateScale( form_widget,
                                "scale",
                                args,
                                n );

        XtManageChild( scale_widget );

        XtAddCallback( scale_widget,
            XmNvalueChangedCallback,
            scale_callback,
            NULL );

        XmStringFree( motif_string );

        /*
         * Attach widget
         */
        n = 0;
        XtSetArg( args[n], XmNtopAttachment, XmATTACH_WIDGET ); n++;
        XtSetArg( args[n], XmNtopWidget, quit_widget ); n++;
        XtSetArg( args[n], XmNleftAttachment, XmATTACH_FORM ); n++;
        XtSetArg( args[n], XmNrightAttachment, XmATTACH_FORM ); n++;
        XtSetArg( args[n], XmNbottomAttachment, XmATTACH_FORM ); n++;

        XtSetValues( scale_widget, args, n );

        XtRealizeWidget( parent );
        XtMainLoop();

}     /* main */

/* end of file */
```

Compiling and Linking the Scale Program

The `scale` program needs just three source files:

```
    push.c  (from Chapter 3)
    scale.c
    string.c  (from Chapter 2)
```

You can compile and link the `scale` program with a UNIX command something like:

```
    cc -o scale push.c scale.c string.c -lXm -lXt -lX11
```

You can use `Makefile` in Appendix C and type:

    make scale

or

    make all

Running the Scale Program

The `scale` program has a quit pushbutton to get rid of the program when you're done. Try using the mouse to drag the scale's slider around. You'll notice the callback, which just prints out the new scale value, doesn't get called until you release the mouse button. That is, you can drag the slider all over the place, but the value hasn't officially changed until you release the mouse button. Play around a bit and have fun. Figure 10-5 shows the `scale` program.

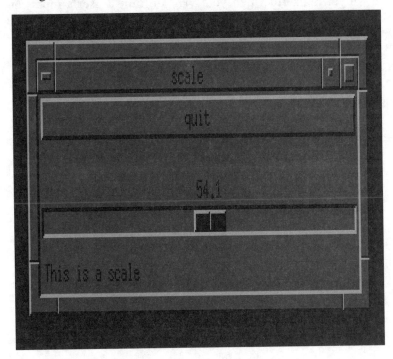

Figure 10-5. The Scale Program.

Notice the extremely helpful title, "This is a scale." Obviously, you'll probably want something better in your programs.

MOTIF FUNCTIONS AND MACROS INTRODUCED IN THIS CHAPTER

The following is a list of Motif functions and macros introduced in this chapter.

```
XmCreateScale()
XmScaleGetValue()
XmScaleSetValue()
```

You should be familiar with these functions and macros before moving on to Chapter 11.

SUMMARY

The scale widget is useful when you want to limit a user's input into a certain numeric range, such as setting temperatures or machine speed for an industrial process-control application, or adjusting a color RGB (i.e., Red, Green, and Blue) value in a color mixing program.

As you've seen in this chapter, the scale widget nicely complements our bag of tricks. Next, Chapter 11 takes a look at using the low-level X library (Xlib) calls from within a Motif program.

# Chapter 11

The Drawing Area Widget

T his chapter covers a very useful technique with Motif: the ability to use Xlib drawing functions with the Motif drawing area widget. The drawing area widget comes in handy when you want the support a widget offers, but find none of the Motif widget classes have the features you need.

A common use of the drawing area widget is for displaying scatter plots of data values, since Motif doesn't really offer a scatter-plot widget. (Of course, you can also write your own widgets. You can do this by inheriting the structure of the closest widget to what you want and then writing the proper code to integrate your widget into the Intrinsics. However, writing widgets is a topic that's far too advanced for a beginning Motif book.)

The drawing area widget provides you with a blank rectangular drawing area that your program can do with as it pleases (using low-level X library calls). Even so, this widget is fully integrated into the Motif toolkit, so you can change resources and set up callbacks. You'll want to set up plenty of callbacks, because that's how you know when to draw into your drawing area. Figure 11-1 shows the drawing area widget.

227

Widget Class	Name Class	Pointer Creation Function
XmDrawingArea	xmDrawingAreaWidgetClass	XmCreateDrawingArea()

Figure 11-1. The Drawing Area Widget.

The drawing area widget include file is Xm/DrawingA.h. You can use XmCreateDrawingArea() to create a drawing area widget:

```
#include <Xm/DrawingA.h>

Widget      parent;
Widget      draw_widget;
String      name;
ArgList     args;
Cardinal    n;

draw_widget = XmCreateDrawingArea( parent,
                 name,
                 args,
                 n );
XtManageChild( draw_widget );
```

DRAWING AREA RESOURCES

In the code below (in the file drawtest.c), we create a drawing area widget and arbitrarily set its width and height, using the width (XmNwidth in C programs) and height (XmNheight in C programs) resources.

The main resource you'll probably want to set is the resizePolicy resource (XmNresizePolicy in C programs). This resource controls whether the widget will grow or shrink. A value of XmRESIZE_NONE means that the drawing area widget will maintain a fixed size. It will not grow or shrink, even if its surrounding parent form or other constraint widget changes size. A value of XmRESIZE_GROW means that the drawing area widget may grow, but won't ever shrink. A value of XmRESIZE_ANY means that the drawing area widget will grow and shrink normally, as the user changes the size of the application's main window, for instance:

```
Arg    args[10];
int    n;

n = 0;
XtSetArg( args[n], XmNresizePolicy, XmRESIZE_ANY ); n++;

/* create the widget... */
```

It's not difficult to create a drawing area widget. The main concern is drawing what you want into the widget. To do this, you need to set up the proper callback functions.

DRAWING AREA CALLBACKS

The drawing area widget offers three main types of callback functions: the expose callback, the input callback, and the resize callback. These callbacks are tied intimately to the X Window System events that are generated on windows. The drawing area widget gives you a raw window under X, and therefore, these callbacks are necessary if you want to draw into the window.

The expose callback function is called when the drawing area widget's window gets an `Expose` event from the X server (or one generated internally by Motif or the Intrinsics). When your application gets an `Expose` event, it means that you need to redraw the portion of the window that was exposed.

The input callback is called whenever the user clicks a mouse button or presses a key inside your drawing area widget's window. The resize callback is called whenever the drawing area widget's window changes size.

All three callbacks get a pointer to an `XmDrawingAreaCallbackStruct` as the call_data parameter. The `XmDrawingAreaCallbackStruct` looks like:

```
typedef struct
        {
        int           reason;
        XEvent        *event;
        Window        window;
        } XmDrawingAreaCallbackStruct;
```

The reason field will be `XmCR_EXPOSE` for expose callbacks, `XmCR_INPUT` for input callbacks and `XmCR_RESIZE` for resize callbacks.

THE XEVENT STRUCTURE

Up to now, we've used the callback structures and pointedly ignored the `XEvent` field of most Motif callback structures. We've ignored it because the event field really hasn't been all that useful—yet. Now, however, we need everything the event field can give us. An X Window `XEvent` structure is a union of many types of events, but the basic structure looks like this:

```
typedef union _XEvent
        {
        int                 type;
        XAnyEvent           xany;
        XKeyEvent           xkey;
        XButtonEvent        xbutton;
        ...
        XExposeEvent        xexpose;
        ...
        XConfigureEvent     xconfigure;
        ...
        long                pad[24];
        } XEvent;
```

We've only included the ones used in drawtest.c. Most Xlib programs include the files X11/Xlib.h and X11/Xutil.h. You may find the types and constants defined in these files of use if you want to do more than what is in the drawtest program.

A Brief Primer on X Window Events

Events are a means for the X server to communicate with X applications. All Motif programs are, under the hood, X applications.

In this chapter, we're going under the hood—luckily the Motif drawing area widget hides much of the complexity of the X library.

An event in X is generated whenever the user presses or releases a key on the keyboard. Events are also generated by mouse clicks. In addition, the X server also generates events on its own. When a window changes size, it sends a ConfigureNotify event. When part of the window needs to be redrawn (due to other windows moving out of the way), the X server sends an Expose event (or more likely, a number of Expose events).

Expose EVENTS

In the X Window System there are no guarantees that what you draw to a window will stay there. The user could very well place another window on top of yours. (Even though we know that your application windows are better than anyone else's, the user is still free to cover up your windows.)

Some window systems, like the AmigaDOS window system, maintain —in memory—the pixels that were in your window, but are now covered up. These pixels are called a *backing store*. In X, you can request that the X server maintain a backing store for your windows, but this is just a request. The X server can ignore your request entirely, or it can run out of memory. In any case, you cannot depend on the X server to maintain the contents of your windows for you. (To be fair, the X documentation clearly points this out, so you're forewarned.)

When your window becomes uncovered (either partially or fully), the X server sends your application an Expose event. You'll also get Expose events when your window first appears on the screen.

Inside the event structure that comes with each Expose event are the coordinates of a rectangle that was exposed (and needs to be redrawn). The first Expose event you get generally is for the whole window and comes down the pike about the time your window is first created. Other Expose events come in batches as the user moves windows about the screen and new windows appear and disappear.

The Expose event part of the XEvent union looks like this:

```
typedef struct
    {
    int             type;              /* Expose */
    unsigned long   serial;
    Bool            send_event;
    Display         *display;
    Window          window;
    int             x, y;              /* location */
    int             width, height;     /* size */
    int             count;             /* zero on end of batch */
    } XExposeEvent;
```

Here, the important fields are the location (x,y) and the size (width, height) of the exposed area and the count field. The count field equals zero (0) when all the Expose events in a batch have come in. This is very useful for some applications.

ConfigureNotify EVENTS for Window Resizes

When a window is resized, it gets a ConfigureNotify event. (Note that a number of other things cause a ConfigureNotify event, too.)

The ConfigureNotify part of the XEvent union looks like:

```
typedef struct
    {
    int             type;              /* ConfigureNotify */
    unsigned long   serial;
    Bool            send_event;
    Display         *display;
    Window          event;
    Window          window;
    int             x, y;              /* new location */
    int             width, height;     /* new size */
    int             border_width;
    Window          above;
    Bool            override_redirect;
    } XExposeEvent;
```

Since we're dealing with resizing only, the fields that matter are the width and height—the new size of the window.

ButtonPress EVENTS

A `ButtonPress` event occurs when the user presses a button on the mouse. A `ButtonRelease` event occurs when the user releases that same button.

The `ButtonPress` and `ButtonRelease` structures look the same:

```
typedef struct
    {
    int                 type; /* ButtonPress, ButtonRelease */
    unsigned long       serial;
    Bool                send_event;
    Display             *display;
    Window              window;
    Window              root;
    Window              subwindow;
    Time                time;
    int                 x, y;
    int                 x_root, y_root;
    unsigned int        state;
    unsigned int        button; /* which button */
    Bool                same_screen;
    } XButtonEvent;
```

The important field here is the button field, which contains a bit-mask that shows which button was pressed or released. The X Window System defines constants for five mouse pointer buttons (although most mice have one, two, or three buttons). These constants are Button1, Button2, Button3, Button4, and Button5. Generally, Button1 is the left-most mouse button, followed by Button2 (middle on a three-button mouse), and then by Button3 (right on a three-button mouse).

The x and y fields are also useful, in that these fields show where—the coordinates—the mouse was in relation to your drawing area window when the mouse button was pressed or released.

KeyPress EVENTS

A `KeyPress` event is generated when the user presses a key on the keyboard. A `KeyRelease` event is generated when the user lifts up on the key that was pressed. Both events arrive with an `XKeyEvent` structure:

```
typedef struct
    {
    int                 type; /* KeyPress, KeyRelease */
    unsigned long       serial;
    Bool                send_event;
```
continued...

232

...from previous page

```
      Display           *display;
      Window            window;
      Window            root;
      Window            subwindow;
      Time              time;
      int               x, y;
      int               x_root, y_root;
      unsigned int      state;
      unsigned int      keycode;    /* which key */
      Bool              same_screen;
      } XKeyEvent;
```

The keycode tells which key was pressed or released. Unfortunately, these keycodes are vendor-specific and inherently nonportable. To make use of the keycode, you really need to translate it into a more portable KeySym or a plain old ASCII string, such as "A" for when the user presses the A key.

Converting the KeyPress EVENT to an ASCII Character

The Xlib function XLookupString() converts a KeyPress event into both a KeySym (a portable key encoding scheme) and an ASCII string (really an ISO Latin-1, but close enough to ASCII):

```
      XKeyEvent         *event;
      char              *string;
      int               max_string_bytes;
      KeySym            *keysym;
      XComposeStatus    *composestatus;
      int               string_length;

      string_length = XLookupString( event,
                            string,
                            max_string_bytes,
                            keysym,
                            composestatus );
```

The event is the event structure that the X server (or in this case, the Motif callback) passed to your application. The string parameter is a normal C string, for which you must allocate bytes to hold the ASCII result. The value max_string_bytes specifies how many characters your code is willing to accept in the string (this value should be smaller than the number of bytes in the variable string, obviously). The keysym is a portable ID, which is useful for keys like function keys (F1, F2, and so on) and special keys like Page Up and Home. The include files X11/keysym.h and X11/keysymdef.h define these keysyms and their families. The F1 function key, for example, has a keysym defined as XK_F1. The F2 key has a keysym of XK_F2 and so on. The Page Up key, though, usually has a keysym of XK_Prior. You can look through the file X11/keysymdef.h for a larger list than you ever wanted to see. The composestatus is intended mainly for future use and probably isn't implemented on your version of the X server. XLookupString() returns the number of bytes actually placed into string.

The two important results from XLookupString() are the string and the keysym. The string will contain an "a" when the user presses the A key ("A" for shift-A) and so on. For those keys where there is no ASCII (ISO Latin-1) equivalent, like F1, the keysym will contain the proper result as a defined constant from the file X11/keysymdef.h.

If the key pressed is in the standard ASCII printable range, its value will be between 32 (ASCII space) and 126 (ASCII ~). Note that officially the encoding is ISO Latin-1, not ASCII, so in European countries, the values between 127 and 255 are probably in use for national symbols like umlauts. Folks in those countries will have to translate the next few lines of code, but it shouldn't be difficult.

With ASCII, you can check if a keysym is printable by comparing the keysym's value with 32 and 126, something like:

```
if (( keysym >= ' ' ) && ( keysym < '~' ))
    {
    /* The value in string is printable... */
    }
```

We could also use the isprint() macro instead of the above code. The key points here are that the keysym contains a standard constant for each character and that the string value may contain a printable string with the character's value.

KeySyms are generally portable, but some vendors, notably Hewlett-Packard, have defined extensions to the base KeySym set, extensions that make your code nonportable. To make matters worse, you can run a program on an Hewlett-Packard workstation, but connect up to the display on an X terminal that has a different set of KeySym extensions. This is a very tough area of X right now, and a lot of solutions aren't available. Anyway, use XLookupString() to convert the nonportable keycode to something more portable. We do this in the input_callback() function in drawtest.c.

This short primer won't make you an Xlib expert. There's so much material in the X library that you could write a book or two on it—which in fact we did (*X Window Applications Programming* and *Advanced X Window Applications Programming*). A great many books have been written about Xlib programming; you should explore your options—especially if you intend to use the drawing area widget in your applications. There's just not enough space to cover Xlib and Motif programming at the same time. So, try out the following example program below. If you have questions, start looking up some Xlib books. You can find a number of them listed in Appendix D.

THE EXPOSE CALLBACK

The function `expose_callback()` is set up to be called back whenever our drawing area widget gets an `Expose` event.

This callback is passed a pointer to an `XmDrawingAreaCallbackStruct`, `draw_struct`. The size of the exposed area is then `draw_struct-> event->xexpose.width` wide by `draw_struct->event->xexpose.height` high. The start of the exposed area is at local coordinates (local to our drawing area widget) `draw_struct->event->xexpose.x` and `draw_struct->event->xexpose.y`. (Remember that the origin is at the top left corner of a window.)

In `expose_callback()`, below, we print out the coordinates of this exposed area as well as draw a line through it and a rectangle around it:

```
void expose_callback( widget, client_data, draw_struct )

Widget                          widget;
caddr_                          client_data;
XmDrawingAreaCallbackStruct     *draw_struct;

{        /*  expose_callback */
         Display *display;

         display = XtDisplay( widget );

         XDrawLine( display,
                 draw_struct->window,
                 drawing_gc,
                 draw_struct->event->xexpose.x,
                 draw_struct->event->xexpose.y,
                 draw_struct->event->xexpose.x +
                 draw_struct->event->xexpose.width,
                 draw_struct->event->xexpose.height );

         XDrawRectangle( display,
                 draw_struct->window,
                 drawing_gc,
                 draw_struct->event->xexpose.x,
                 draw_struct->event->xexpose.y,
                 draw_struct->event->xexpose.width,
                 draw_struct->event->xexpose.height );

         XFlush( display );

         /*
          * Print size of area exposed
          */
```

continued...

...from previous page

```
            printf( "Expose (%d,%d) to (%d,%d) \n",
                    draw_struct->event->xexpose.x,
                    draw_struct->event->xexpose.y,
                    draw_struct->event->xexpose.x +
                    draw_struct->event->xexpose.width,
                    draw_struct->event->xexpose.y +
                    draw_struct->event->xexpose.height );

}           /* expose_callback */
```

DRAWING LINES WITH THE X LIBRARY

The function XDrawLine() is one of the X library (or Xlib) line-drawing functions:

```
    Display     *display;
    Window      window;
    GC          gc;
    int         x1, y1;            /* start location */
    int         x2, y2;            /* end location */

    XDrawLine( display,
               window,
               gc,
               x1, y1,
               x2, y2 );
```

XDrawLine() will draw a line from (x1,y1) to (x2,y2) in the given window and using the given graphics context (GC; more on GCs below). Note that the window parameter can be a pixmap as well, but we won't go into that here. Check out a book on Xlib programming for more information on Xlib drawing functions. See Appendix D for a list of these books.

DRAWING RECTANGLES WITH THE X LIBRARY

XDrawRectangle() draws the outline of a rectangle:

```
    Display     *display;
    Window      window;
    GC          gc;
    int         x, y;             /* start location */
    int         width, height;    /* size of rectangle */
```

continued...

...from previous page

```
XDrawRectangle( display,
          window,
          gc,
          x, y,
          width, height );
```

You'll quickly note that all rectangular shapes in the X Window System are defined by a location (x,y) and a size (width, height). The location is the upper left corner.

SENDING OUT THE DRAWING COMMANDS

When you're done drawing, call XFlush() to send out all the queued drawing requests out to the X server (usually over a network link):

```
Display *display;

XFlush( display );
```

Normally, the Motif toolkit takes care of this task for you, but if you use Xlib functions, you should always call XFlush() after drawing.

CREATING A GRAPHICS CONTEXT

Before you can draw anything with Xlib, you need to create a graphics context, or GC. A GC contains values like the current pen color and width of lines. Your application can have multiple GCs, but each one uses memory in the X server, so you don't want to create thousands of GCs, or you'll bog down the X server.

XCreateGC() will create a new graphics context for you:

```
Display          *display;
Window           window;
GC               drawing_gc;
unsigned long    mask;
XGCValues        *xgcvalues;

drawing_gc = XCreateGC( display,
                  window,
                  mask,
                  xgcvalues );
```

The `display` is the display connection pointer, and the `window` is the drawing area widget's window (more on both of these below).

There are a host of options for the `mask` and `xgcvalues` parameters, both of which are simply not needed for the simple graphics context you're going to create. In the code below, we create a GC for drawing:

```
Widget        drawing_widget;
Display       *display;
Window        window;
GC            drawing_gc;

display       = XtDisplay( drawing_widget );
window        = XtWindow( drawing_widget );

drawing_gc    = XCreateGC( display,
                 window,
                 0L,
                 (XGCValues *) NULL );
```

Note that in `drawtest.c` the `drawing_gc` is a global variable, so it's available to all our callback functions.

GETTING THE DISPLAY POINTER

We need a display pointer to call just about any Xlib function. This display pointer is first created when we set up a connection to an X server. In all the example programs in this book, the function `XtInitialize()` hides the opening of a display connection, so we usually never see (and never have to deal with the hassles of) a display pointer. `XtDisplay()`, an Xt Intrinsics function introduced in Chapter 1, returns the display pointer associated with a given widget:

```
Display       *display;
Widget        widget;

display = XtDisplay( widget );
```

We've used this function a lot in `drawtest.c` and in the examples above. Note that in our applications, we are only connecting to one display, so calling `XtDisplay()` on any widget should result in the same pointer being returned.

GETTING THE WINDOW ID

Just as `XtDisplay()` returns the display pointer for a given widget, we can call `XtWindow()`, another Xt Intrinsics function, to return the window ID associated with the given widget. In this case, most widgets create their own window, so for different widgets, `XtWindow()` should return different window IDs:

```
Widget          widget;
Window          window;

window = XtWindow( widget );
```

Note that until `XtRealizeWidget()` is called to realize a widget hierarchy, the window IDs in that widget hierarchy will probably not be valid. So, you'll have to get the window IDs after the widgets are created, managed, and realized.

THE INPUT CALLBACK

The function `input_callback()` is called on `KeyPress`, `KeyRelease`, `ButtonPress` and `ButtonRelease` events. The first thing we do is use a switch statement to switch off the event type in the `XEvent` event field of the `XmDrawingAreaCallbackStruct` structure:

```
void input_callback( widget, client_data, draw_struct )

Widget                          widget;
caddr_t                         client_data;
XmDrawingAreaCallbackStruct *draw_struct;

{ /* input_callback */
    char                string[31];
    XComposeStatus      composestatus;
    KeySym          keysym;

    switch( draw_struct->event->type )
            {
            case ButtonPress:
                printf( "Button Press at (%d,%d)\n",
                    draw_struct->event->xbutton.x,
                    draw_struct->event->xbutton.y );
                break;
            case ButtonRelease:
                printf( "Button Release at (%d,%d)\n",
                    draw_struct->event->xbutton.x,
                    draw_struct->event->xbutton.y );
                break;
            case KeyPress:
                XLookupString( draw_struct->event,
                    string,
                    30,
                    &keysym,
```

continued...

...from previous page

```
                &composestatus );

    /*
     * Note: this is a
     * US-ASCII test.
     * You'll need to
     * change this in other
     * countries.
     */
     if (( keysym >= ' ' ) && ( keysym < '~' ))
            {
            string[1] = '\0';
            }
     else
            {
            string[0] = '\0';
            }
     printf( "KeyPress %s keysym 0x%x\n",
            string,
            keysym );
     break;
case KeyRelease:
     XLookupString( draw_struct->event,
            string,
            30,
            &keysym,
            &composestatus );
     if (( keysym >= ' ' ) && ( keysym < '~' ))
            {
            string[1] = '\0';
            }
     else
            {
            string[0] = '\0';
            }
     printf( "KeyRelease %s keysym 0x%x\n",
            string,
            keysym );
     break;
default:
     printf( "Other event %d\n",
     draw_struct->event->type );
}

}       /* input_callback */
```

THE RESIZE CALLBACK

The `resize_callback()` function is called when the drawing area widget's window changes size. On some systems, the event field of the `XmDrawingAreaCallbackStruct` structure was sometimes `NULL`, causing problems when we tried to access that field's width and height members (to get the new window size). Hence the check:

```
if ( draw_struct->event != (XEvent *) NULL )
    {
    ...
    }
```

```
void resize_callback( widget, client_data, draw_struct )

Widget                      widget;
caddr_t                     client_data;
XmDrawingAreaCallbackStruct  *draw_struct;

{ /*  resize_callback */

  if ( draw_struct->reason == XmCR_RESIZE )
      {
      printf( "resize_callback(): Reason is XmCR_RESIZE\n" );
      }

  if ( draw_struct->event != (XEvent *) NULL )
      {
      printf( "Resize to %d,%d\n",
                      draw_struct->event->xconfigure.width,
                      draw_struct->event->xconfigure.height );
      }
  else
      {
      /*
       * Certain systems often send a NULL event
       */
      printf( "Resize with a NULL event!\n" );
      }

} /*  resize_callback */
```

THE DRAWTEST PROGRAM

The `drawtest` program places a quit pushbutton widget in a form to quit the program. Beneath the quit pushbutton is a drawing area widget. The drawing area widget and its associated callbacks form the meat of the program. The hierarchy of the `drawtest` program is as follows:

> * Top-level Shell
> > * Form Widget
> > > * Pushbutton Widget (Quit)
> > > * Drawing Area Widget

The `expose_callback()` function will draw a line and a box in the exposed area, whenever `Expose` events arrive. The `expose_callback()` function will also print out the coordinates of the exposed area. The `resize_callback()` function will print out the new size of the window, and the `input_callback()` function will print out that a mouse button or a key was pressed, translating the keycodes into something a bit more understandable.

Source Code for Drawtest.c

Virtually all of the `drawtest` program lies within the file `drawtest.c`:

```
/*
 *              drawtest.c
 *              Motif DrawingArea widget test
 *
 *              Written for Power Programming Motif
 *
 */

#include     <X11/Intrinsic.h>
#include     <X11/StringDefs.h>
#include     <Xm/Xm.h>
#include     <Xm/Form.h>
#include     <Xm/DrawingA.h>

/*
 *              Global to hold our graphic context
 */
GC           drawing_gc;

void quit_callback( widget, client_data, call_data )

Widget       widget;
caddr_t      client_data;
caddr_t      call_data;
```

continued...

...from previous page
```
/*
 *      quit_callback() is the callback for the
 *      Motif quit button. This function
 *      terminates the program by calling exit().
 */

{       /* quit_callback */

        XtCloseDisplay( XtDisplay( widget ) );
        exit( 0 );

}       /* quit_callback */

void expose_callback( widget, client_data, draw_struct )

Widget                          widget;
caddr_t                         client_data;
XmDrawingAreaCallbackStruct *draw_struct;

/*
 *      An XmDrawingAreaCallbackStruct looks like:
 *
 *      typedef struct
 *          {
 *          int             reason;
 *          XEvent          *event;
 *          Window          window;
 *          } XmDrawingAreaCallbackStruct;
 *
 */

{       /* expose_callback */
        Display *display;

        /*
         * draw_struct->reason should be XmCR_EXPOSE
         */

        display = XtDisplay( widget );

        XDrawLine( display,
            draw_struct->window,
            drawing_gc,
            draw_struct->event->xexpose.x,
            draw_struct->event->xexpose.y,
            draw_struct->event->xexpose.x +
            draw_struct->event->xexpose.width,
            draw_struct->event->xexpose.y +
            draw_struct->event->xexpose.height );
```

continued...

...from previous page

```
        XDrawRectangle( display,
            draw_struct->window,
            drawing_gc,
            draw_struct->event->xexpose.x,
            draw_struct->event->xexpose.y,
            draw_struct->event->xexpose.width,
            draw_struct->event->xexpose.height );

        XFlush( display );

        /*
         * Print size of area exposed
         */
        printf( "Expose (%d,%d) to (%d,%d) \n",
            draw_struct->event->xexpose.x,
            draw_struct->event->xexpose.y,
            draw_struct->event->xexpose.x +
            draw_struct->event->xexpose.width,
            draw_struct->event->xexpose.y +
            draw_struct->event->xexpose.height );

}       /* expose_callback */

void input_callback( widget, client_data, draw_struct )

Widget                          widget;
caddr_t                         client_data;
XmDrawingAreaCallbackStruct *draw_struct;

/*
 *      An XmDrawingAreaCallbackStruct looks like:
 *
 *      typedef struct
 *          {
 *          int             reason;
 *          XEvent          *event;
 *          Window          window;
 *          } XmDrawingAreaCallbackStruct;
 *
 */

{       /*  input_callback */
        char                    string[31];
        XComposeStatus          composestatus;
        KeySym                  keysym;

        /*
         * draw_struct->reason should be XmCR_INPUT
         */
        switch( draw_struct->event->type )
```

continued...

...from previous page

```
        {
    case ButtonPress:
        printf( "Button Press at (%d,%d)\n",
                draw_struct->event->xbutton.x,
                draw_struct->event->xbutton.y );
        break;
    case ButtonRelease:
        printf( "Button Release at (%d,%d)\n",
                draw_struct->event->xbutton.x,
                draw_struct->event->xbutton.y );
        break;
    case KeyPress:
        XLookupString( draw_struct->event,
                string,
                30,
                &keysym,
                &composestatus );

    /*
     * Note: this is a
     * US-ASCII test.
     * You'll need to
     * change this in other
     * countries.
     */
        if (( keysym >= ' ' ) && ( keysym < '~' ))
                {
                string[1] = '\0';
                }
        else
                {
                string[0] = '\0';
                }
        printf( "KeyPress %s keysym 0x%x\n",
                string,
                keysym );
        break;
    case KeyRelease:
        XLookupString( draw_struct->event,
                string,
                30,
                &keysym,
                &composestatus );
        if (( keysym >= ' ' ) && ( keysym < '~' ))
                {
                string[1] = '\0';
                }
        else
                {
                string[0] = '\0';
                }
```

continued...

...from previous page

```
            printf( "KeyRelease %s keysym 0x%x\n",
                    string,
                    keysym );
        break;
    default:
        printf( "Other event %d\n",
                draw_struct->event->type );
    }

}       /* input_callback */

void resize_callback( widget, client_data, draw_struct )

Widget                                widget;
caddr_t                               client_data;
XmDrawingAreaCallbackStruct *draw_struct;

/*
 *      An XmDrawingAreaCallbackStruct looks like:
 *
 *      typedef struct
 *          {
 *          int             reason;
 *          XEvent          *event;
 *          Window          window;
 *          } XmDrawingAreaCallbackStruct;
 *
 */

{       /*  resize_callback */

        /*
         * draw_struct->reason should be XmCR_RESIZE
         */
        if ( draw_struct->reason == XmCR_RESIZE )
            {
            printf( "resize_callback(): Reason is XmCR_RESIZE\n" );
            }

        if ( draw_struct->event != (XEvent *) NULL )
            {
            printf( "Resize to %d,%d\n",
            draw_struct->event->xconfigure.width,
            draw_struct->event->xconfigure.height );
            }
        else
            {
        /*
         * Certain systems often send a NULL event
         */
```

continued...

...from previous page

```
        printf( "Resize with a NULL event!\n" );
        }

}       /* resize_callback */

main( argc, argv )

int     argc;
char    *argv[];

{       /* main */
        Widget          parent, form_widget;
        Widget          quit_widget, CreatePushButton(); /* push.c */
        Widget          drawing_widget;
        Arg             args[ 10 ];
        int             n;
        Display         *display;
        Window          window;

        /*
         * Initialize Xt Intrinsics
         */
        parent = XtInitialize( argv[0],
            "Drawtest",
            NULL,
            0,
            &argc,
            argv );

        n = 0;
        XtSetArg( args[n], XmNallowShellResize, True ); n++;
        XtSetValues( parent, args, n );

        /*
         * Create a form widget,
         * using an arbitrary size
         */
        n = 0;
        XtSetArg( args[n], XmNwidth, 300 ); n++;
        XtSetArg( args[n], XmNheight, 250 ); n++;

        form_widget = XtCreateManagedWidget( "form",
            xmFormWidgetClass,
            parent,
            args,
            n );

        /*
         * Create the quit-button widget
         */
        n = 0;
```

continued...

...from previous page

```
        XtSetArg( args[n], XmNtopAttachment, XmATTACH_FORM ); n++;
        XtSetArg( args[n], XmNleftAttachment, XmATTACH_FORM ); n++;
        XtSetArg( args[n], XmNrightAttachment, XmATTACH_FORM ); n++;

        quit_widget = CreatePushButton( form_widget,
            "quit",
            args,
            n,
            quit_callback );

        /*
         * Create DrawingArea widget
         */
        n = 0;
        XtSetArg( args[n], XmNwidth, 300 ); n++;
        XtSetArg( args[n], XmNheight, 220 ); n++;
        XtSetArg( args[n], XmNresizePolicy, XmRESIZE_ANY ); n++;

        drawing_widget = XmCreateDrawingArea( form_widget,
                    "draw",
                    args,
                    n );

        XtManageChild( drawing_widget );

        n = 0;
        XtSetArg( args[n], XmNtopAttachment, XmATTACH_WIDGET ); n++;
        XtSetArg( args[n], XmNtopWidget, quit_widget ); n++;
        XtSetArg( args[n], XmNleftAttachment, XmATTACH_FORM ); n++;
        XtSetArg( args[n], XmNrightAttachment, XmATTACH_FORM ); n++;
        XtSetArg( args[n], XmNbottomAttachment, XmATTACH_FORM ); n++;

        XtSetValues( drawing_widget, args, n );

        /*
         * Set up callbacks
         */
        XtAddCallback( drawing_widget,
            XmNexposeCallback,
            expose_callback,
            NULL );

        XtAddCallback( drawing_widget,
            XmNinputCallback,
            input_callback,
            NULL );

        XtAddCallback( drawing_widget,
            XmNresizeCallback,
            resize_callback,
            NULL );
```

continued...

...from previous page
```
        XtRealizeWidget( parent );

        /*
         * Create a graphics context
         * You MUST do this AFTER the
         * widget hierarchy is Realized!
         */
        display      = XtDisplay( drawing_widget );
        window       = XtWindow( drawing_widget );

        drawing_gc = XCreateGC( display,
            window,
            0L,
            (XGCValues *) NULL );

        XtMainLoop();

}           /* main */

/* end of file */
```

Compiling and Linking the Drawtest Program

The `drawtest` program needs the following source files:

```
    drawtest.c   (from Chapter 3)
    push.c   (from Chapter 3)
    string.c   (from Chapter 2)
```

You can compile and link the `drawtest` program with a UNIX command like:

```
    cc -o drawtest drawtest.c push.c string.c -lXm -lXt -lX11
```

You can use `Makefile` in Appendix C and type:

```
    make drawtest
```

or

```
    make all
```

Running the Drawtest Program

When you run the `drawtest` program, you'll see a window like the one shown in Figure 11-2.

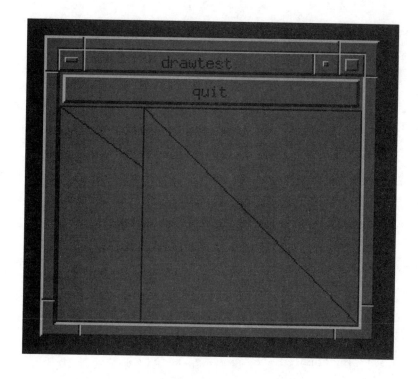

Figure 11-2.   The Drawtest Program.

As the program gets Expose events, you'll see new lines in the drawing area widget. You'll also see something akin to the output in the xterm window from which you run the drawtest program, as shown in Figure 11-3.

```
Expose (0,0) to (204,156)
Expose (105,0) to (204,156)
resize_callback(): Reason is XmCR_RESIZE
Resize with a NULL event!
Expose (0,83) to (204,114)
resize_callback(): Reason is XmCR_RESIZE
Resize with a NULL event!
Expose (0,0) to (204,21)
Expose (0,114) to (204,160)
Expose (0,0) to (204,160)
Expose (105,0) to (204,160)
Expose (0,0) to (204,160)
Expose (57,0) to (204,160)
Expose (57,0) to (204,160)
```

Figure 11-3.   Expose and Resize Output from the Drawtest Program.

If you click a mouse button or press a key in the drawing area widget, you'll see the characters you type printed to the xterm window, as shown in Figure 11-4.

```
Button Press at (111,99)
Button Release at (111,99)

KeyPress p keysym 0x70
KeyRelease p keysym 0x70
KeyPress a keysym 0x61
KeyRelease a keysym 0x61
KeyPress u keysym 0x75
KeyRelease u keysym 0x75
KeyPress l keysym 0x6c
KeyRelease l keysym 0x6c
KeyPress  keysym 0x20
KeyRelease  keysym 0x20
KeyPress i keysym 0x69
KeyRelease i keysym 0x69
KeyPress s keysym 0x73
KeyReleaase s keysym 0x73
KeyPress  keysym 0x20
KeyRelease  keysym 0x20
KeyPress d keysym 0x64
KeyRelease d keysym 0x64
KeyPress e keysym 0x65
KeyRelease e keysym 0x65
KeyPress a keysym 0x61
KeyRelease a keysym 0x61
KeyPress d keysym 0x64
KeyRelease d keysym 0x64
KeyPress ! keysym 0x21
KeyRelease ! keysym 0x21
```

Figure 11-4. ButtonPress and KeyPress Events in the Drawtest Program.

Note that each `ButtonPress` event corresponds to a `ButtonRelease` event, and that each `KeyPress` event corresponds to a `KeyRelease` event.

MOTIF FUNCTIONS AND MACROS INTRODUCED IN THIS CHAPTER

The following is a list of Motif functions and macros introduced in this chapter.

```
XmCreateDrawingArea()
```

You should be familiar with this function before you move on to Chapter 12.

251

X TOOLKIT FUNCTIONS AND MACROS INTRODUCED IN THIS CHAPTER

The following is a list of X Toolkit functions and macros introduced in this chapter.

```
XtWindow()
```

You should be familiar with this function before you move on to Chapter 12.

X LIBRARY FUNCTIONS AND MACROS INTRODUCED IN THIS CHAPTER

The following is a list of X Library functions and macros introduced in this chapter.

```
XCreateGC()
XDrawLine()
XDrawRectangle()
XFlush()
XLookupString()
```

You should be familiar with these functions and macros before you move on to Chapter 12.

SUMMARY

When the Motif widget set doesn't offer what you need, you have three options:

1) You can dump Motif and get something else (but you wouldn't have read this far if that was a viable option, would you?).

2) You can write your own widget, which may be necessary, but something newcomers to Motif want to avoid at all costs.

3) You can use the Motif drawing area widget, a widget designed to meet those cases when a regular widget isn't enough.

If you use the drawing area widget, you should learn about the X library (Xlib) and its set of function calls and events—the drawing area widget basically provides you a raw window in the X environment.

Appendix D lists a number of Xlib programming books you may want to check out.

# Chapter 12

Background Processing

C hapter 11 showed a set of X library functions that you can tie into Motif. This chapter takes this concept one step further and demonstrates the use of Xt Intrinsics functions for background processing.

FOREGROUND AND BACKGROUND PROCESSING

X Window applications, including Motif applications, are essentially event-driven. That is, these applications await events from the X server that are generated by users or the server itself, then act on these events. Event-driven applications tend to put the user in charge, as the application is always waiting to process a user command. Instead of the application controlling the user, the user controls the application.

Most event-driven programs have a central event loop somewhere—we're using the event loop in `XtMainLoop()`. In this event loop, the application awaits a new event, then acts on it. Because of this, event-driven applications are waiting a lot of the time if events are coming in few and far between. If events are coming in with great frequency, then the application is very busy.

An application writer may want to put the potential dead time to good use. A spreadsheet writer, for example, may want the spreadsheet to recalculate in the background while the application is not busy. Or, a designer of a LISP or Smalltalk system may want to perform incremental garbage collection during the dead time.

The key here, though, is incremental. The application must respond quickly to any events that arrive, in order to provide interactive feedback with good performance.

So, the designers of the Xt Intrinsics added the concept of work procedures. You can register a procedure—really a C callback function—and have your function called when the system is idle. To maintain a good interactive performance your work callback must execute all the way through in well under a second. That means to make use of work procedures, you'll have to divide up any large tasks into very tiny blocks that can be executed in work callbacks.

ADDING A WORK PROCEDURE

You can add a work callback function with `XtAddWorkProc()` as shown below:

```
XtWorkProc      work_callback;
XtPointer       client_data;
XtWorkProcId    work_proc_id;

work_proc_id = XtAddWorkProc( work_callback,
                client_data );
```

The `client_data` (really a `caddr_t` type) contains a pointer to any data you want to pass to your work callback function.

The work callback function itself looks something like the following:

```
Boolean work_callback( client_data )

caddr_t client_data;

{       /* work_callback */

        return( False );

}       /* work_callback */
```

The callback needs to return a value (one of the few Xt or Motif callbacks that return a value). The callback should return `True` if it has successfully completed its work. (That is, if it's done.) If so, your callback will not be called back again. If your function still has work to do (that is, it still wants to be called again), then the function should return `False`.

X11 Release 4

In Release 4 of the X Window System, a new function, `XtAppAddWorkProc()`, replaces the older `XtAddWorkProc()`. The new `XtAppAddWorkProc()` takes the following parameters. `XtAddWorkProc()` is obsolete in Release 4.

```
XtAppContext      app_context;
XtWorkProc        work_callback;
XtPointer         client_data;
XtWorkProcId      work_proc_id;

work_proc_id = XtAppAddWorkProc( app_context,
                work_callback,
                client_data );
```

Just like all the App functions, this function is available only on Release 4 systems. Unfortunately, you again have the classic conversion dilemma. Should you use `XtAddWorkProc()` or `XtAppAddWorkProc()`? As in all these choices, you really don't have much choice. We recommend you use what works, being pragmatists rather than purists (which is probably considered heresy in the same circles of people who think that everyone has at least 24 megabytes of RAM and 35+ MIPS in their workstations).

THE WORK PROCEDURE CALLBACK

Even on a "slow" 386-based machine, we were pleasantly surprised at how often our work callback got called. So, we created a very simple, dumb callback just to demonstrate the use of `XtAddWorkProc()`.

In the `work_callback()` function, shown below, we print out a "Work" message every five hundred (500) times our function is called. After one hundred thousand (100,000) times, the `work_callback()` shuts itself off, by returning `True`. (Up to that time, it returns `False` to continue callbacks.) The 100,000 times end up being quicker than you'd expect.

Thus, work procedures are perfect for tasks like incrementally recalculating a spreadsheet:

```
int                  work_count = 0;
unsigned long        work_called = 0L;

Boolean work_callback( client_data )

caddr_t client_data;

{          /* work_callback */

           work_count++;       /* global */
           work_called++;      /* global */

           if ( work_count > 499 )
                 {
                 printf( "Work %ld\n", work_called );
                 work_count = 0;
                 }

           /*
            * if your work-proc returns
            * True, it won't be called
            * again. If it returns False
            * it will be called again.
            */
           if ( work_called > 100000L )
                 {
                 work_called = 0L;
                 printf( "Work reset\n" );
                 return( True );
                 }
           else
                 {
                 return( False );
                 }
}          /* work_callback */
```

REMOVING A WORK PROCEDURE

If you don't want a work procedure from executing again, you can remove it by using XtRemoveWorkProc():

```
XtWorkProcId     work_proc_id;

XtRemoveWorkProc( work_proc_id );
```

You need to pass the ID returned by `XtAddWorkProc()`, or `XtAppAddWorkProc()`, to remove the right work callback. After calling `XtRemoveWorkProc()`, your work callback will no longer be called back.

You can also stop (remove) a work procedure by having your work function return `True`. If your work function returns `True`, it will not be called again.

TIMING OUT MOUSE CLICKS

There's another type of pseudo-background processing you can set up with the Xt Intrinsics called timers. You can set up a timer to go off (in technical terms, this is called "timing out") and then call a function when the timer times out. Timers are perfect for the task of detecting double (or triple, etc.) clicks on the mouse.

Since X has no inherent ability to detect a double-click, the usual procedure is to set up a timer on the first click of a mouse with some arbitrary short time period. If you get a second click of the mouse before the timer times out, then you have a certified double-click. (You probably also want to check that the mouse hasn't moved out of a small area between the clicks, because the second click could signify a totally different purpose.) If the timer times out, then you only have a single click. (In addition, you have to worry about asynchronous network delays, but that's another matter.)

ADDING TIMEOUTS

You can add a timeout with `XtAddTimeOut()`:

```
unsigned longtimer_interval;
XtTimerCallbackProc       timer_callback;
XtPointer                 client_data;
XtIntervalId timer_id;

timer_id = XtAddTimeOut( timer_interval,
        timer_callback,
        client_data );
```

The `client_data` (really a `caddr_t` type) is a pointer to any data you want to pass to your callback function. The `timer_interval` is the amount of time before the timer times out, in milliseconds. The `timer_callback()` function should look something like this:

```
void timer_callback( client_data, id )

caddr_t        client_data;
XtIntervalId   *id;

{              /* timer_callback */
}              /* timer_callback */
```

Unlike the work procedures, the time outs will be only called once, when the given time period runs out.

The `timer_id` is an ID number that you can use to later remove the time out.

X11 Release 4

We bet you guessed this one, right? In Release 4 of the X Window System, `XtAppAddTimeOut()` replaces `XtAddTimeOut()`, just like `XtAppAddWorkProc()` replaces `XtAddWorkProc()`. Even so, the concepts are still the same, and you still have the same dilemma as to which function to use.

```
XtAppContext            app_context;
unsigned long           timer_interval;
XtTimercallbackProc     timer_callback;
XtPointer               client_data;
XtIntervalId            timer_id;

timer_id = XtAppAddTimeOut( app_context,
            timer_interval,
            timer_callback,
            client_data );
```

REMOVING TIMEOUTS

You can remove a timeout procedure before it is triggered, by calling `XtRemoveTimeOut()`. Once the timeout procedure is called, it is removed anyway:

```
XtIntervalId    timer_id;

XtRemoveTimeOut( timer_id );
```

You'll want to call XtRemoveTimeOut() if the reason you started the timer is no longer valid, such as in the case of checking for a double click. If you get the second click before the timer has expired, then you'll want to stop the timer by calling XtRemoveTimeOut().

DETECTING DOUBLE CLICKS WITH TIMEOUTS

In the worktest program, we use a timer callback to detect a double click of the mouse (in a very primitive manner), to demonstrate the use of XtAddTimeOut(). If a mouse click occurs (a ButtonPress event, just like we described in the last chapter), then a timer is set up with XtAddTimeOut(). We include a lot of time to allow for slow users (like us) to click again. We set a global variable, time_state, to maintain whether we have received the first click or not.

If a second click arrives, then we remove the timer with XtRemoveTimeOut().

The function input_callback() is modified from the same function in the last chapter and is an input callback for a drawing area widget. Just the relevant portions of the function are as follows:

```
void input_callback( widget, client_data, draw_struct )

Widget                          widget;
caddr_t                         client_data;
XmDrawingAreaCallbackStruct *draw_struct;

{       /* input_callback */

    switch( draw_struct->event->type )
         {
         case ButtonPress:
             /*
             * On the first click, we
             * start a timeout. The
             * timeout will be removed if
             * a second click comes in
             * in time. Normally, if you
             * wanted to check for a double-click,
             * you'd use a timeout AND
             * check that the mouse hasn't moved
             * (at least not very far).
             */
             if ( time_state == False )
                 {
                 click_id = XtAddTimeOut( 1600L,
```

continued...

...from previous page

```
                                      timer_callback,
                                      NULL );
                            time_state = True;
                            printf( "Try to click again.\n" );
                            }
                      else
                            {
                            /*
                             * Timed out
                             */
                            XtRemoveTimeOut( click_id );
                            time_state = False;
                            }
                   break;
            ...
            }

      }        /*  input_callback */
```

THE TIMER CALLBACK FUNCTION

We've made the timer callback function do nothing more than print out a message
that the user was too slow for a double click. This is shown below:

```
void timer_callback( client_data, id )

caddr_t        client_data;
XtIntervalId   *id;

{                /* timer_callback */

      printf( "Timed out! You lose, so there!\n" );

}                /* timer_callback */
```

THE WORKTEST PROGRAM

The `worktest` program uses the drawing area widget introduced in the previous
chapter. Instead of drawing lines this time, the `worktest` program starts a timer on
`ButtonPress` events, and starts a work procedure on `KeyPress` events. You'll
notice a striking similarity to the `drawtest` program presented in Chapter 11.

Source Code for Worktest.c

The following is the source code for the `worktest.c` program.

```
/*
 *      worktest.c
 *      Motif test program for
 *              XtAddWorkProc()
 *              XtAddTimeOut()
 *
 *      Written for Power Programming Motif *
 */

#include         <X11/Intrinsic.h>
#include         <X11/StringDefs.h>
#include         <Xm/Xm.h>
#include         <Xm/Form.h>
#include         <Xm/DrawingA.h>

XtIntervalId            click_id;
Boolean                 time_state = False;
Boolean                 work_state = False;
int                     work_count = 0;
unsigned long  work_called = 0L;

Boolean work_callback( client_data )

caddr_t client_data;

/*
 * Background-processing function set up
 * by XtAddWorkProc(). This should execute
 * in much less than a second.
 */

{      /* work_callback */

        work_count++;   /* global */
        work_called++; /* global */

        if ( work_count > 499 )
                {
                printf( "Work %ld\n", work_called );
                work_count = 0;
                }

        /*
         * if your work-proc returns
         * True, it won't be called
         * again. If it returns False
         * it will be called again.
         */
```

continued...

...from previous page

```
        if ( work_called > 100000L )
                {
                work_called = 0L;
                printf( "Work reset\n" );
                return( True );
                }
        else
                {
                return( False );
                }

}    /* work_callback */

void timer_callback( client_data, id )

caddr_t         client_data;
XtIntervalId    *id;

/*
 * Called when a timer times out.
 */

{    /* timer_callback */

    printf( "Timed out! You lose, so there!\n");

}    /* timer_callback */

void quit_callback( widget, client_data, call_data )

Widget          widget;
caddr_t         client_data;
caddr_t         call_data;

/*
 *    quit_callback() is the callback for the
 *    Motif quit button. This function
 *    terminates the program by calling exit().
 */

{    /* quit_callback */

    XtCloseDisplay( XtDisplay( widget ) );
    exit( 0 );

}    /* quit_callback */

void input_callback( widget, client_data, draw_struct )

Widget                          widget;
caddr_t                         client_data;
XmDrawingAreaCallbackStruc *draw_struct;
```

continued...

...from previous page

```
{       /* input_callback */

     /*
      * draw_struct->reason should be XmCR_INPUT
      */
     switch( draw_struct->event->type )
              {
              case ButtonPress:
                   /*
                    * On the first click, we
                    * start a timeout. The
                    * timeout will be removed if
                    * a second click comes in
                    * in time. Normally, if you
                    * wanted to check for a double-click,
                    * you'd use a timeout AND
                    * check that the mouse hasn't moved
                    * (at least not very far).
                    */
                   if ( time_state == False )
                        {
                        click_id = XtAddTimeOut( 1600L,
                             timer_callback,
                             NULL );
                        time_state = True;
                        printf( "Try to click again.\n" );
                        }
                   else
                        {
                        /*
                         * Timed out
                         */
                        XtRemoveTimeOut( click_id );
                        time_state = False;
                        }
                   break;
              case KeyPress:
                   /*
                    * Start background work
                    * on a key press
                    */
                   if ( work_state == False )
                        {
                        XtAddWorkProc( work_callback,
                                  NULL );
                        work_state = True;
                        printf( "Start work\n" );
                        }
                        break;
                   default:;
                   }
```

continued...

...from previous page

```
}     /* input_callback */

main( argc, argv )

int    argc;
char   *argv[];

{     /* main */
      Widget    parent, form_widget;
      Widget    quit_widget, CreatePushButton(); /* push.c */
      Widget    drawing_widget;
      Arg       args[ 10 ];
      int       n;

      /*
       * Initialize Xt Intrinsics
       */
      parent = XtInitialize( argv[0],
               "Worktest",
               NULL,
               0,
               &argc,
               argv );

      n = 0;
      XtSetArg( args[n], XmNallowShellResize, True ); n++;
      XtSetValues( parent, args, n );

      /*
       * Create a form widget,
       * using an arbitrary size
       */
      n = 0;
      XtSetArg( args[n], XmNwidth, 300 ); n++;
      XtSetArg( args[n], XmNheight, 250 ); n++;

      form_widget = XtCreateManagedWidget( "form",
               xmFormWidgetClass,
               parent,
               args,
               n );

      /*
       * Create the quit-button widget
       */
      n = 0;
      XtSetArg( args[n], XmNtopAttachment, XmATTACH_FORM ); n++;
      XtSetArg( args[n], XmNleftAttachment, XmATTACH_FORM ); n++;
      XtSetArg( args[n], XmNrightAttachment, XmATTACH_FORM ); n++;

      quit_widget = CreatePushButton( form_widget,
```
continued...

...from previous page

```
                    "quit",
                    args,
                    n,
                    quit_callback );

    /*
     * Create DrawingArea widget
     */
    n = 0;
    XtSetArg( args[n], XmNwidth, 300 ); n++;
    XtSetArg( args[n], XmNheight, 220 ); n++;
    XtSetArg( args[n], XmNresizePolicy, XmRESIZE_ANY ); n++;

    drawing_widget = XmCreateDrawingArea( form_widget,
                    "draw",
                    args,
                    n );

    XtManageChild( drawing_widget );

    n = 0;
    XtSetArg( args[n], XmNtopAttachment, XmATTACH_WIDGET ); n++;
    XtSetArg( args[n], XmNtopWidget, quit_widget ); n++;
    XtSetArg( args[n], XmNleftAttachment, XmATTACH_FORM ); n++;
    XtSetArg( args[n], XmNrightAttachment, XmATTACH_FORM ); n++;
    XtSetArg( args[n], XmNbottomAttachment, XmATTACH_FORM ); n++;
    XtSetValues( drawing_widget, args, n );

    /*
     * Set up callback
     */
    XtAddCallback( drawing_widget,
            XmNinputCallback,
            input_callback,
            NULL );

    XtRealizeWidget( parent );
    XtMainLoop();

}     /* main */

/* end of file */
```

Compiling and Linking the Worktest Program

The `worktest` program needs the following source files:

```
worktest.c
push.c (from Chapter 3)
string.c (from Chapter 2)
```

You can compile and link the `worktest` program with a UNIX command like:

```
cc -o worktest worktest.c push.c string.c -lXm -lXt -lX11
```

You can use `Makefile` in Appendix C and type:

```
make worktest
```

or

```
make all
```

Running the Worktest Program

At first glance, the `worktest` program looks a lot like the `drawtest` program from Chapter 11. Figure 12-1 shows the `worktest` program.

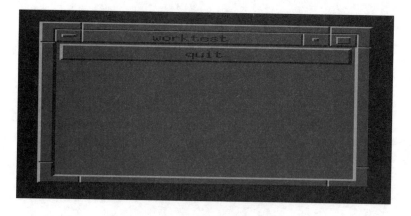

Figure 12-1. The Worktest Program.

Try clicking a mouse button in the drawing area widget's window. You'll see:

Try to click again.

printed out on the xterm window you called the `worktest` program from. If you don't click fast enough, you'll see

Timed out! You lose, so there!

If you press a key, such as "X", then the `worktest` program will start printing out work messages every 500 calls to the `work_callback()` function. After 100,000 times, the `work_callback()` function will shut itself down, ready to go again. Figure 12-2 shows sample output (edited for brevity).

```
Try to click again.
Timed out! You lose, so there!
Try to click again.
Try to click again.
Try to click again.

Start work
Work 500
Work 1000
Work 1500
Work 2000
    . . .
Work 99000
Work 99500
Work 100000
Work reset
```

Figure 12-2. Sample Output of the Worktest Program.

Click on the quit button and the program will quit.

X TOOLKIT FUNCTIONS AND MACROS INTRODUCED IN THIS CHAPTER

The following is a list of Xtoolkit functions and macros introduced in this chapter.

```
XtAppAddTimeOut()
XtAppAddWorkProc()
XtAddTimeOut()
XtAddWorkProc()
XtRemoveTimeOut()
XtRemoveWorkProc()
```

You should be familiar with these functions and macros before moving on to Chapter 13.

SUMMARY

This chapter introduced background processing with work procedures and time-out callbacks using Xt Intrinsics functions.

The next section, Section III, covers a very important feature of Motif and X toolkit programming—X resources. You'll learn how to create resource files and how to use those files to customize your Motif applications.

Using Resources

Section III introduces the concept of setting Motif resources outside of programs. Users (and developers) can customize a Motif application using external resources and resource files.

Chapter 13 covers how to customize your applications using resources. This chapter introduces the syntax of resource files and tells you where to look for these files.

Chapter **13**

Setting Motif Resources

This chapter covers the setting of resource values outside of your Motif applications. Setting resources externally has many advantages, but it becomes confusing when you try to figure out the dizzying array of options available to set resources values. Because of all the options, this is an advanced topic.

Note that most of the discussion in this chapter applies to the X Window System in general, and only somewhat specifically to Motif. Since Motif applications are really X applications too (the Motif toolkit resides on top of the X Window System), this applies to Motif programs and fits into our book on Motif. You can apply most of this chapter to X programs written with other toolkits (such as xterm, written using the Athena widget set) as well as to Motif applications. Since this is a Motif book, it concentrates on the Motif-related issues.

Every Motif widget has a number of resources that modify its behavior. These resources control whether scroll bars appear (and where they appear), how wide borders around objects are, what colors text is drawn in, and so on.

So far in this book, just about every time we've created a widget we've set up the values for these resources in our example programs, using code something like this:

```
Arg        args
int        n;
n=0;

XtSetArg ( args[n],XmNresourceName, resource_value) ; n++;

/* create the widget... */
```

That is, we've used XtSetArg() to set up an Arg array, and then passed this array to a widget creation function, like XmCreatePushButton(), or XtSetValues(). Now this is a perfectly valid way to set resources, but it means that all the resource values are hard-coded.

You don't have to hard-code all your resource values though. You can use resource files or command-line parameters to set these values. The primary advantage to setting resource values is to allow the end user to customize your Motif applications. The end user can do this without access to the source code to your applications, and can change customizations every time your applications are run (with a dizzying array of options).

This means that end users can set resources to maintain system-wide consistency between applications. So the user can invert the foreground and background colors or use different colors instead of the default blue backgrounds or, perhaps, a vision-impaired user would change to a very large font for better visibility.

There's a hitch. The end users can only customize your Motif applications for those resources that you don't hard-code within your programs. This is because the hard-coded resource values take precedence over the externally set resources values.

Up to now, we've hard-coded all resource values we've used. We did this to show how to set resources from within a Motif program (still a useful technique) and to avoid having to explain resource files at the same time we were introducing the Motif toolkit.

In this chapter we'll fill in the blanks and concentrate on methods to modify resource values outside of your programs.

SETTING RESOURCE VALUES

There are five basic ways to set resource values and four of them are external to your programs (warning: This is going to become fairly confusing):

1) In a user-resource file. This is a text file that contains resource-setting commands. These files are called "user" resource files since they are usually set up by the user. These files can reside in a number of places which we'll describe later. The resource-setting commands in these files can apply to any and all X and Motif applications.

2) In a class-resource file. This is also a text file that contains resource-setting commands, only those commands just apply to one application class. Usually these files are used to set resources on an application-wide basis. That is, you may want to set up all `xterm` programs to act in a certain way. To do this, use a class resource file.

3) In the `RESOURCE_MANAGER` property on the root window. This property is created by the standard X Window program called `xrdb`. You can use `xrdb` to add the resource values you want to this `RESOURCE_MANAGER` property. If you've never read about properties before or never dealt with `xrdb` before, don't worry, as you won't need to delve into `xrdb` for anything in this chapter. (One reason you may want to use `xrdb`, though, is if you're using an X terminal that doesn't have its own file system.)

4) In command-line parameters passed to the program.

5) Inside a program using the hard-coding techniques we've used so far in all the program examples.

HARD-CODING RESOURCES: THE GOOD, THE BAD, AND THE UGLY

Some advantages to hard-coding resource values do exist. You don't have to worry about installing extra resource files in their particular locations. You don't have to worry about UNIX environment variables, and you don't have to mess with file permissions. You don't have to teach the obscure, obtuse resource-setting syntax to end-users who only want to use a spreadsheet and don't want to be victimized by their graphical interface.

In addition, with hard-coded resource values, there's not a lot the user can do to trip up your program. It doesn't matter that the user didn't install your resource file properly—if your program doesn't work right you'll be to blame anyway.

That's the good. The bad is that Motif allows you to create highly customizable applications. If you don't allow your users to take advantage of this feature, then you've defeated a major design goal of the Motif toolkit. You've already paid for the dynamic resource-setting code by the size of your applications when you link in the Motif and X libraries, and in the complexity of the Motif toolkit. It would be a shame if you added all this code to your application and never bothered to use it.

The ugly is that many users want their environment customized in a certain way. Perhaps they want to always use a particular font with every Motif application. If you hard-code the resources in your program, then you're defeating your own users. For example, users in Germany may want the text messages in your program to be in German. If you use hard-coded messages (such as `labelString` resources in your label widgets), then you've effectively prevented your applications from being internationalized in this way.

SPECIFYING RESOURCE VALUES

There are a number of ways to specify resource values outside of a program. There are three parts to a standard resource specification: the name of what we want to set, a colon, and the value. This is shown below:

```
name_what_we_want_to_set : value_to_set
```

All resource setting is done using text strings. The hardest part is properly naming what we want to set. This leads to Rule Number 1, which is as follows:

Rule Number 1: When setting resources, errors are ignored, usually silently. You lose.

If you make a mistake you may have a very hard time figuring out what went wrong. This makes the already tough process of resource setting tougher. Another tough part is naming exactly what to set.

NAMING THE RESOURCES TO SET

Widgets are created in a hierarchy. We begin with a top-level shell and then we create a main window or a form or a `RowColumn` or whatever container widget. After the container widget, we create a number of child widgets.

If we want to set a resource in a child widget, we have to name the full widget path to that child, usually by widget names. Start with the name of the top-level shell (just coincidentally the application name), then put a period and then put in the name of the next widget down, and so on. For example, let's say we create a program with the widget hierarchy listed as follows:

```
* Top-Level Shell—"restest"
    * RowColumn Widget, to hold the other widgets—"rowcolumn"
        * Label Widget—"label"
        * Push Button Widget—"quit"
```

The widget names (the names we pass to the `XmCreateWhatever` functions) are listed after the type of widget. We want to set the text that the label widget above displays. The resource for the text message is the `labelString` resource, which we've used since Chapter 2. To name this resource we go down the tree until we hit the widget's name, then we add the name of the actual resource to set:

```
restest.rowcolumn.label.labelString
```

To set the text label to display, "This is a new label," on the label widget, we'd need a resource-setting command:

```
restest.rowcolumn.label.labelString:    This is a new label
```

In Figure 13-1, the window on the left has a `labelString` resource value of "This is our new label." The window on the right uses the default resource settings.

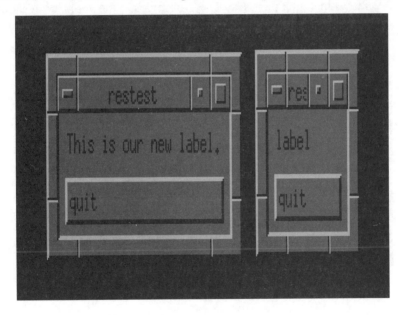

Figure 13-1. Setting the labelString Resource.

In this case, the period means that the resource specification is exactly as listed. This isn't so bad in a simple test program, but this can get tedious, especially in a complex Motif application with a large widget hierarchy. It can also get worse because if you decide to change the widget hierarchy, your resource-setting commands may fail. The solution to this is to use wildcards in setting resources, as described in the next section.

Wildcards in Setting Resources

An asterisk (*) is used as a wildcard in naming resources. You can use a wildcard in place of a full resource path name, but be careful. The resource setting command in the previous section can be written as:

```
restest*label.labelString:        This is a new label
```

This means that in the restest application (restest is the name of the parent top-level widget), the widgets named "label" will have their labelString resource set. Be careful when using wildcards. For example, if you use the following command you'll see what can go wrong:

```
restest*labelString:     This is a new label
```

Figure 13-2 shows that all labelString resources in the application should be set to "This is our new label." We didn't really intend to set the labelString on the push button, but we did anyway by accident.

Figure 13-2. Using Wildcards without Care.

Another example is shown by using the following command:

```
*labelString:        This is a new label
```

This would set the labelString resource on every widget that had a labelString, in every application.

Rule number 2 is then as follows:

Rule Number 2: Be careful with wildcards in setting resource values.

Using Class Names Instead of Widget Names

Instead of using each widget's name, you can also use its class name. The label widget above has a name (chosen by us and put into a C program) of "label" (the name could just as well be "foo"). Label widgets in Motif have a class name of XmLabel, so you could use the following resource-setting command:

```
restest*XmLabel.labelString:      This is our new label.
```

In a resource-setting command, commands that begin with capital letters normally indicate widget classes. Commands that begin with lowercase letters indicate widget and resource names. (The names of the actual resources also normally begin with a lowercase letter. If there is more than one word, as in "fontList," the next words begin with a capital letter. There are no spaces in resource names.)

For another example, you could set the labelString resource in the push-button widget this time, using a class-based specification of:

```
restest*XmPushButton.labelString:        This is a push button
```

Figure 13-3 uses class names to set the labelString resources.

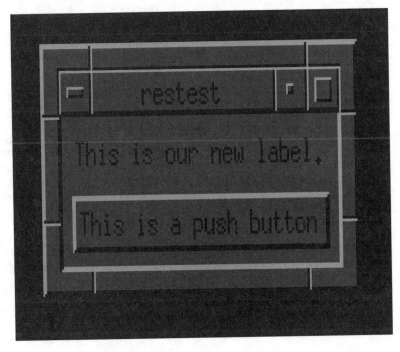

Figure 13-3. Setting the labelString Resources Using Class Names.

277

Use caution when you use the widget class names. All widgets of the same class will be modified. If you have three or more label widgets, you may not want all of them to have the same message. Refer back to Rule Number 2.

Note that resource names also have class names. The class names are usually the resource name with the first letter capitalized, such as `Foreground`, the class name for the resource foreground. This is shown below:

```
restest*XmLabel.Foreground: red
```

Note that specific names take precedence over the class names.

FINDING OUT WHAT RESOURCES CAN BE SET

You can find out the resources for a given Motif widget by looking up the widget class names in the *OSF/Motif Programmer's Reference Manual*. The class name for a label widget, for example, is `XmLabel`. Look up `XmLabel` and you'll see a host of resources. We've already covered the most important ones in Chapter 2. You'll probably want the *OSF/Motif Programmer's Reference Manual* constantly by your side when you write Motif programs.

The main way to use these resource-setting commands is to put them in a resource file. This is described in the next section.

RESOURCE FILES

Resource files contain resource-setting commands. That is, a resource file is an ASCII (ISO Latin-1 actually) text file that contains resource-setting commands. To be useful, a resource file needs to be in a place that your applications (actually, the Xt Intrinsics that sit underneath Motif that sits underneath your applications) will look for it. This is a key requirement, obviously. What isn't so obvious is where all the possible places that resource files can reside.

Note that instead of covering every permutation of all the resource files and locations, we're going to concentrate more on the syntax of resource-setting commands. You can then use these resource-setting commands with methods 1 to 4 mentioned at the beginning of the chapter).

There are two basic types of resource files: class and user. These are described in the following sections.

Class Resource Files

Class resource files pertain to applications of the same class. Usually this really means that class resource files pertain to separate applications since most applications have their own class.

For example, the `xterm` application that most X users use all the time has a class of `XTerm` (note that most classes begin with a capital letter). A class resource file for the `XTerm` class would only pertain to the `xterm` application. For example, if you wanted all `xterms` to have a black background and a white foreground (commonly called reverse video), you could create an `XTerm` class file called "XTerm". The class name here is the file name. Inside the `XTerm` class file, you could set whatever resources you wanted to apply to all `xterm` programs you run. (Most X users typically run two or three `xterms` at a time).

Class resource files only apply to just one application. In the sample program later in this chapter, we're going to create a `restest` program which will have a class of "Restest." Any class resource files for this application, would then have a file name of "Restest."

Most class resource files reside in the directory `/usr/lib/X11/app-defaults`. This is typically where system wide application default files (class resource files) are stored. Normally, regular users don't have permission to change these files, as they are meant to apply system wide.

Some example files you will find in `/usr/lib/X11/app-defaults` include:

XTerm	for the `xterm` application
XCalc	for the `xcalc` calculator application
XLoad	for the `xload` application
XClock	for the `xclock` clock application

Note that your system may have the `app-defaults` directory some other place if your X Window System isn't installed in the standard directories. If you suspect this (especially if you don't find a `/usr/lib/X11/app-defaults` directory), ask your system administrator.

You can create a local applications default file (class resource file) in your home directory. Your Motif applications will also recognize that file. For example, if the class name of your application is `Restest` (as it will be in the sample application shown below), the proper file name for this file would also be "Restest."

In UNIX parlance, this file should be located in:

```
$HOME/Restest
```

If you want, you can jump ahead and type in the C program `restest.c`, shown later in the chapter and create a file named "Restest" in your home directory. Include the following line in that file:

```
Restest*XmPushButton.labelString:        This is in Restest
```

Run the `restest` program to see the results. This is shown in Figure 13-4.

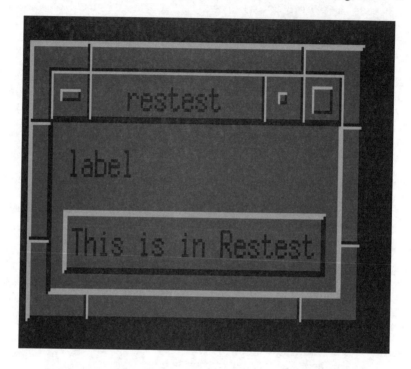

Figure 13-4. Using a Class Resource File in Your Home Directory.

THE XAPPLRESDIR Environment Variable

Your home directory isn't the only place you can set up a class resource file. You can also use an environment variable, `XAPPLRESDIR` (which stands for X APPLication RESource file DIRectory). The `XAPPLRESDIR` environment variable tells `XtInitialize()` where to find your (application) class resource files. Note that `XAPPLRESDIR` must end in a UNIX forward slash ("/") to be a complete directory name. This means that the file `Restest`, for example, could be located at `$XAPPLRESDIRRestest`.

Let's say that your class resource file, `Restest`, is located in the directory `/users/erc`. In that case, the environment variable `XAPPLRESDIR` would be set to: "`/users/erc/`". In the UNIX C shell, you could use the following command:

```
setenv XAPPLRESDIR /users/erc/
```

There are now three standard places where a class resource file can go. Using the example of the `Restest` file, these three are:

```
/usr/lib/X11/app-defaults/Restest
$APPLRESDIRRestest
$HOME/Restest
```

Remember that we haven't even introduced user resource files yet!

User Resource Files

User resource files contain resource-setting commands for anything you care to put into them. While class resource files just apply to one application class, user resource files apply to anything under X and Motif. Inside one of these user resource files, you place the same resource-setting commands. The only difference is that these commands can apply to all application classes (that is, to all applications).

The .Xdefaults File

The traditional user resource file is the `.Xdefaults` file. The `.Xdefaults` file, in your home directory (`$HOME/.Xdefaults`) is the traditional place for you to customize your X Window (and Motif) environment. You can set resources for any and all your X and Motif applications in this file.

The Host .Xdefaults Files

Some systems also support host-based `.Xdefaults` files. In such a case, the resource file for a machine named "`nokomis`" would be:

```
.Xdefaults-nokomis
```

Check your X Window user manuals for more information on this, but don't worry too much about this now.

The XENVIRONMENT Environment Variable

In addition to the `.Xdefaults` file, user resource files can be located anywhere. What you need to do is tell your X and Motif applications where the resource file is. You can do this with the `XENVIRONMENT` environment variable. `XENVIRONMENT` is the full, complete path name for a resource file.

For example, if you create a user resource file named "`foo`" in the `/users/erc/resources` directory, then you should set the `XENVIRONMENT` environment variable to:

```
/users/erc/resources/foo
```

In the UNIX C shell, you can use the following command:

```
setenv XENVIRONMENT /users/erc/resources/foo
```

Note that `XENVIRONMENT` points to a file, while `XAPPLRESDIR` points to a directory in which to look for files.

Resource File Locations

The following are traditional places where your X Window (this includes Motif) resource files may reside.

```
/usr/lib/X11/app-defaults/Class
$APPLRESDIRClass
$HOME/Class
$HOME/.Xdefaults
$XENVIRONMENT
```

"`Class`" is the name of an application class.

In a resource file, a exclamation mark indicates a comment to the end of the current line. Comments are ignored when the resource file is loaded in.

The following would make a valid resource file:

```
! is a comment
Restest*XmPushButton.labelString: This is in Restest
! is also a comment
```

We will now take a break from this and intoduce a program to test ways to set up resource values.

THE RESTEST PROGRAM

To test out all the resource-setting we're going to do, we've put together a simple example program. This will give us an excuse to more formally introduce the `RowColumn` widget.

The hierarchy of the `restest` program is as follows:

```
* Top-Level Shell
    * RowColumn Widget (to hold the other widgets)
        * Label Widget
        * Push Button Widget (quit)
```

The `restest` program puts up a `RowColumn` widget with two simple child widgets: a label and a push button. The main feature of this program is that we explicitly try to avoid hard-coding resources in the `restest` program. That way, there are a lot more resources free that we can set externally to the `restest` program (using resource files and whatnot).

The `restest` program uses a `RowColumn` widget to hold other widgets. The RowColumn widget is a easy-to-use container widget as shown in Figure 13-5.

Widget Class Name	Class Pointer	Creation Function
`XmRowColumn`	`xmRowColumnWidgetClass`	`XmCreateRowColumn()`

Figure 13-5. The RowColumn Widget.

The include file for the `RowColumn` widget is `Xm/RowColumn.h`.

We've seen the `RowColumn` widget before, especially in menus and menu bars. So far, we haven't explicitly created one. An example of one is as follows:

```
#include <Xm/RowColumn.h>

Widget        row_widget, parent;
String        name;
ArgList       args;
Cardinal      n;

row_widget = XmCreateRowColumn( parent,
                "rowcolumn",
                 args,
                n );

XtManageChild( row_widget );
```

The `RowColumn` widget is a container widget: it holds child widgets inside. RowColumn widgets don't give you nearly as many options like the form has (for attachments and so on).

RowColumn WIDGET RESOURCES

When you look up `XmRowColumn` in the *OSF/Motif Programmer's Reference Manual,* prepare to be confused. Since the `RowColumn` widget is used for so many things (menu bars, pop-up menus, pulldown menus, and for holding radio buttons in addition to a plain old container), there are a host of confusing resources that you can set. Most of them won't apply at any one time, unless you are using the `RowColumn` widget for a special purpose, like a menu.

One resource you may want to look at is the orientation resource (XmNorientation in C programs). This resource can have a value of XmVERTICAL or XmHORIZONTAL. The following code sets up the RowColumn to align its children horizontally:

```
Arg      args[10];
int      n;

n = 0;
XtSetArg( args[n], XmNorientation, XmHORIZONTAL ); n++;

/* create the widget... */
```

The packing resource (XmNpacking in C programs) can be one of the following:

```
XmPACK_COLUMN
XmPACK_NONE
XmPACK_TIGHT
```

With the packing resource set to XmPACK_COLUMN, all child widgets are placed as if they were the same size. That is, each child widget is placed in a bounding box, with the bounding box the size of the largest child widget.

The child widgets are placed in the RowColumn widget in the direction of the orientation resource (that is, horizontally or vertically). The value of the numColumns resource determines how many columns (horizontal) or rows (vertical) there are.

With the packing resource set to XmPACK_TIGHT, then child widgets are placed on after the other in the proper direction (in the orientation resource). If there are too many child widgets, the RowColumn will "wrap around" and start a new column or row.

The numColumns resource (XmNnumColumns in C programs) specifies how many columns (or rows, depending on the orientation) you want the RowColumn widget to try to create. The numColumns resource only applies if the packing resource is set to XmPACK_COLUMN.

Source Code for Restest.c

The major part of the restest program is in the file restest.c. All that's done is to create a few widgets and then realize the widget hierarchy. We've avoided hard-coding most resources, so you can try the resource-setting commands we'll get to in a bit. The code is as follows:

```
/*
 *    restest.c
 *    A Motif program to help show how resource files
continued...
```

...from previous page

```
 *    work.
 *
 *    Written for Power Programming Motif
 */

#include      <X11/Intrinsic.h>
#include      <X11/StringDefs.h>
#include      <Xm/Xm.h>
#include      <Xm/Label.h>
#include      <Xm/RowColumn.h>

void quit_callback( widget, client_data, call_data )

Widget        widget;
caddr_t       client_data;
caddr_t       call_data;

/*
 *    quit_callback() is the callback for the
 *    Motif quit push button. This function
 *    terminates the program by calling exit().
 */

{     /* quit_callback */

      XtCloseDisplay( XtDisplay( widget ) );
      exit( 0 );

}     /* quit_callback */

main( argc, argv )

int   argc;
char  *argv[];

{     /* main */
      Widget   parent, row_widget;
      Widget   label_widget;
      Widget   quit_widget, CreatePushButton(); /* push.c */
      Arg      args[ 10 ];
      int      n;

      /*
       * Initialize Xt Intrinsics
       */
      parent = XtInitialize( argv[0],
                             "Restest",
                             NULL,
                             0,
                             &argc,
                             argv );
```

continued...

...from previous page

```
      n = 0;
      XtSetArg( args[n], XmNallowShellResize, True ); n++;
      XtSetValues( parent, args, n );

      /*
       * Create a RowColumn,
       * using no arbitrary size
       * or hard-coded resource values.
       */
      n = 0;
      row_widget = XmCreateRowColumn( parent,
                                  "rowcolumn",
                                  args,
                                  n );

      XtManageChild( row_widget );

      /*
       * Create label widget
       */
      n = 0;

      label_widget = XtCreateManagedWidget( "label",
                                  xmLabelWidgetClass,
                                  row_widget,
                                  args,
                                  n );

      /*
       * Create the quit-button widget
       */
      n = 0;
      quit_widget = CreatePushButton( row_widget,
                                  "quit",
                                  args,
                                  n,
                                  quit_callback );

      XtRealizeWidget( parent );
      XtMainLoop();

}     /* main */

/* end of file */
```

Compiling and Linking the Restest Program

The restest program needs only two C source files:

```
push.c (Chapter 3)
restest.c
```

You can compile and link the `restest` program with the following UNIX command:

```
cc -o restest push.c restest.c -lXm -lXt -lX11
```

You can use `Makefile` in Appendix C and type:

```
make restest
```

or

```
make all
```

To really make use of the `restest` program, though, you'll need to set up some resources external to the program.

Running the Restest Program

We'll run this simple `restest` program over and over in the next few examples. Each example will test out a different way to set resources externally to the `restest` program. Figure 13-6 shows the `restest` program without setting any resource values. Note that the `restest` program isn't very interesting at all without some resource values.

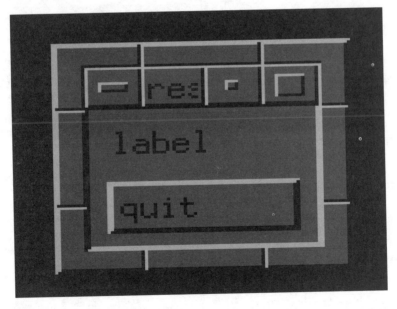

Figure 13-6. The Restest Program without Setting any Resources.

287

We've covered a number of methods for setting resource values previously and we will now try using command-line parameters.

SETTING RESOURCES WITH COMMAND-LINE PARAMETERS

You can set some common resources with standard X Window command-line parameters. For example, `fg` stands for the foreground color. You can set the foreground color (usually the color the text is drawn in) to green with the command:

```
restest -fg green
```

Some Common Command-Line Parameters

Some common command-line parameters include:

```
-display        display_name
-geometry       WidthxHeight+Xorigin+Yorigin
-bg             background_color
-fg             foreground_color
-xrm            X resource_manager_string
```

Note that Motif uses a number of background colors together to form its 3D shadow effects.

You've also probably seen the `-display`, `-geometry` `-bg` and `-fg` options already. The real interesting one is the `-xrm` option.

The `resource_manager_string` is a valid command to send to the X resource manager. The syntax of this command is basically the same as the syntax for inside a resource file.

Using the xrm Command-Line Option

You can set resource options of an application from the command line by sending the values to the X resource manager. The `-xrm` option allows you to do this. For example, to set a value of the `fontList` resource (globally—but in this case only globally for the application), the syntax in a resource file would be:

```
*fontList:      variable
```

The command line would be:

```
restest -xrm "*fontList: variable"
```

The above command would run the `restest` program and set its `fontList` resource (for all widgets in the `restest` program) to the font " variable". The syntax "`*fontList:`" usually means globally for all applications, but resources set with the `-xrm` option only affect the application you send this command-line parameter to.

You could also try:

```
restest -xrm "restest*fontList: variable"
```

This is shown in Figure 13-7. (Note that the "variable" font is not available on every X server. For a list of the fonts available on your server, use the `xlsfonts` program.)

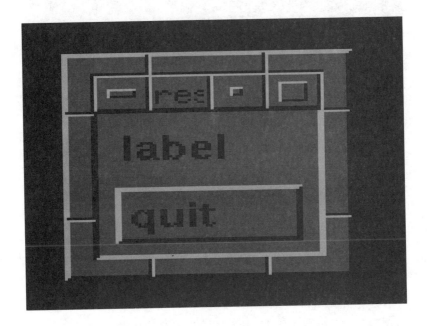

Figure 13-7. The Restest Program with a fontList of "Variable".

With the `-xrm` command-line option, you can basically set any resource values that you can in a resource file, only you don't need to create a resource file to do it. Unfortunately, you do need to be a good typist. If you have more than a few options, you'll probably want to create a resource file.

Using xrm to Set Resources Application-wide

Try the following command to launch the `restest` program:

```
restest -xrm "restest*fontList: variable"     \
    -xrm "restest*foreground: red" \
    -xrm "restest*shadowThickness: 8"
```

This command uses wildcards (the "*") to set resource values application-wide. Figure 13-8 shows the use of multiple -xrm options. You can also use -xrm options to set resource values for one widget.

Figure 13-8. Using Multiple -xrm Options.

Using xrm to Set Resources for One Widget

Try the following command:

```
restest -xrm "restest*label.fontList: variable" \
    -xrm "restest*quit.fontList: cursor" \ -xrm
    "restest*quit.shadowThickness: 8"
```

You'll notice that the cursor font is used for the quit pushbutton. The cursor font normally contains X Window cursor shapes (like arrows and cross-hairs), but it is still a full-fledged X Window font. You'll note that using the cursor font makes for a very visible outcome as shown in Figure 13-9. We mention this because it can help in debugging resource files. If you set up a resource value to something that is instantly recognized, then you'll notice right away whether your resource-setting syntax worked.

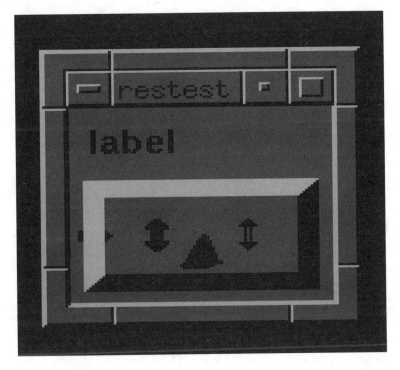

Figure 13-9. Using the Cursor Font with the Pushbutton Widget.

Using the .Xdefaults File to Set Resources

You can also create a file in your home directory called ".Xdefaults" and fill the .Xdefaults file with the resource-setting commands above, such as:

```
!
! These are our resource-setting test commands
!
restest*label.fontList: variable
restest*quit.fontList: cursor
restest*quit.shadowThickness: 8
continued...
```

291

...from previous page

```
!
! end of restest resources
!
!
```

Note that you probably already have a file named .Xdefaults in your home directory.

USING AN APPLICATION DEFAULTS FILE

You can also create an application defaults file, named in our example "Restest". Inside the Restest file you can place any resource-setting commands that apply to the restest application. You can place this file in any of the class resource file locations:

```
/usr/lib/X11/app-defaults/Class
$APPLRESDIRClass
$HOME/Class
```

Note that Class is the name of an application class (in our case "Restest").

In the next three sections of this chapter, we're going to practice setting resource values in our Motif applications. We'll start out by setting resource values for all applications, and then gradually zero in on application-wide resources and resources specific to one widget. By trying out a number of examples, we hope to show how resource-setting commands work. This is a tough topic, so don't get too concerned if things don't work out the first time. Just keep trying and eventually it will all make sense.

STEP 1: Setting Resources Globally

To set resources globally, you need to use a user resource file, like the .Xdefaults we talked about above (or use the xrdb program) .

Try placing the following resource-setting commands in your .Xdefaults file (or whatever equivalent file you want to use):

```
!
! Resource test step 1
!
*fontList:          variable
*marginTop:         24
*borderWidth:       2
!
! end of resource test step 1
!
```

We've chosen the resource values to generate some very visible results—you probably won't want these for everyday use in your applications. This is shown in Figure 13-10.

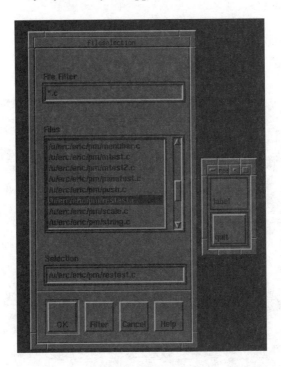

Figure 13-10. Setting Resource Values for Multiple Applications.

Note that there is a leading asterisk wildcard ("*"). If you purchased the source code diskette, these values are in the file "ch13stp1.txt" (for Chapter 13, Step 1). You'll note that these resource-settings apply to all Motif applications.

STEP 2: Setting Resources Application -wide

Next, we're going to zero in on the restest application. Step 2 works with resource-setting commands that just modify the restest program. Try the following resource-setting commands instead of the commands in Step 1.

```
!
!       Resource test step 2
!
restest*labelString:        Step 2
restest*width:              200
restest*height:             225
restest*shadowThickness:    10
```
continued...

...from previous page
```
restest*borderWidth:          10
restest*fontList:             *times-bold-r-normal--*-140-*-*-*
!
! end of resource test step 2
!
```

This is shown in Figure 13-11.

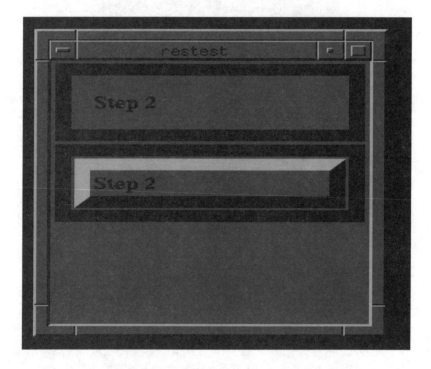

Figure 13-11. Setting Resource Values Application-wide.

These commands are in the file "`ch13stp2.txt`"on the source-code diskette. You may not have the given font installed in your system, but you can just choose another. Most X Window systems have different sets of available fonts that differ by X release number—2, 3, or 4—as well as by vendor.

STEP 3: Setting Resources for Individual Widgets

In Step 3 we concentrate on setting resource values for individual widgets:

```
!
! Resource test step 3
!
! We can use wildcards...
!
restest*quit.labelString:  Push Me to Quit
restest*quit.shadowThickness:     10
restest*quit.fontList:                  *charter-bold-r-normal—*-180-*-*-*
!
! or the exact widget path.
!
restest.rowcolumn.quit.shadowThickness: 12
restest.rowcolumn.quit.borderWidth: 1


!
! Now set up values for the label widget
!
restest*label.labelString: One small step in coding...
restest*label.borderWidth: 35
restest*label.fontList:         *helvetica-bold-r-normal--*-240-*-*-*
!
! and now apply to the top-level shell.
!
restest.width:            370
restest.height:           350
!

! end of resource test step 3
!
```

This is shown in Figure 13-12.

Figure 13-12. Setting Resources for Individual Widgets.

These commands are in the file "ch13stp3.txt" on the source-code diskette. You may not have either of the fonts listed above installed in your particular system (so you may need to come up with two new font names that are available on your system—don't worry about it—we're not really concerned with fonts here, just setting resources).

SPECIFIC RULES VS GENERAL RULES

We will now introduce Rule Number 3 which is:

Rule Number 3: Specific Commands Take Precedence Over General Commands.

If you try the two resource-setting commands listed below, you'll notice that Rule Number 3 is true:

```
restest*fontList:                          cursor
restest.rowcolumn.quit.fontList:           variable
```

Figure 13-13 shows that specific resource-setting commands take precedence over general commands.

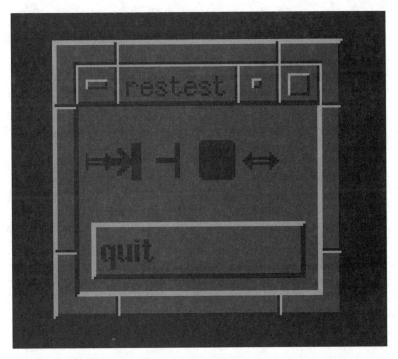

Figure 13-13. Specific Resource-Setting Commands Take Precedence over General Commands.

The quit button will not have the globally set font of "cursor" but instead will use the font "variable". The label widget, though, will use the font "cursor", which makes for an unintelligible label.

RESOURCE-SETTING ETIQUETTE

There's a debate now about which resources you should set with your application default files and which resources you should leave to your users to set in their user resource files.

The idea here is that you don't want your applications to override a user's carefully (and painfully) set-up resources. The most agreement seems to be in the area of fonts. Your applications shouldn't override a default font setting. Other than that, try to think about your resources and allow the user as much flexibility as possible.

MOTIF FUNCTIONS AND MACROS INTRODUCED IN THIS CHAPTER

The following is a list of motif functions and macros introdcued in this chapter.

```
XmCreateRowColumn()
```

You should be familiar with this function before moving on to Chapter 14.

SUMMARY

To understand how to use resources, you're going to want to play around with all the examples presented in this chapter. This stuff is complex, and the designers of the X Window System realize this. In fact, a better way to edit resources is being developed for Release 5 of X. Until then, you'll want to try out different ways to set resources, until you feel comfortable with the process.

There are five main ways to set values into widget resources.

1) In a user resource file.

2) In a class resource file, also called an application defaults file.

3) In the RESOURCE_MANAGER property on the root window. This property is created by the standard X Window program called xrdb.

4) In command-line parameters passed to the program.

5) Inside a program using the hard-coding techniques we've used so far in all the previous program examples.

Resource Quick Reference

!   starts a comment

.   (a period) separates widget names or classes, if you are specifying the widget hierarchy exactly.

*   is a wildcard. The wildcard can separate widget names or classes, without specifying the widget hierarchy exactly. We recommend using wildcards, but be careful, as it's easy to set the resources of too many widgets.

A resource-setting command looks like:

```
name_what_we_want_to_set : value_to_set
```

Some examples:

```
*labelString:            This is a new label
restest*fontList:        *times-bold-r-normal--*-140-*-*-*
restest.rowcolumn.quit.borderWidth: 1
```

The following are traditional places where your X Window (this includes Motif) resource files may reside.

```
/usr/lib/X11/app-defaults/Class
$APPLRESDIRClass
$HOME/Class
$HOME/.Xdefaults
$XENVIRONMENT
```

Class is the name of an application class.

Following the Motif Style

Section IV covers some of the main areas of the *OSF/Motif Style Guide*—especially the sections on menu and dialog design. One of the prime benefits of the Motif toolkit is application consistency. Motif applications tend to look and act like other Motif applications. Far from being boring (when has the X Window System ever been boring?), this helps users transfer skills from one application to another.

Chances are most of your users really don't care about Motif or X—they just want to get work done. The more the user interface provides consistency and easy-to-use features, the better it is for the users. Motif applications can help this by conforming to the *OSF/Motif Style Guide,* which provides a set of rules for writing Motif applications.

Chapter 14 covers the Motif rules for pulldown menus and lists the standard menus your applications should support. Chapter 15 covers the Motif rules for dialogs, especially custom dialogs. Chapter 16 creates a custom Motif dialog as an example of the rules in Chapter 15.

Motif Menus

The Motif toolkit comes with the *OSF/Motif Style Guide*, a document that is the official "look and feel" arbiter for well-behaved Motif applications (until you obtain a license from the Open Software Foundation). Since we won't cover everything from the manual in the following chapters, you will need to read through this manual.

This chapter covers the *Style Guide's* rules and guidelines for application menus—especially the menus that pull down from the menu bar. We will give you a head start at actually implementing an application that follows the Motif style. That's the difficult part.

The first part of the Motif style specifies a menu bar at the top of your application's main window and what menus should appear.

STANDARD MOTIF MENUS AND MENU CHOICES

In the menu bar at the top of your application's main window, you should plan for at least five menus: File, Edit, View, Options, and Help (you can certainly add more). The Motif style allows you a little leeway here, but we think that consistency is good when designing graphical applications—inconsistency defeats the purpose of a graphical interface. Unless you have a really good reason, you should use the naming conventions set up in the *OSF/Motif Style Guide*. Figure 14-1 shows a standard Motif menu bar.

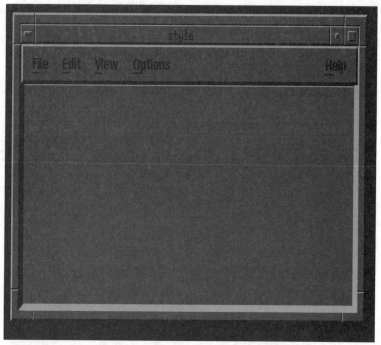

Figure 14-1 . A Standard Motif Menu Bar.

Menus on the menu bar should have mnemonics, as shown in Figure 14-2.

Menu Name	Mnemonic
File	F
Edit	E
View	V
Options	O
Help	H

Figure 14-2. Menu bar Mnemonics.

If you've ever used a Macintosh or ran applications under Microsoft Windows, Presentation Manager, or DECwindows, the menu choices presented below will look very familiar. The basics are all here, starting with the File menu.

The File Menu

The File menu should always be the first menu on the menu bar. This menu has choices that obviously pertain to files, including loading, saving, and printing files. This, of course, assumes your application deals with files (which most do, including spreadsheets, word processors, and database managers). Figure 14-3 shows the file menu.

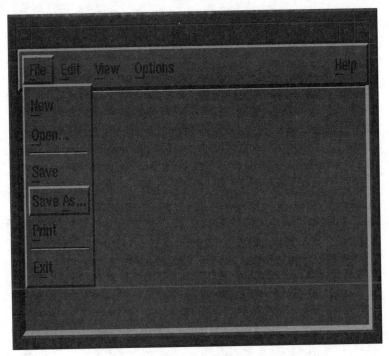

Figure 14-3 . The File Menu.

Figure 14-4 shows the file menu choices.

Name	Mnemonic	Purpose
New	N	Creates an empty new file for the user to act on.
Open...	O	Opens a file that already exists. Note the "..." after the "Open". The "..." means that this menu choice will call up a dialog and requires further action from the user. Normally, a file selection dialog will appear so that the user can choose a file.
Save	S	Saves the current file to its current name. That is, if you use the "Open..." choice to open a file named "foobar", the "Save" choice would save your work back to the file "foobar".
Save As...	A	Saves the current file to a different name. Note that the "..." implies a dialog will appear—again a file selection dialog.
Print	P	This choice can be "Print" or "Print...", depending whether a print dialog appears or not (to perhaps choose the printer, the print quality and paper size).
Exit	X	Quits your application. If work needs to be saved, your application should prompt the user to save the work.

Figure 14-4. The File Menu Choices.

Even if your application has nothing to do with files, you probably want to include a File menu with just one choice—the Exit choice—to maintain consistency. One of the primary advantages of Motif is application consistency. It's nice to know that the last choice in the File menu is always an Exit choice. Users tend to feel safer using a program if they can easily quit that program.

The Edit Menu

The Edit menu essentially provides a menu-driven cut and paste mechanism. The Edit menu should come second on the menu bar and is probably the hardest to actually implement—especially the Undo choice. Figure 14-5 shows the Edit Menu.

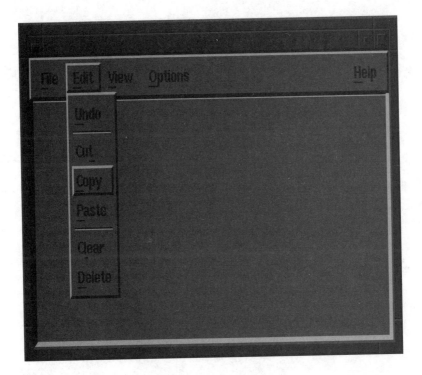

Figure 14-5 . The Edit Menu.

Figure 14-6 shows the standard Edit menu choices.

Name	Mnemonic	Purpose
Undo	U	This is normally the toughest menu choice to implement. Undo should undo the last thing the user did. The *OSF/Motif Style Guide* also recommends that the "Undo" text be changed to indicate what can be undone, such as "Undo Paste" to undo a paste operation and "Undo Typing" to undo the last text that was entered.
Cut	T	Removes the selected (highlighted) material and places that material (text, spreadsheet cells, whatever) into the Motif clipboard.
Copy	C	Copies the selected material to the Motif clipboard, but doesn't remove the material from where it was originally.
Paste	P	Pastes the contents of the clipboard at the current "location" (usually where an insertion cursor is).
Clear	l	This optional choice removes the selected material but doesn't copy the material to the clipboard—potentially a dangerous operation. The Clear choice is supposed to leave a gap where the old material was.
Delete	D	This optional choice wipes out the selected material.

Figure 14-6. The Edit Menu Choices.

The View Menu

The View menu controls "views" of the data. That is, the View menu allows the user to adjust what is viewing the in main window of your application. Some examples of this include choosing how to sort the data, if the data should be sorted at all and how much detail to show. An outlining application for example, could use the view menu to control how many levels of the outline are visible at one time.

View menus are highly dependent on what your application actually does. A spreadsheet view menu will look a lot different than the view menu on an SQL query-by-forms application.

We've used the example View menu from the *OSF/Motif Style Guide* in Figure 14-7 to give you a flavor of what the view menu should look like.

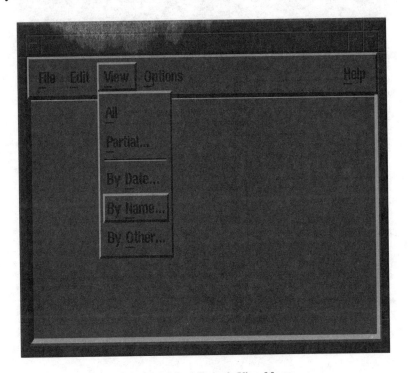

Figure 14-7. A Sample View Menu.

The Options Menu

The Options menu is essentially a miscellaneous menu. Various choices go into this menu and allow the user to customize the application, such as choosing the colors As with the View menu, the Options menu is highly dependent on what your application actually does, as shown in Figure 14-8.

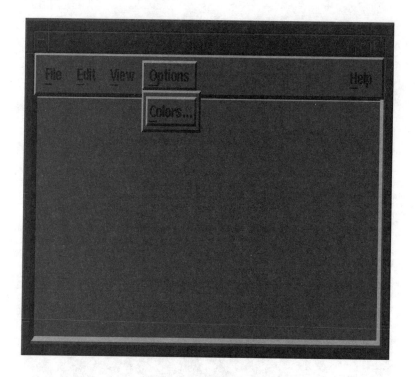

Figure 14-8. A Sample Options Menu.

The Help Menu

Helping the user is often neglected, especially in UNIX-based software. The help menu, however, is essential, especially for graphical software. Once users see windows and pulldown menus, their expectations on user-friendliness increase. Adding a good on-line help system is an effective way to improve productivity with software you create. Figure 14-9 shows the Help Menu.

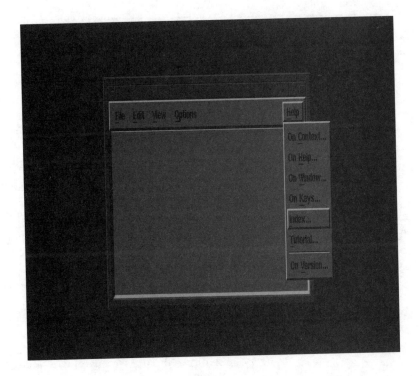

Figure 14-9 . The Help Menu.

Like the View and Options menus, the Help menu is also very application-specific. Some sample choices are listed in Figure 14-10.

Name	Mnemonic	Purpose
On Context...	C	This choice should provide help on the current context—that is, on what the user is currently trying to do. The idea is to provide context-sensitive help. (Personally, we think the "On Context.." name is wretched. The name here should change with the context of what the user is doing. For example, if the user is drawing valves in a factory automation package, the "On Context..." choice should instead be an "On Drawing Valves..." choice.)
On Help...	H	This choice shows how to use the help system. We really hope your help isn't very tough to learn—otherwise it won't be much help.
On Window...	W	Describes the window from which help was requested, including the standard ways to interact with that window.
On Keys...	K	Provides help on the special keys used in the application, especially on the mnemonics. Motif uses quite a few keyboard accelerators and allows the user to customize quite a bit more.
Index...	I	Should provide an Index to help topics.
Tutorial...	T	You'll really be lucky if you ever see this in an application. If you create a quality online tutorial your users will love you.
On Version...	V	This is the fun choice. Just look at Macintosh applications with their "About..." box equivalent. The "On Version..." choice, which we'll go into more detail below, should display information including the name of the application and any version numbers associated with the application. Macintosh applications especially have fun with this choice, as the designers include things like fireworks and animated dogs.

Figure 14-10 . Sample Help Menu Choices.

Providing "On Version" Help

The "On Version..." help message should contain information about the version of the program, such as the version number, the date the program was created, the authors, and any copyright information you want to place in the box.

You can create the "On Version..." help message by using a dialog such as those introduced in Chapter 4. This time, though, we'll use a message-box dialog, which is a very simple form of dialog.

The message box dialog, as shown in Figure 14-11, gives use a message area and the three standard dialog pushbuttons: OK, Cancel and Help.

Figure 14-11. The Message Box Dialog.

The Message-Box Dialog. You can create a message-box dialog with `XmCreateMessageDialog()`:

```
#include <Xm/MessageB.h>

Widget               parent, widget;
String               name;
ArgList              args;
Cardinal             n;

widget = XmCreateMessageDialog( parent,
                              name,
                              args,
                              n );
```

This time, though, we won't manage the dialog right away with XtManageChild(). Instead, we'll let a callback function on the Help menu manage the dialog. The OK button will then be set to have a callback unmanage the dialog, using XtUnmanageChild(), which was also covered in Chapter 4.

Creating "On Version" Help. In the function AboutBox(), below, you create a message-box dialog to present information about the version of the program. In this case, we're just using a simple message-box dialog. In your applications, though, this version information may get complex (with cute graphics). Because of this, we don't want to create a new dialog each time the "On Version..." Help menu choice is made (this is the technique used in most of Chapter 4). Instead, we'll let the version_callback() function manage the dialog, and the unversion_call-back() function unmanage the dialog.

Here's the code to the AboutBox() function:

```
Widget        version_dialog;     /* global dialog widget */

AboutBox( parent, message )

Widget parent; char message[];

{       /* AboutBox */
        Widget      simple_menu_call();    /* menugad.c */
        XmString    motif_string;
        XmString    Str2XmString();        /* string.c */
        Arg         args[10];
        int         n;

        /*
         * Create an About version...box
         */
        motif_string = Str2XmString( message );

        n = 0;
        XtSetArg( args[n], XmNmessageString, motif_string ); n++;
```

continued...

...from previous page

```
/*
 * version_dialog is a global widget
 */
version_dialog = XmCreateMessageDialog( parent,
                    "About Version...", args, n );


/*
 * Callback to unmanage dialog
 */
XtAddCallback( version_dialog,
          XmNokCallback,
          unversion_callback, NULL );

/*
 * Get rid of unwanted children.
 * See dialog.c for more information
 * on this.
 */
XtUnmanageChild( XmMessageBoxGetChild( version_dialog,
          XmDIALOG_CANCEL_BUTTON ) );

XtUnmanageChild( XmMessageBoxGetChild( version_dialog,
          XmDIALOG_HELP_BUTTON ) );

XmStringFree( motif_string );


/*
 * Set up menu item
 */
simple_menu_call( parent, "On Version...", 'V',
          True, version_callback );

}       /* AboutBox */
```

Note that we're using a global widget for the `version_dialog`. This means we can only have one about box.

Note also the call to the function `simple_menu_call()` in the code above. This function creates a push-button gadget on a menu and links in the given callback function (we'll fully introduce this function below).

The function `version_callback()` is set up as the callback for the Help menu's "On Version..." menu choice. This function checks if the about box is managed, using a simple global status value.

If the version_dialog is not already managed, `version_callback()` calls `XtManageChild()` to manage (or pop up) the dialog:

```
Boolean version_up = False;    /* global status */

void version_callback( widget, client_data, call_data )

Widget      widget;
caddr_t     client_data;
caddr_t     call_data;

{            /* version_callback */

        if( version_up == False )
                {
                XtManageChild( version_dialog ):
                version_up = True;
                }

}            /* version_callback */
```

The AboutBox() function also sets up the OK button to call back the function unversion_callback(). This function checks if the version_dialog widget is managed, and if so, calls XtUnmanageChild() to unmanage (or pop down) the about box dialog. Again, we use the global status version_up.

```
void unversion_callback( widget, client_data, call_data )

Widget      widget;
caddr_t     client_data;
caddr_t     call_data;

{        /* unversion_callback */
if( version_up == True )
            {
            XtUnmanageChild( version_dialog );
            version_up = False;
            }

}            /* unversion_callback */
```

Note that we assume you can write a much more efficient means of keeping track of this status. We're merely trying to show this manage-unmanage technique as simply as possible.

SOURCE CODE FOR ABOUT.C

The file about.c contains the following code to support an about box and the "On Version..." menu choice in the Help menu of an application.

```
/*
 *      about.c
 *      Motif "On Version..." About box.
 *
 *      Written for Power Programming Motif
 */

#include       <X11/Intrinsic.h>
#include       <X11/StringDefs.h>
#include       <Xm/Xm.h>
#include       <Xm/MessageB.h>

/*
 *      Globals for On Version dialog.
 */
Widget          version_dialog;                 /*  dialog  widget  */
Boolean         version_up = False;             /* Is the dialog managed? */

void    version_callback( widget, client_data, call_data )

Widget          widget;
caddr_t         client_data;
caddr_t         call_data;

/*
 * Callback to manage About... dialog.
 * If the dialog is not yet managed, then
 * manage it and set a global status to that
 * effect.
 */

{       /* version_callback */

        if( version_up == False )
                {
                XtManageChild( version_dialog );
                version_up = True;
                }

}       /* version_callback */

void unversion_callback( widget, client_data, call_data )

Widget          widget;
caddr_t         client_data;
caddr_t         call_data;

/*
 * Callback to unmanage About... dialog.
 * If the version_dialog is managed, then unmanage
 * it (to make the dialog disappear, and set
 * a global status.
 */
```

continued...

...from previous page

```
{       /* unversion_callback */

        if( version_up == True )
                {
                XtUnmanageChild( version_dialog );
                version_up = False;
                }

}       /* unversion_callback */

AboutBox( parent, message )

Widget          parent;
char            message[];

/*
 * Create the "On Version.." help menu choice
 * and a dialog widget to display a message
 * about the current version of the program.
 */

{       /* AboutBox */
        Widget simple_menu_call();    /* menugad.c */
        XmString        motif_string;
        XmString        Str2XmString();         /* string.c */
        Arg             args[10];
        int             n;

        /*
         * Create an About version...box
         */
        motif_string = Str2XmString( message );

        n = 0;
        XtSetArg( args[n], XmNmessageString, motif_string ); n++;

        /*
         * version_dialog is a global widget
         */
        version_dialog = XmCreateMessageDialog( parent,
                    "About Style...", args, n );

        /*
         * Callback to unmanage dialog
         */
        XtAddCallback( version_dialog,
              XmNokCallback,
              unversion_callback, NULL );
```

continued...

...from previous page

```
   /*
    * Get rid of unwanted children.
    * See dialog.c for more information
    * on this.
    */
   XtUnmanageChild( XmMessageBoxGetChild( version_dialog,
         XmDIALOG_CANCEL_BUTTON ) );

   XtUnmanageChild( XmMessageBoxGetChild( version_dialog,
         XmDIALOG_HELP_BUTTON ) );

   XmStringFree( motif_string );

   /*
    * Set up menu item
    */
   simple_menu_call( parent, "On Version...", 'V',
         True, version_callback );

}       /* AboutBox */

/* end of file */
```

USING GADGETS TO IMPROVE MENU PERFORMANCE

In the function AboutBox() a new function, simple_menu_call(), was used to create a menu choice using gadgets. As discussed in chapters 2 and 6, the designers of Motif created gadgets for performance reasons.

Most Motif menus use pushbutton widgets or pushbutton gadgets for the actual choices on a menu. In this example, we'll use gadgets.

You can generally treat gadgets like widgets, except that sometimes gadgets need special gadget-based functions to access their internal values. Luckily, in the following examples, that isn't the case.

PUSHBUTTON GADGETS FOR MENU CHOICES

You can create a pushbutton gadget with XmCreatePushButtonGadget():

```
#include      <Xm/PushBG.h>

Widget          parent, widget;
String          name;
ArgList         args;
Cardinal        n;

widget = XmCreatePushButtonGadget( parent,
                name,
                args,
                n );

XtManageChild( widget );
```

Note the "G" (for gadget) on the name of the include file, Xm/PushBG.h.

MNENOMICS FOR MENU CHOICES

You can add mnemonics for gadget menu choices just like you did for widget menu choices by using the mnemonic resource (XmNmnemonic in C programs). To set up 'V' as a mnemonic, you could use:

```
Arg           args[10];
int           n;

n = 0;
XtSetArg( args[n], XmNmnemonic, 'V' ); n++;
/* create the widget */
```

We've used mnemonics before for triggering menu bar items (like pull-down menus) from the keyboard for those who wish to avoid using a mouse. In the menu bar, the default is to press the Meta key and the mnemonic at the same time (see Chapter 5 for more on the Meta key). Once a menu is pulled down, you can press Meta and another menu's mnemonic to pull down that menu.

However, the default for the choices in the actual menu is to press just the mnemonic key. In the File menu above, the "Exit" choice has a mnemonic of 'x'. Once the File menu is pulled down, you can press the 'x' key (just the one letter x) to choose the "Exit" choice. You don't use the Meta key for the mnemonics within the menu to pull down menus on the menu bar.

Since Motif applications are highly configurable, you could configure yourself into and out of this, but the basic (default) idea is to use the Meta key with the mnemonic key to pull down a menu and just use the mnemonic key (without the Meta key) to choose a choice within that pulled-down menu.

In the `style` program below, you can press `Meta-F` to pull down the File menu and then press x to exit the program (actually, to choose the "Exit" choice). This takes a while to get used to, but it isn't really all that confusing in practice.

Just like you're using gadgets for pushbutton-based menu choices, you can also use gadgets for the menu separator lines.

SEPARATOR GADGETS

Separator gadgets work basically like separator widgets. You can use `XmCreateSeparatorGadget()` to create a separator gadget:

```
#include    <Xm/SeparatoG.h>

Widget          parent, widget;
String          name;
ArgList         args;
Cardinal        n;

widget = XmCreateSeparatorGadget( parent,
                name,
                args,
                n );

XtManageChild( widget );
```

Note the "G" (for gadget) on the name of the include file, `Xm/SeparatoG.h`.

Now, to pull all this together, we need to flesh out a menu by adding menu choices.

Creating a Simple Menu Item Using Gadgets

The function `simple_menu_item()` adds a menu choice to a given menu widget. It creates a pushbutton gadget for the choice, and optionally, a leading separator gadget (that is, a separator before the choice). This function also sets up a mnemonic for the actual menu choice. The `simple_menu_item()` function returns the pushbutton gadget:

```
Widget simple_menu_item( menu_widget, name, mnemonic,
NeedsSeparator )

Widget          menu_widget;
char            *name;
int             mnemonic;
Boolean         NeedsSeparator; /* == True if you want a leading
separator                           */
```
continued...

...from previous page

```
{       /* simple_menu_item */
        Widget          widget, sep;
        Arg             args[10];
        int             n;

        if ( NeedsSeparator == True )
                {
                sep = XmCreateSeparatorGadget( menu_widget,
                        "sep", NULL, 0 );

                XtManageChild( sep );
                }

        n = 0;
        XtSetArg( args[n], XmNmnemonic, mnemonic ); n++;

        widget = XmCreatePushButtonGadget( menu_widget,
                name, args, n );

        XtManageChild( widget );

        return( widget );

}       /* simple_menu_item */
```

Adding a Callback to a Simple Menu Item

The function `simple_menu_item()` creates a very simple, gadget-based menu choice, but doesn't do anything about setting up a callback for that menu choice. The function `simple_menu_call()`, shown below, adds a callback function. `simple_menu_call()` calls `simple_menu_item()` to set up the menu-choice gadgets, and then calls `XtAddCallback()` to set up the callback function:

```
Widget simple_menu_call( menu_widget, name, mnemonic,
NeedsSeparator, callback )

Widget      menu_widget;
char        *name;
int         mnemonic;
Boolean     NeedsSeparator; /* == True if you want a leading
separator                   */
void    (*callback)();

{       /* simple_menu_call */
        Widget          widget;
```

continued...

...from previous page
```
        widget = simple_menu_item( menu_widget, name,
                mnemonic, NeedsSeparator );

        XtAddCallback( widget,
            XmNactivateCallback,
            callback, NULL );

        return( widget );

}       /* simple_menu_call */
```

In a real application, every menu choice will have a callback function. However, when you're prototyping or simply want to demonstrate what the proper menus look like you don't need the callback functions.

Source Code for Menugad.c

The file `menugad.c` contains a set of functions for creating menus and menu choices using gadgets where possible.

To round out our set of simple gadget-based menu functions, we added `simple_menu()`, below, which creates a pulldown menu:

```
/*
 *      menugad.c
 *      Simple Menu gadget functions
 *
 *      Written for Power Programming Motif
 *
 */

#include     <X11/Intrinsic.h>
#include     <X11/StringDefs.h>
#include     <Xm/Xm.h>
#include     <Xm/CascadeB.h>
#include     <Xm/PushBG.h>
#include     <Xm/RowColumn.h>
#include     <Xm/SeparatoG.h>

Widget simple_menu( menu_bar, name, mnemonic )

Widget       menu_bar; /* parent */
char         *name;
int          mnemonic;

/*
 *      Creates a simple pull-down menu.
```
continued...

...from previous page
```
 *     Uses as few hard-coded resources
 *     as possible.
 */

{      /* simple_menu */
       Widget cascade_button;
       Widget menu_widget;
       Arg           args[10];
       int           n;
       char          new_name[ 400 ];

       n = 0;
       XtSetArg( args[n], XmNmnemonic, mnemonic ); n++;

       cascade_button = XmCreateCascadeButton( menu_bar,
                          name, args, n );

       XtManageChild( cascade_button );

       /*
        * Check if Help, if so then
        * set up this widget for the
        * menu bar's help.
        */
       if ( strcmp( name, "Help" ) == 0 )
             {
             n = 0;
             XtSetArg( args[n], XmNmenuHelpWidget, cascade_button ); n++;
             XtSetValues( menu_bar, args, n );
             }

       /*
        * Create a new name for the
        * actual menu.
        */
       strcpy( new_name, name );
       strcat( new_name, "Menu" );

       n = 0;
       menu_widget = XmCreatePulldownMenu( menu_bar, new_name, args, n );

       n = 0;
       XtSetArg( args[n], XmNsubMenuId, menu_widget ); n++;
       XtSetValues( cascade_button, args, n );

       return( menu_widget );
```

continued...

...from previous page
```
}      /* simple_menu */

Widget  simple_menu_item( menu_widget,  name,  mnemonic,
NeedsSeparator )

Widget          menu_widget;
char            *name;
int             mnemonic;
Boolean         NeedsSeparator; /* == True if you want a leading
separator                                    */

/*
 * Creates a push button gadget and optionally
 * a separator gadget (if NeedsSeparator == True)
 * to add to a simple menu.
 */

{      /* simple_menu_item */
       Widgetwidget, sep;
       Arg           args[10];
       int           n;

       if ( NeedsSeparator == True )
                     {
                     sep = XmCreateSeparatorGadget( menu_widget,
                     "sep", NULL, 0 );

                     XtManageChild( sep );
                     }

       n = 0;
       XtSetArg( args[n], XmNmnemonic, mnemonic ); n++;

       widget = XmCreatePushButtonGadget( menu_widget,
                     name, args, n );

       XtManageChild( widget );

       return( widget );

}      /* simple_menu_item */

Widget  simple_menu_call( menu_widget,  name,  mnemonic,
NeedsSeparator, callback )

Widget          menu_widget;
char            *name;
int             mnemonic;
Boolean         NeedsSeparator; /* == True if you want a leading
separator                                    */
void            (*callback)();
```
continued...

...from previous page

```
/*
 * Creates a push button gadget and optionally
 * a separator gadget (if NeedsSeparator == True),
 * using simple_menu_item(). Then, this routine
 * adds in a callback function for the menu choice.
 */

{       /* simple_menu_call */
        Widget widget;

        widget = simple_menu_item( menu_widget, name,
                    mnemonic, NeedsSeparator );

        XtAddCallback( widget,
                    XmNactivateCallback,
                    callback, NULL );

        return( widget );

}       /* simple_menu_call */

/* end of file */
```

This function is a closer match to the Motif style than `CreatePulldownMenu()` in `menu.c`. You could easily use either function to create your pulldown menus.

THE STYLE PROGRAM

We've created `style`, a program that demonstrates how to put together a standard Motif menu bar and menus. This program has a rather complex widget hierarchy, even though the program really does nothing. This hierarchy is as follows:

```
* Top-Level Shell
    * Main Window
        * Menu Bar
            * Cascade Button (File Menu)
            * Pulldown Menu (File)
                * Pushbutton Gadget ("New" Choice)
                * Pushbutton Gadget ("Open" Choice)
                * Separator Gadget
```

```
            * Pushbutton Gadget ("Save" Choice)
            * Pushbutton Gadget ("Save As" Choice)
            * Pushbutton Gadget ("Print" Choice)
            * Separator Gadget
            * Pushbutton Gadget ("Exit" Choice)
    * Cascade Button (Edit Menu)
    * Pulldown Menu (Edit)
            * Pushbutton Gadget ("Undo" Choice)
            * Separator Gadget
            * Pushbutton Gadget ("Cut" Choice)
            * Pushbutton Gadget ("Copy" Choice)
            * Pushbutton Gadget ("Paste" Choice)
            * Separator Gadget
            * Pushbutton Gadget ("Clear" Choice)
            * Pushbutton Gadget ("Delete" Choice)
    * Cascade Button (View Menu)
    * Pulldown Menu (View)
            * Pushbutton Gadget ("All" Choice)
            * Pushbutton Gadget ("Partial" Choice)
            * Separator Gadget
            * Pushbutton Gadget ("By Date" Choice)
            * Pushbutton Gadget ("By Name" Choice)
            * Pushbutton Gadget ("By Other" Choice)
    * Cascade Button (Options Menu)
    * Pulldown Menu (Options)
            * Pushbutton Gadget ("Colors" Choice)
    * Cascade Button (Help Menu)
    * Pulldown Menu (Help)
            * Pushbutton Gadget ("On Context" Choice)
            * Pushbutton Gadget ("On Help" Choice)
            * Pushbutton Gadget ("On Window" Choice)
            * Pushbutton Gadget ("On Keys" Choice)
            * Pushbutton Gadget ("Index" Choice)
            * Pushbutton Gadget ("Tutorial" Choice)
            * Pushbutton Gadget ("On Version" Choice)
             * Message Dialog (About box)
                * Pushbutton (OK on Message Dialog)
```

Source Code for Style.c

The file `style.c` contains the `main()` function for the `style` program (note that we again try to hard-code as few resource values as possible, so that users can customize the application with resource files):

```
/*
 *   style.c
 *   Menu bar skeleton that follows the
 *   Motif Style Guide
 *
 *   Written for Programming Motif
 */
#include        <X11/Intrinsic.h>
#include        <X11/StringDefs.h>
#include        <Xm/Xm.h>
#include        <Xm/CascadeB.h>
#include        <Xm/MainW.h>
#include        <Xm/MessageB.h>
#include        <Xm/RowColumn.h>

/*
 * Message for about box
 */
#define MSG "Motif Style Guide Menus\nby Johnson and Reichard\nver. 1.0"

void quit_callback( widget, client_data, call_data )

Widget          widget;
caddr_t         client_data;
caddr_t         call_data;

/*
 *   Callback to quit program
 */

{    /* quit_callback */

    XtCloseDisplay( XtDisplay( widget ) );

    exit( 0 );

}    /* quit_callback */

main( argc, argv )

int             argc;
char            *argv[];

{    /* main */
    Widget   parent;
    Widget   main_window;
    Widget   menu_bar;
    Widget   simple_menu();                      /* menugad.c */
    Widget   simple_menu_item();                 /* menugad.c */
```
continued...

...from previous page

```
    Widget    simple_menu_call();              /* menugad.c */
    Widget    file_menu, edit_menu, view_menu;
    Widget    options_menu, help_menu;
    Arg       args[10];
    int       n;

    parent = XtInitialize( argv[0],
                "Style",
                NULL,
                0,
                &argc,
                argv );

    n = 0;
    XtSetArg( args[n], XmNallowShellResize, True ); n++;
    XtSetValues( parent, args, n );

    /*
     * Create a main window without
     * setting too many resources.
     */
    n = 0;
    XtSetArg( args[n], XmNshadowThickness, 4 ); n++;
    XtSetArg( args[n], XmNshowSeparator, True ); n++;

    main_window = XmCreateMainWindow( parent,
                        "main",
                        args,
                        n );

    XtManageChild( main_window );

    /*
     * Create a menu bar
     */
    n = 0;
    menu_bar = XmCreateMenuBar( main_window,
                "menu_bar",
                args,
                n );

    XtManageChild( menu_bar );

    /*
     * File menu
     */
    file_menu = simple_menu( menu_bar, "File", 'F' );
```

continued...

...from previous page

```
    simple_menu_item( file_menu, "New",       'N', False );
    simple_menu_item( file_menu, "Open...",   'O', False );
    simple_menu_item( file_menu, "Save",      'S', True  );
    simple_menu_item( file_menu, "Save As..."'A', False );
    simple_menu_item( file_menu, "Print",     'P', False );

    simple_menu_call( file_menu, "Exit", 'x', True,  quit_callback );

    /*
     * Edit menu
     */
    edit_menu = simple_menu( menu_bar, "Edit", 'E' );

    simple_menu_item( edit_menu, "Undo",      'U', False );
    simple_menu_item( edit_menu, "Cut",       't', True  );
    simple_menu_item( edit_menu, "Copy",      'C', False );
    simple_menu_item( edit_menu, "Paste",     'P', False );
    simple_menu_item( edit_menu, "Clear",     'l', True  );
    simple_menu_item( edit_menu, "Delete",    'D', False );

    /*
     * View menu
     */
    view_menu = simple_menu( menu_bar, "View", 'V' );

    simple_menu_item( view_menu, "All",         'A', False );
    simple_menu_item( view_menu, "Partial...",  'P', False );
    simple_menu_item( view_menu, "By Date...",  'D', True  );
    simple_menu_item( view_menu, "By Name...",  'N', False );
    simple_menu_item( view_menu, "By Other...", 'O', False );

    /*
     * Options menu
     */
    options_menu = simple_menu( menu_bar, "Options", 'O' );

    simple_menu_item( options_menu, "Colors...", 'C', False );

    /*
     * Help menu
     */
    help_menu = simple_menu( menu_bar, "Help", 'H' );

    simple_menu_item( help_menu,    "On Context...", 'C', False );
    simple_menu_item( help_menu,    "On Help...",    'H', False );
    simple_menu_item( help_menu,    "On Window...",  'W', False );
    simple_menu_item( help_menu,    "On Keys...",    'K', False );
    simple_menu_item( help_menu,    "Index...",      'I', False );
    simple_menu_item( help_menu,    "Tutorial...",   'T', False );
```

continued...

...from previous page

```
/*
 * On version box
 */
AboutBox( help_menu, MSG );

XmMainWindowSetAreas( main_window,
        menu_bar,
        (Widget) NULL,
        (Widget) NULL,
        (Widget) NULL,
        (Widget) NULL );

XtRealizeWidget( parent );
XtMainLoop();

}   /* main */

/* end of file */
```

Compiling and Linking the Style Program

The `style` program needs the following C source files:

```
about.c
menugad.c
string.c (from chapter 2)
style.c
```

You can compile and link the `style` program with a UNIX command like:

```
cc -o style about.o menugad.o string.o style.o -lXm -lXt -lX11
```

With `Makefile` in Appendix C, you can use:

```
make style
```

or

```
make all
```

The `style` program is shown in Figure 14-12.

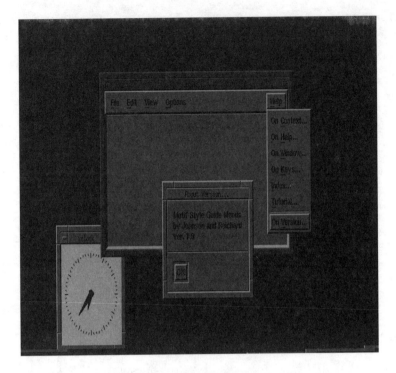

Figure 14-12 . The Style Program.

A Resource File for the Style Program

The file `Style.ad` shown below, contains a few resource definitions for the `style` program. Feel free to change the definitions as much as you like:

```
!
!       Style.ad (note capital "S"),
!       a Motif resource file for the
!       style program in chapter 14.
!
style*fontList:              variable
style.width:                 400
style.height                 225
!
!       end of file
!
```

We named this file "`Style.ad`" for Style application defaults. The ".ad" extension is fairly common in the X Window and Motif community. You will most likely need to give this file another name if you want to treat the file as an application defaults file. Rename this file to `Style` and then place in your home directory (`$HOME` in UNIX parlance) or in a place where other application default files go, such as `/usr/lib/X11/app-defaults`. See Chapter 13 for for more information on where resource files can be placed.

Running the Style Program

The `style` program mainly serves to demonstrate the standard Motif menus—most of the menu choices do nothing at all. The "On Version..." choice from the Help menu, though, calls up a version information dialog. You should experiment with the resource file by setting different fonts and other resources to see what happens.

MOTIF FUNCTIONS AND MACROS INTRODUCED IN THIS CHAPTER

The following is a list of motif functions and macros introduced in this chapter.

```
XmCreateMessageDialog()
XmCreatePushButtonGadget()
XmCreateSeparatorGadget()
```

You should be familiar with these functions and macros before moving on to Chapter 15.

SUMMARY

The *OSF/Motif Style Guide* describes the look and feel for well-behaved Motif programs. There is a lot of flexibility within the Style Guide, but your applications should start out with a menu bar and the five standard menus: File, Edit, View, Options and Help. You really don't want to deviate too far from the Style Guide unless you have a good reason. One of the goals of a toolkit like Motif is to provide the users with a consistent, easy-to-use set of application software. A message dialog can be used to implement the "On Version..." Help menu choice. You can create a message dialog with `XmCreateMessageDialog()`.

Using gadgets to replace widgets in menus can improve the performance of your Motif applications. Use `XmCreatePushButtonGadget()` to create a pushbutton gadget and `XmCreateSeparatorGadget()` to create a separator gadget. Remember to include the proper include files (which have a "G" in their names).

Chapter 15 extends the Motif style discussion by introducing dialog design.

Chapter 15

Custom Dialogs

C hapter 14 covered the *OSF/Motif Style Guide's* rules on menus. This chapter extends that discussion by going into the Motif style guidelines for dialogs, especially the customized, complex dialogs that you are likely to need in any real application.

Once again, we're going to start with the *OSF/Motif Style Guide*. We won't cover everything in the style guide on dialogs—instead, we'll focus on the basic rules for dialogs. In the next chapter, you'll learn how to create a fairly complex custom dialog. A custom dialog is shown in Figure 15-1.

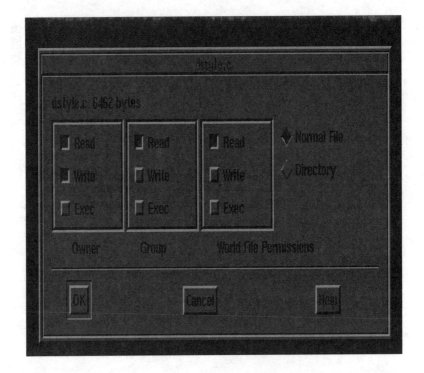

Figure 15-1 . A Custom Dialog.

Chapter 4 covered the standard Motif dialogs—this chapter focuses on creating dialogs, especially using the bulletin-board widget.

COMMON PUSHBUTTONS IN DIALOGS

In the standard Motif dialogs used so far, you've only seen the OK, the Cancel, and the Help pushbuttons. Motif allows for a number of standard pushbuttons beyond these as shown in Figure 15-2.

Pushbutton	Function
Apply	Applies the changes the user made in the dialog. The dialog window remains on the screen.
Cancel	Officially, this combines the Reset and Close operations.
Close	Makes the dialog go away. Usually Close is part of a combined operation like Cancel or OK.
Help	Presents help on the dialog (usually by popping up another dialog, a help dialog). Help should always be the rightmost push button, just like a Help menu is always the rightmost menu. It's a good idea to offer help on dialogs, especially complex dialogs.
No	Answers no to the given question. Note that it is very easy to confuse yes and no in certain questions, so be very careful when using Yes and No push buttons. "Are you sure you don't want to continue?" is an example of a bad yes/no question.
OK	Officially, this combines the Apply and Close operations.
Reset	Resets the values displayed in the dialog to the values when the dialog first appeared.
Retry	Attempt to perform a task again. This could be used to retry to print after encountering a printer error (such as out of paper).
Stop	Ends whatever task is in progress. Your application may wait until a convenient stopping point to actually stop the operation.
Yes	Answers yes to the given question. Again, note that it is very easy to confuse yes and no in certain questions, so use caution when using Yes and No pushbuttons.

Figure 15-2. Pushbutton Functions.

If you use a standard name, like "Apply," then you should implement the Apply button as defined in figure 15-2, otherwise, your Motif applications will be inconsistent.

Note that you are free to define your own buttons if they make sense, such as "Log Out" or "Format Disk." In general, the more specific the pushbutton titles are, the better, because the user will get a better idea of what will happen when the button is "pushed."

Generally, the pushbuttons should go at the bottom of the dialog like the standard Motif dialogs—the working dialog and error dialog—introduced in Chapter 4. Do not use too many pushbuttons in a dialog.

When creating your own dialogs, you should group like components together, so that the user doesn't have to search for the available choices. It is often a good idea to group components by placing a frame widget around a set of controls in a dialog. We'll do this in the dstyle program in the next chapter.

MAKING DISABLED CHOICES UNAVAILABLE

Choices that are invalid or unavailable should be greyed out and set to be insensitive to the keyboard and the mouse input. You can do this in your C programs by using the X toolkit function XtSetSensitive():

```
Widget widget;
Boolean state;

XtSetSensitive( widget, state );
```

If the state is False, then the widget will no longer receive keyboard or mouse events. If the state is True, then the widget is restored to receiving keyboard and mouse events.

You'll use XtSetSensitive() to set a help button on our custom dialog to insensitive (since we're not offering on-line help on the dialog) in the file fileinfo.c, in Chapter 16.

USING THE BULLETIN BOARD DIALOG FOR CUSTOM DIALOGS

You now know a number of Motif dialog types, including the information and file-selection dialogs in Chapter 4 and the message-box dialog in Chapter 14. When you're creating a custom dialog, you'll probably have the best luck using a form dialog or a bulletin-board dialog. Both of these dialogs provide a flexible area in which to create and place your own widgets.

Chapter 3 introduced the form widget—most of that material applies to a form dialog as well. This chapter introduces the bulletin-board dialog, as it is used more often than not to create a custom dialog.

THE BULLETIN-BOARD WIDGET

The bulletin-board widget is like a real bulletin board; you can place things in it at certain locations. This widget is a container widget that manages any number of child widgets, but does not provide as complex placement control as the form widget. In fact, most of the time you use a bulletin board widget, you'll place your child widgets by hand and then just keep the child widgets locked in place. This may not seem like it offers enough, but the bulletin-board widget, as the parent class of other dialog widgets, provides a number of services that aid in creating your own dialogs.

Creating the Bulletin-Board Dialog

You create a bulletin-board dialog with XmCreateBulletinBoardDialog(). XmCreateBulletinBoardDialog() will create a XmBulletinBoard widget as a child of a DialogShell widget and do everything else that is necessary to have a simple dialog. The include file is Xm/BulletinB.h:

```
#include     <Xm/BulletinB.h>

Widget       parent, widget;
String       name;
ArgList      args;
Cardinal     n;

widget = XmCreateBulletinBoardDialog( parent,
                  name,
                  args,
                  n );
```

Again, as in the previous chapter, you won't manage the dialog immediately with XtManageChild(). Instead, you'll let a callback function on the menu that calls up the dialog manage the widget. You'll do this as you did in Chapter 14 with the "About version..." box.

Managing and Unmanaging the Bulletin-Board Dialog

When you create a bulletin-board dialog, you probably don't want to manage it immediately. Use a menu or another pushbutton callback to manage the dialog. Then, in at least one pushbutton at the bottom of your custom dialog, set up a callback to unmanage the bulletin board dialog. You don't have to use this strategy—you can use the strategy in the Chapter 4 example programs. If you do decide to manage and unmanage the bulletin-board dialog on your own, you'll need to set the autoUnmanage resource (XmNautoUnmanage in C programs) to False:

```
Arg      args[10];
int      n;

n = 0;
XtSetArg( args[n], XmNautoUnmanage, False ); n++;

/* create the widget... */
```

Setting the `autoUnmanage` resource to `False` tells the bulletin board to keep its hands off and allow your program to explicitly manage and unmanage the dialog.

Placing Widgets in a Bulletin-Board Dialog

Child widgets are placed in a bulletin-board dialog by setting the x (XmNx in C programs) and y (XmNy in C programs) resources on the child widgets. This tells the bulletin-board widget (the parent) where you'd like the child widgets to go. The bulletin board does not support attachments like the form widget, but we think you'll find the ability to place items works well enough for creating dialogs.

In fact, in Chapter 16, you'll use resource-setting commands in resource files to place the widgets in a custom bulletin-board dialog. This allows you to dynamically place the child widgets. You can use the resource file as a prototyping aid when laying out your dialog.

Controlling Resizing of a Bulletin-Board Dialog

If you place child widgets at a given x,y location within a bulletin-board dialog, you probably don't want your placements changed. One way to avoid this is to control the ability of the user to resize your dialog. If the user cannot change the size of your dialog, then all your items will always remain visible(assuming your users have a screen large enough to show your entire dialog).

The `noResize` resource (XmNnoResize in C programs) controls whether the bulletin-board dialog will allow itself to be resized. If you are running the Motif window manager, mwm, you won't see the resize handles on the window's border, as shown in Figure 15-3.

Figure 15-3 . The Top of a Dialog Window without Resize Handles.

If you set the `noResize` resource to `True`, then the user will not be able to resize your dialog (provided the window manager cooperates):

```
Arg        args[10];
int        n;

n = 0;
XtSetArg( args[n], XmNnoResize, True ); n++;

/* create the widget... */
```

A Function to Create a Bulletin-Board Dialog

In the function CreateBulletinDialog(), below, we've combined the code above to make a utility function for creating bulletin-board dialogs:

```
Widget        CreateBulletinDialog( parent, name )

Widget        parent;
char          name[];

{      /* CreateBulletinDialog */
       Widget          bulletin;
       Arg             args[10];
       int             n;

       /*
        * Create a bulletin board dialog, but don't
        * manage it. A callback will manage
        * it later.
        */
       n = 0;
       XtSetArg( args[n], XmNautoUnmanage, False ); n++;
       XtSetArg( args[n], XmNnoResize, True ); n++;

       bulletin = XmCreateBulletinBoardDialog( parent,
                                 name,
                                 args,
                                 n );

       return( bulletin );

}      /* CreateBulletinDialog */
```

Default Buttons

Dialogs can have a default button—a button that is triggered when the Return key is pressed. You must not use the default pushbutton for a destructive action. You wouldn't want your users accidentally pressing the Return key and erasing their 100=gigabyte hard disk.

In many Motif dialogs, you'll see an extra shadow effect around one pushbutton. This signifies that the pushbutton is the default button for the dialog. When the user presses the Return key in the dialog, the default button will be activated. In Figure 15-4, the OK button is the default button for the dialog.

Figure 15-4. The OK Button as the Default Button.

There are two steps needed to set up a default button. First, you need to add the extra shadow effect to the pushbutton. You do this by setting the showAsDefault resource (XmNshowAsDefault in C programs) on the pushbutton widget, the pushbutton that you want to make the default button. We've found a value of 1 works fine:

```
Arg        args[10];
int        n;

n = 0;
XtSetArg( args[n], XmNshowAsDefault, 1 ); n++;

/* create push button widget */
```

Remember, this is a resource set on the actual pushbutton widget itself, and not on the bulletin-board widget. Look up XmPushButton in the *OSF/Motif Programmer's Reference* manual for more information.

The second step is to tell the bulletin-board dialog which pushbutton widget is the default button. It is a very good idea to use the same pushbutton widget to which you added the extra shadow effect (with the showAsDefault resource).

You can tell a bulletin-board dialog which pushbutton child widget is the default button by setting the defaultButton resource (XmNdefaultButton in C programs). The defaultButton resource requires the widget ID for the pushbutton widget:

```
Widget    bulletin; /* bulletin board Dialog */
Widget    button; /* default push button widget */
Arg       args[10];
int       n;

n = 0;
XtSetArg( args[n], XmNdefaultButton, button ); n++;

XtSetValues( bulletin, args, n );
```

Since this is a common task (you'll need to do this for every bulletin-board dialog you create), we put together BulletinDefaultButton(), a utility function to handle this:

```
Widget        bulletin;
Widget        button;

{       /* BulletinDefaultButton */
        Arg  args[10];
        int  n;

        /*
         * Set button as default
         */
        n = 0;
        XtSetArg( args[n], XmNdefaultButton, button ); n++;

        XtSetValues( bulletin, args, n );

}       /* BulletinDefaultButton */
```

Setting the Window Title

You can change the title of a bulletin-board dialog by setting the `dialogTitle` resource (`XmNdialogTitle` in C programs).

You can set this from a resource file, for example:

```
application*bulletin_name.dialogTitle:   File Information
```

or, you can set this in your C code:

```
XmString        motif_string;
Arg             args[10];
int             n;

n = 0;
XtSetArg( args[n], XmNdialogTitle, motif_string ); n++;

/* create the widget or call XtSetValaues()... */

XmStringFree( motif_string );
```

In the `dstyle` program in the next chapter, we'll set the title of the dialog to be the name of the file the dialog is presenting. Note that the title string must be a Motif `XmString`.

The function `BulletinDialogTitle()` on the next page, handles the task of converting a C string into a `XmString` and then sets the `dialogTitle` resource for the given bulletin-board widget:

```
BulletinDialogTitle( bulletin, title )

Widget      bulletin;
char        title[];

{           /* BulletinDialogTitle */
            XmString            motif_string;
            XmString            Str2XmString(); /* string.c */
            Arg                 args[10];
            int                 n;

            motif_string = Str2XmString( title );

            n = 0;
            XtSetArg( args[n], XmNdialogTitle, motif_string ); n++;

            XtSetValues( bulletin, args, n );

            XmStringFree( motif_string );

}           /* BulletinDialogTitle */
```

Source Code for Bulletin.c

The file bulletin.c has three utility functions for working with bulletin-board dialogs:

```
/*
 *    bulletin.c
 *    Utility functions for the Motif Bulletin Board Dialog.
 *
 * Written for Power Programming Motif. */

#include       <X11/Intrinsic.h>
#include       <X11/StringDefs.h>
#include       <Xm/Xm.h>
#include       <Xm/BulletinB.h>

BulletinDefaultButton( bulletin, button )

Widget         bulletin;
Widget         button;

/*
 *    BulletinDefaultButton() sets the given bulletin board
 *    dialog to have the given push button as its default
 *    button (the one that is triggered when the user presses
 *    the Return key).
 */
```

continued...

345

...from previous page

```
{       /* BulletinDefaultButton */
        Arg         args[10];
        int         n;

        /*
         *          Set button as default
         */
        n = 0;
        XtSetArg( args[n], XmNdefaultButton, button ); n++;

        XtSetValues( bulletin, args, n );

}       /* BulletinDefaultButton */


BulletinDialogTitle( bulletin, title )

Widget          bulletin;
char title[];

/*
 *     BulletinDialogTitle() sets the title of
 *     the given bulletin board dialog.
 */

{       /* BulletinDialogTitle */
        XmString        motif_string;
        XmString        Str2XmString();
        Arg             args[10];
        int             n;

        /*
         * Set up title of dialog box
         */
        motif_string = Str2XmString( title );

        n = 0;
        XtSetArg( args[n], XmNdialogTitle, motif_string ); n++;

        XtSetValues( bulletin, args, n );

        XmStringFree( motif_string );

}       /* BulletinDialogTitle */


Widget CreateBulletinDialog( parent, name )

Widget          parent;
char            name[];
```
continued...

...from previous page

```
/*
 *    CreateBulletinDialog() creates a bulletin board
 *    dialog, but does not manage it. The dialog
 *    is set up to forbid resizes.
 */

{      /* CreateBulletinDialog */
       Widget      bulletin;
       Arg         args[10];
       int         n;

/*
 * Create a bulletin board dialog, but don't
 * manage it. A callback will manage
 * it later.
 */
n = 0;
XtSetArg( args[n], XmNautoUnmanage, False ); n++;
XtSetArg( args[n], XmNnoResize, True ); n++;

bulletin = XmCreateBulletinBoardDialog( parent,
                          name,
                          args,
                          n );

       return( bulletin );

}      /* CreateBulletinDialog */

/* end of file */
```

MOTIF FUNCTIONS AND MACROS INTRODUCED IN THIS CHAPTER

The following is a list of Motif functions and macros introduced in this chapter.

```
XmCreateBulletinBoardDialog()
```

You should be familiar with this function before moving on to Chapter 16.

X TOOLKIT FUNCTIONS AND MACROS INTRODUCED IN THIS CHAPTER

The following is a list of Xtoolkit functions and macros introduced in this chapter.

```
XtSetSensitive()
```

You should be familiar with this function before moving on to Chapter 16.

SUMMARY

This chapter covered the basic rules for Motif dialogs and introduced the bulletin-board dialog which is commonly used to create custom dialogs.

The Xt function `XtSetSensitive()` can be used to make a pushbutton widget insensitive. That is, `XtSetSensitive()` can make a pushbutton choice unavailable to the user. The choice text is greyed out and the widget will no longer accept keyboard or mouse input.

In the next chapter, you'll learn how to use the utility functions in `bulletin.c` and create a complex custom dialog using the bulletin-board dialog.

Chapter 16

Building a Custom Motif Dialog

C hapter 15 presented rules for building dialogs using the Motif toolkit and introduced the bulletin-board dialog. This chapter shows how to create a custom dialog using the bulletin-board dialog.

Almost every serious application you create requires a custom dialog of one sort or another. Most word processors, for example, need a dialog to control printing options (like paper size and number of copies) or to adjust style sheets. Most other applications, too, have dialog needs that go far beyond the standard Motif set, like working and file-selection dialogs. So, you'll probably have to build a custom dialog at some point.

BUILDING A CUSTOM DIALOG

To build a custom dialog, start out with a form dialog or a bulletin-board dialog. The latter is used more often and is generally easier to deal with, so it is used here.

The following code creates a custom dialog that presents information about a file in a graphical fashion. This type of dialog is a good start in creating a graphical Motif file browser or a similar application.

The dialog shows the file name, its size in bytes, as well as the access permissions for the file. (Following a UNIX model, there are read, write, and execute permissions for the file: the owner; every member of the group the owner is in; and for everyone else who is not in the same group as the owner. Those who have read permission, for example, are allowed to read the given file). A custom file information dialog is shown in Figure 16-1.

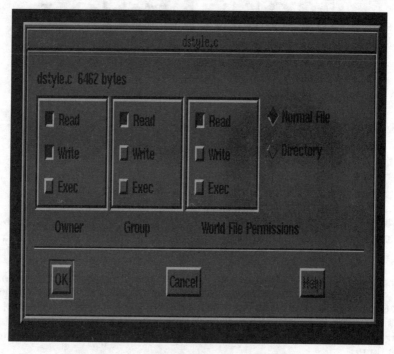

Figure 16-1 . A Custom File Information Dialog.

The custom dialog could be extended to allow the user to set the file permissions.

To create your dialog, the basic strategy is to create a bulletin-board dialog and then fill in the dialog with our widgets in the specified locations. (We'll use a resource file to specify the child widget locations.) The child widgets will mostly be `RowColumn` container widgets, which will hold toggle-button children.

Here is the widget hierarchy used just in the custom file information dialog:

        * Bulletin Board ("fileinfo")—parent for the dialog
            * Label (for file name and size)
            * RowColumn (horizontal) for main information area ("mainrow")
                * Frame ("frame") for grouping
                    * RowColumn (vertical, for owner "permissions")
                        *Toggle Button ("Read")
                        *Toggle Button ("Write")
                        *Toggle Button ("Exec")
                * Frame ("frame") for grouping
                    * RowColumn (vertical, for group "permissions")
                        *Toggle Button ("Read")
                        *Toggle Button ("Write")
                        *Toggle Button ("Exec")
                * Frame ("frame") for grouping
                    * RowColumn (vertical, for world "permissions")
                        *Toggle Button ("Read")
                        *Toggle Button ("Write")
                        *Toggle Button ("Exec")
                * RowColumn (vertical, radio box for "file_dir")
                    * Radio Toggle Button ("normal")
                    * Radio Toggle Button ("directory")
            * Label ("owner")
            * Label ("group")
            * Label ("world")
            * Separator Gadget ("fileinfosep")
            * Pushbutton ("OK")—the default button
            * Pushbutton ("Cancel")
            * Pushbutton ("Help")—later made insensitive

There are a lot of widgets to create. We could cut down on the number of widgets, but this layout tries to organize the widgets into groups. Note how we use frame widgets to group together the toggles (which are managed by a `RowColumn` widget). The frames add a bounding box that physically groups these like items together.

MANAGING AND UNMANAGING THE CUSTOM FILE INFORMATION DIALOG

Since this is such a complex dialog (and since we may want to dynamically change the information in the dialog on the fly), you'll only allow one copy of this dialog to be active at a time. Because of this, you can use the manage/unmanage scheme introduced in Chapter 14 for the "About Version..." box. That is, one callback (set up for a "File Info..." menu choice) will manage the global file info dialog. Another callback (set up for both the OK and Cancel pushbuttons on the dialog) will unmanage the file info dialog. In both cases, a status variable is checked to prevent errors. (You don't really have to use global variables—it's just an easy way to concentrate on the task at hand.)

The function `fileinfo_callback()` is set up on a menu choice to manage the dialog (remember that you do have to create the dialog before you manage it):

```
Widget            file_info_widget;              /* file information dialog */
Boolean           file_info_managed = False; /* status */

void fileinfo_callback( widget, client_data, call_data )

Widget            widget;
caddr_t           client_data;
caddr_t           call_data;

{       /* fileinfo_callback */

        if ( file_info_managed == False )
                {
                XtManageChild( file_info_widget );
                file_info_managed = True;
                }

}       /* fileinfo_callback */
```

The function `unfileinfo_callback()` unmanages the dialog if it has been managed:

```
void unfileinfo_callback( widget, client_data, call_data )

Widget            widget;
caddr_t           client_data;
caddr_t           call_data;
```

continued...

352

...from previous page

```
/*
 *      Pops down, or unmanages the file information
 *      dialog, if it is already managed.
 */

{       /* unfileinfo_callback */

        if ( file_info_managed == True )
                {
                XtUnmanageChild( file_info_widget );
                file_info_managed = False;
                }

}       /* unfileinfo_callback */
```

CREATING CHILD WIDGETS FOR THE DIALOG

The function FileInformationDialog() below creates your file information dialog, with the widget hierarchy shown earlier (this is a rather long function, since it has a lot of work to do).

FileInformationDialog(), shown below, uses a number of global variables to allow the file information to be set up. This is normally done in the function FillFileInformation(), contained in the file fileinfo.c:

```
/*
 *      Globals for the file information custom dialog
 */
Widget      file_info_widget;    /* file information dialog */
Boolean     file_info_managed = False;
Widget      file_info_label;
Widget      read_perms[ 4 ];
Widget      write_perms[ 4 ];
Widget      exec_perms[ 4 ];
Widget      file_or_dir[ 3 ];
```

The first thing FileInformationDialog() does is to create a bulletin-board dialog widget, using the function CreateBulletinDialog() in the file bulletin.c (introduced in Chapter 15).

After that, you start creating a number of label widgets and a RowColumn widget to manage the main information area. The RowColumn is set up as a column-based horizontal (XmHORIZONTAL) widget. This way, the four child widgets (three frames and another RowColumn) will be aligned in columns horizontally. Using a RowColumn here isn't necessary, but it eliminates much of the work of placing all the child widgets.

The `CreateFilePermissions()` function creates the following widgets from our widget hierarchy:

> * Frame ("frame") for grouping
> > * RowColumn (vertical, for "permissions")
> > > *Toggle Button ("Read")
> > > *Toggle Button ("Write")
> > > *Toggle Button ("Exec")

We'll cover `CreateFilePermissions()` later in this chapter.

Other important widgets include a `RowColumn` set up as a radio box and toggle button widgets. Functions to create these are in the file `toggle.c`, which are described later in this chapter.

At the end of `FileInformationDialog()`, you create a separator gadget to draw a line and then create three pushbutton widgets, one each for OK, Cancel, and Help. Since the OK pushbutton is the default button for this dialog, you set that up by using the technique described in Chapter 15. And, since we don't offer any help on this dialog (normally a no-no), we make the Help pushbutton unavailable with the `XtSetSensitive()` X toolkit function.

Here's the code for `FileInformationDialog()`:

```
Widget        FileInformationDialog( parent, name, callback_func )

Widget        parent;
char          name[];
void          (*callback_func)();

{      /* FileInformationDialog */
       Widget main_row, sep;
       Widget CreateBulletinDialog();          /* bulletin.c */
       Widget CreateLabelWidget();    /* label.c */
       Widget CreatePushButton();     /* push.c */
       Widget CreateRadioBox();            /* toggle.c */
       Widget CreateToggle();              /* toggle.c */
       Widget CreateFilePermissions();
       Widget ok, cancel, help, file_dir_box;
       Arg           args[10];
       int           n;

       /*
        * Create a bulletin board dialog, but don't
        * manage it. A callback will manage
        * it later.
        */
       file_info_widget = CreateBulletinDialog( parent, name );
continued...
```

...from previous page

```
/*
 * Create a label for the file name
 */
n = 0;
file_info_label = CreateLabelWidget( file_info_widget,
                 "label", "label", args, n );

n = 0;
(void) CreateLabelWidget( file_info_widget,
                 "owner", "Owner", args, n );

n = 0;
(void) CreateLabelWidget( file_info_widget,
                 "group", "Group", args, n );

n = 0;
(void) CreateLabelWidget( file_info_widget,
                 "world",
                 "World File Permissions",
                 args, n );

/*
 * Row column for main information area.
 */
n = 0;
XtSetArg( args[n],  XmNorientation, XmHORIZONTAL ); n++;
XtSetArg( args[n],  XmNpacking,     XmPACK_COLUMN ); n++;

main_row = XmCreateRowColumn( file_info_widget,
           "mainrow",
           args,
           n );

XtManageChild( main_row );

/*
 * Create RowColumn children, enclose each child
 * RowColumn within a frame to group like items.
 */
(void) CreateFilePermissions( main_row, 0, callback_func );
(void) CreateFilePermissions( main_row, 1, callback_func );
(void) CreateFilePermissions( main_row, 2, callback_func );

/*
 * Radio box for file or directory
 */
file_dir_box = CreateRadioBox( main_row, "file_dir" );
```

continued...

...from previous page

```
     file_or_dir[ 0 ] = CreateToggle( file_dir_box,
                               "normal",
                               "Normal File",
                               True,
                               XmONE_OF_MANY, /* diamond */
                               callback_func );

     file_or_dir[ 1 ] = CreateToggle( file_dir_box,
                               "directory",
                               "Directory",
                               False,
                               XmONE_OF_MANY, /* diamond */
                               callback_func );

     /*
      * Separator
      */
     n = 0;
     sep = XmCreateSeparatorGadget( file_info_widget,
             "fileinfosep", args, n );

     XtManageChild( sep );


     /*
     .* Create push buttons in dialog.
      * The OK button is the default
      * for the dialog.
      */
     n = 0;
     XtSetArg( args[n], XmNshowAsDefault, 1 ); n++;

     ok = CreatePushButton( file_info_widget, "OK", args, n,
             unfileinfo_callback );
     /*
      * Set OK button as default
      */
     BulletinDefaultButton( file_info_widget, ok );

     n = 0;
     cancel = CreatePushButton( file_info_widget, "Cancel", args, n,
             unfileinfo_callback );

     n = 0;
     help = CreatePushButton( file_info_widget, "Help", args, n,
             unfileinfo_callback );
```

continued...

...from previous page

```
      /*
       * Since we're not offering help, we should
       * make the help button greyed out.
       */
      XtSetSensitive( help, False );

      return( file_info_widget );

}      /* FileInformationDialog */
```

Refer back to the widget for clarification on this function.

GROUPING RELATED WIDGETS UNDER A 3D FRAME WIDGET

The function `CreateFilePermissions()` creates three toggle-button widgets, one each for the read, write, and execute file permissions. The hierarchy for `CreateFilePermissions()` is as follows:

> * Frame ("frame") for grouping
> > * RowColumn (vertical, for "permissions")
> > > *Toggle Button ("Read")
> > > *Toggle Button ("Write")
> > > *Toggle Button ("Exec")

A vertically oriented `RowColumn` widget makes sure these toggle buttons are displayed in the right order and one on top of the other. A 3D frame widget provides a means to group these like items. You'll find the frame widget is handy to use when you want to group widgets together in a box.

`CreateFilePermissions()` uses a number of global variables, which are used to ease the task of updating these widgets later:

```
Widget      read_perms[ 4 ];
Widget      write_perms[ 4 ];
Widget      exec_perms[ 4 ];

Widget      CreateFilePermissions( parent, which_one, callback_func )

Widget      parent;
int         which_one;
void        (*callback_func)();
```

continued...

...from previous page

```
{       /* CreateFilePermissions */
        Widget          rowcolumn, frame;
        Widget          CreateRadioBox();   /* toggle.c */
        Widget          CreateToggle();     /* toggle.c */
        Arg             args[10];
        int             n;

        /*
         * Create a bounding frame to group
         * the three toggle buttons together.
         */
        n = 0;
        XtSetArg( args[n], XmNshadowThickness, 4 ); n++;

        frame = XmCreateFrame( parent, "frame", args, n );

        XtManageChild( frame );

        /*
         * Create a RowColumn widget to
         * manage three child widgets.
         */
        n = 0;
        XtSetArg( args[n], XmNorientation, XmVERTICAL ); n++;

        rowcolumn = XmCreateRowColumn( frame,
                        "permissions", args, n );

        XtManageChild( rowcolumn );

        read_perms[ which_one ] = CreateToggle( rowcolumn,
                                        "Read",
                                        "Read",
                                        True,
                                        XmN_OF_MANY, /* square */
                                        callback_func );

        write_perms[ which_one ] = CreateToggle( rowcolumn,
                                        "Write",
                                        "Write",
                                        True,
                                        XmN_OF_MANY, /* square */
                                        callback_func );

        exec_perms[ which_one ] = CreateToggle( rowcolumn,
                                        "Exec",
                                        "Exec",
                                        False,
                                        XmN_OF_MANY, /* square */
                                        callback_func );
```

continued...

358

...from previous page

```
                return( frame );

}               /* CreateFilePermissions */
```

The `CreateToggle()` function is in the file `toggle.c`, which is covered later in this chapter.

PLACING THE CHILD WIDGETS IN THE DIALOG

We are using a bulletin-board dialog to place each immediate child of the bulletin board by hand. We determine a good x,y location and then place the widget there.

This is a tedious process at best, but it allows you to make a dialog that looks exactly as you want it. To speed things up, though, we've used a resource file to place most of these widgets. Not only does this allow you (and your users) to customize the (custom) dialog, but it allows you to prototype different locations for the various widgets to find the design we think is the easiest to use and which looks the best.

Here's the part of the resource file, `Dstyle.ad`, that pertains to the dialog widget placement and size:

```
!
!       FileInfo Custom Dialog Resources
!
!
!       size of the dialog
!
dstyle*fileinfo.width:               450
dstyle*fileinfo.height:              160
!
!       default title for the dialog
!
dstyle*fileinfo.dialogTitle:         File Information
!
!       file name and size label location
!
dstyle*label.x:                      0
dstyle*label.y:                      0
dstyle*label.width:                  450
!
!       mainrow is the main row column widget
```

continued...

...from previous page

```
dstyle*mainrow.x:                         0
dstyle*mainrow.y:                         32
!
!       Set up the separator gadget line.
!       The width should match the width of
!       the file info dialog.
!
dstyle*fileinfosep.x:                     0
dstyle*fileinfosep.y:                     150
dstyle*fileinfosep.width:                 450
!
!       OK push button
!
dstyle*OK.x:                              30
dstyle*OK.y:                              160
!
!       Cancel push button
!
dstyle*Cancel.x:                          190
dstyle*Cancel.y:                          165
!
!       Help push button
!
dstyle*Help.x:                            370
dstyle*Help.y:                            165
!
!       RowColumn for owner file permissions
!
dstyle*owner.x:                           35
dstyle*owner.y:                           125
!
!       RowColumn for group file permissions
!
dstyle*group.x:                           130
dstyle*group.y:                           125
!
!       RowColumn for world file permissions
!
dstyle*world.x:                           235
dstyle*world.y:                           125
```

Note that the name of our program is "dstyle".

PLACING FILE-SPECIFIC INFORMATION

The function FillFileInformation() takes a file name and then gets information on that file. This information is fed into the global widgets that are set up for the file-information dialog. That way, you could pop up the file info dialog and then keep changing the file you are looking at (and presenting information about). This has a lot of uses if you plan to write a graphical file and directory browser (which, coincidentally, we do in the next few chapters).

Note that you may have to port this function to your operating system (such as VMS or AmigaDOS), as it is somewhat UNIX-specific. This shouldn't be difficult, though.

The SetToggle() function sets the state of the toggle-button widgets used in the dialog.

```
FillFileInformation( filename )

char  filename[];

{      /* FillFileInformation */
       struct stat            file_info;
       char                   string[400];

       /*
        * Get information on the file.
        */
       if ( stat( filename, &file_info )  != 0 )
                      {
                      return( False );
                      }

       /*
        * Set up label to present file name
        */
       sprintf( string, "%s  %ld bytes",
                      filename,
                      file_info.st_size );

       SetLabel( file_info_label, string );

       /*
        * Owner permissions
        */
       SetToggle( read_perms [0],      file_info.st_mode & S_IRUSR );
       SetToggle( write_perms[0],      file_info.st_mode & S_IWUSR );
       SetToggle( exec_perms [0],      file_info.st_mode & S_IXUSR );

       /*
        * Group permissions
        */
       SetToggle( read_perms [1],      file_info.st_mode & S_IRGRP );
       SetToggle( write_perms[1],      file_info.st_mode & S_IWGRP );
       SetToggle( exec_perms [1],      file_info.st_mode & S_IXGRP );
```
continued...

...from previous page

```
/*
 * World permissions
 */
SetToggle( read_perms [2],    file_info.st_mode & S_IROTH );
SetToggle( write_perms[2],    file_info.st_mode & S_IWOTH );
SetToggle( exec_perms [2],    file_info.st_mode & S_IXOTH );

/*
 * The file either is, or isn't a directory.
 */
SetToggle( file_or_dir[0], !(file_info.st_mode & S_IFDIR) );
SetToggle( file_or_dir[1], file_info.st_mode & S_IFDIR );

/*
 * Set up title of dialog box
 */
BulletinDialogTitle( file_info_widget, filename );

return( True );

}    /* FillFileInformation */
```

SOURCE CODE FOR FILEINFO.C

The file `fileinfo.c` does most of the work in creating your custom dialog. As you can tell, this involves a lot of work on the part of the programmer. We tried to use a resource file to take care of placing most of our file-information dialog widget's children. This way, you can customize the dialog and adjust the placement of its widgets without having to recompile your code—yet another advantage for resource files. Here is the source code for `fileinfo.c`:

```
/*
 *     fileinfo.c
 *     A custom-built file information
 *     dialog demonstrating the use of
 *     radio toggle buttons. Some of this
 *     file in UNIX-specific, but you should
 *     be able to easily port this code
 *     to other operating systems.
 *
 *     Written for Power Programming Motif
 */
```

continued...

...from previous page

```
/*
 *      Include files for the stat() function
 */
#include          <stdio.h>
#include          <sys/types.h>
#include          <sys/stat.h>

/*
 *      X and Motif include files
 */
#include          <X11/Intrinsic.h>
#include          <X11/StringDefs.h>
#include          <Xm/Xm.h>
#include          <Xm/Frame.h>
#include          <Xm/MessageB.h>
#include          <Xm/RowColumn.h>
#include          <Xm/SeparatoG.h>
#include          <Xm/ToggleB.h>

/*
 *      Globals for the file information custom dialog
 */
Widget            file_info_widget;       /* file information dialog */
Boolean           file_info_managed = False;
Widget            file_info_label;
Widget            read_perms[ 4 ];
Widget            write_perms[ 4 ];
Widget            exec_perms[ 4 ];
Widget            file_or_dir[ 3 ];

void fileinfo_callback( widget, client_data, call_data )

Widget            widget;
caddr_t           client_data;
caddr_t           call_data;

/*
 *      Pops up the file information dialog,
 *      if it isn't up already.
 */

{       /* fileinfo_callback */

        if ( file_info_managed == False )
                {
                XtManageChild( file_info_widget );
                file_info_managed = True;
                }

}       /* fileinfo_callback */
```

continued...

...from previous page
```
void unfileinfo_callback( widget, client_data, call_data )

Widget          widget;
caddr_t         client_data;
caddr_t         call_data;

/*
 *      Pops down, or unmanages the file information
 *      dialog, if it is already managed.
 */

{       /* unfileinfo_callback */

        if ( file_info_managed == True )
                {
                XtUnmanageChild( file_info_widget );
                file_info_managed = False;
                }
}       /* unfileinfo_callback */

Widget          FileInformationDialog( parent, name, callback_func )

Widget          parent;
char            name[];
void            (*callback_func)();

/*
 *      Creates a custom dialog for presenting
 *      information about a file.
 */

{       /* FileInformationDialog */
        Widget  main_row, sep;
        Widget  CreateBulletinDialog(); /* bulletin.c */
        Widget  CreateLabelWidget();    /* label.c */
        Widget  CreatePushButton();     /* push.c */
        Widget  CreateRadioBox();       /* toggle.c */
        Widget  CreateToggle();         /* toggle.c */
        Widget  CreateFilePermissions();
        Widget  ok, cancel, help, file_dir_box;
        Arg     args[10];
        int     n;

/*
 * Create a bulletin board dialog, but don't
 * manage it. A callback will manage
 * it later.
 */
file_info_widget = CreateBulletinDialog( parent, name );
```

continued...

...from previous page

```
/*
 * Create a label for the file name
 */
n = 0;
file_info_label = CreateLabelWidget( file_info_widget,
                "label", "label", args, n );

n = 0;
(void) CreateLabelWidget( file_info_widget,
                "owner", "Owner", args, n );

n = 0;
(void) CreateLabelWidget( file_info_widget,
                "group", "Group", args, n );

n = 0;
(void) CreateLabelWidget( file_info_widget,
                "world",
                "World File Permissions",
                args, n );

/*
 * Row column for main information area.
 */
n = 0;
XtSetArg( args[n], XmNorientation, XmHORIZONTAL ); n++;
XtSetArg( args[n], XmNpacking, XmPACK_COLUMN ); n++;

main_row = XmCreateRowColumn( file_info_widget,
                "mainrow",
                args,
                n );

XtManageChild( main_row );

/*
 * Create RowColumn children, enclose each child
 * RowColumn within a frame to group like items.
 */
(void) CreateFilePermissions( main_row, 0, callback_func );
(void) CreateFilePermissions( main_row, 1, callback_func );
(void) CreateFilePermissions( main_row, 2, callback_func );

/*
 * Radio box for file or directory
 */
file_dir_box = CreateRadioBox( main_row, "file_dir" );

file_or_dir[ 0 ] = CreateToggle( file_dir_box,
                                "normal",
                                "Normal File",
```

continued...

365

...from previous page

```
                             True,
                             XmONE_OF_MANY, /* diamond */
                             callback_func );

file_or_dir[ 1 ] = CreateToggle( file_dir_box,
                             "directory",
                             "Directory",
                             False,
                             XmONE_OF_MANY, /* diamond */
                             callback_func );

/*
 * Separator
 */
n = 0;
sep = XmCreateSeparatorGadget( file_info_widget,
                "fileinfosep", args, n );

XtManageChild( sep );

/*
 * Create push buttons in dialog.
 * The OK button is the default
 * for the dialog.
 */
n = 0;
XtSetArg( args[n], XmNshowAsDefault, 1 ); n++;

ok = CreatePushButton( file_info_widget, "OK", args, n,
                unfileinfo_callback );

/*
 * Set OK button as default
 */
BulletinDefaultButton( file_info_widget, ok );

n = 0;
cancel = CreatePushButton( file_info_widget, "Cancel", args, n,
                unfileinfo_callback );

n = 0;
help = CreatePushButton( file_info_widget, "Help", args, n,
                unfileinfo_callback );

/*
 * Since we're not offering help, we should
 * make the help button greyed out.
 */
XtSetSensitive( help, False );
```
continued...

...from previous page

```
        return( file_info_widget );

}       /* FileInformationDialog */

FillFileInformation( filename )

char    filename[];

/*
 *      Fills in information about a file
 *      into the custom FileInformation dialog.
 *      This function uses the UNIX stat()
 *      function to get the information on
 *      the file. You may need to port this
 *      to your operating system.
 */

{       /* FillFileInformation */
        struct stat             file_info;
        char                    string[400];

        /*
         * Get information on the file.
         */
        if ( stat( filename, &file_info )  != 0 )
                {
                return( False );
                }

        /*
         * Set up label to present file name
         */
        sprintf( string, "%s  %ld bytes",
                filename,
                file_info.st_size );

        SetLabel( file_info_label, string );

        /*
         * Owner permissions
         */
        SetToggle( read_perms [0],  file_info.st_mode & S_IRUSR );
        SetToggle( write_perms[0],  file_info.st_mode & S_IWUSR );
        SetToggle( exec_perms [0],  file_info.st_mode & S_IXUSR );

        /*
         * Group permissions
         */
```

continued...

...from previous page

```
        SetToggle( read_perms [1],  file_info.st_mode & S_IRGRP );
        SetToggle( write_perms[1],  file_info.st_mode & S_IWGRP );
        SetToggle( exec_perms [1],  file_info.st_mode & S_IXGRP );

        /*
         * World permissions
         */
        SetToggle( read_perms [2],  file_info.st_mode & S_IROTH );
        SetToggle( write_perms[2],  file_info.st_mode & S_IWOTH );
        SetToggle( exec_perms [2],  file_info.st_mode & S_IXOTH );

        /*
         * The file either is, or isn't a directory.
         */
        SetToggle( file_or_dir[0], !(file_info.st_mode & S_IFDIR) );
        SetToggle( file_or_dir[1],   file_info.st_mode & S_IFDIR );

        /*
         * Set up title of dialog box
         */
        BulletinDialogTitle( file_info_widget, filename );

        return( True );

}       /* FillFileInformation */

Widget  CreateFilePermissions( parent, which_one, callback_func
)

Widget          parent;
int             which_one;
void            (*callback_func)();

/*
 *      Creates a RowColumn widget to hold three
 *      toggle widgets, one for read, on for write
 *      and one for execute permission bits. The
 *      RowColumn is surrounded by a 3D frame widget.
 */

{       /* CreateFilePermissions */
        Widget    rowcolumn, frame;
        Widget    CreateRadioBox();   /* toggle.c */
        Widget    CreateToggle();     /* toggle.c */
        Arg       args[10];
        int       n;

        /*
         * Create a bounding frame to group
         * the three toggle buttons together. */
```

continued...

...from previous page

```
        n = 0;
        XtSetArg( args[n], XmNshadowThickness, 4 ); n++;

        frame = XmCreateFrame( parent, "frame", args, n );

        XtManageChild( frame );

        /*
         * Create a RowColumn widget to
         * manage three child widgets.
         */
        n = 0;
        XtSetArg( args[n], XmNorientation, XmVERTICAL ); n++;

        rowcolumn = XmCreateRowColumn( frame,
                    "permissions", args, n );

        XtManageChild( rowcolumn );

        read_perms[ which_one ] = CreateToggle( rowcolumn,
                                    "Read",
                                    "Read",
                                    True,
                                    XmN_OF_MANY, /* square */
                                    callback_func );

        write_perms[ which_one ] = CreateToggle( rowcolumn,
                                    "Write",
                                    "Write",
                                    True,
                                    XmN_OF_MANY, /* square */
                                    callback_func );

        exec_perms[ which_one ] = CreateToggle( rowcolumn,
                                    "Exec",
                                    "Exec",
                                    false,
                                    XmN_OF_MANY, /* square */
                                    callback_func );


        return( frame );

}       /* CreateFilePermissions */

/* end of file */
```

THE TOGGLE BUTTON WIDGET

You've used a number of toggle button utility functions in the `fileinfo.c` code. Figure 16-2 shows the XmToggleButton widget.

Widget Class Name	Class Pointer	Creation Function
XmToggleButton	xmToggleButtonWidgetClass	XmCreateToggleButton()

Figure 16-2. The XmToggleButton Widget.

A toggle button is a boolean selector: it can be in or out, on or off, or `True` or `False`. When the user clicks the mouse button 1 in a toggle, the toggle changes state, from `True` to `False`, or `False` to `True`.

Creating a Toggle Button Widget

You can create a toggle button widget with `XmCreateToggleButton()`. The toggle button include file is `Xm/ToggleB.h`:

```
#include <Xm/ToggleB.h>

Widget          widget;
Widget          parent;
String          name;
ArgList         args;
Cardinal        n;

widget = XmCreateToggleButton( parent,
            name,
            args,
            n );

XtManageChild( widget );
```

Each toggle button can have a box or diamond that clicks in and out, as well as a text label. You can omit the box or diamond if you want, using the indicatorOn resource (XmNindicatorOn in C programs). Set indicatorOn to True and the box or diamond will appear. Set indicatorOn to False and the box or diamond will not appear:

```
Arg          args[10];
int          n;

n = 0;
XtSetArg( args[n], XmNindicatorOn, True ); n++;
/* create the toggle widget */
```

The toggle widget's text string is a Motif XmString and is stored in the labelString resource (XmNlabelString in C programs):

```
Arg          args[10];
int          n;
XmString     motif_string;

n = 0;
XtSetArg( args[n], XmNlabelString, motif_string ); n++;
/* create the toggle widget */

XmStringFree( motif_string );
```

The shape displayed with the toggle-button widget can be a box or a diamond, called an XmN_OF_MANY (box) and XmONE_OF_MANY (diamond). In the *OSF/Motif Style Guide,* the diamond shape (XmONE_OF_MANY) is reserved for radio buttons.

You can control the shape with the indicatorType resource (XmNindicatorType in C programs). This code sets up the indicatorType to be a box:

```
Arg     args[10];
int     n;

n = 0;
XtSetArg( args[n], XmNindicatorType, XmN_OF_MANY ); n++;
/* create the toggle widget */
```

Figure 16-3 shows XmN_OF_MANY (left and right indicators).

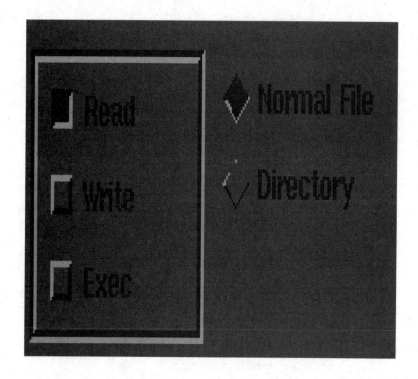

Figure 16-3 . XmN_OF_MANY (left) and XmONE_OF_MANY (right) Indicators.

The Toggle Button Widget Callback Function

The toggle widget allows you to set up a function to be called back whenever the toggle's value changes (from `True` to `False` or `False` to `True`). This callback is called the `valueChangedCallback` (`XmNvalueChangedCallback` in C programs):

```
Widget      toggle_widget;
void        (*callback_func)();
caddr_t     client_data;

XtAddCallback( toggle_widget,
        XmNvalueChangedCallback,
        callback_func,
        client_data );
```

The `valueChangedCallback` sets up your callback function to receive a pointer to an `XmToggleButtonCallbackStruct` structure as the call data. This `XmToggleButtonCallbackStruct` structure looks like:

```
typedef struct
     {
     int        reason       /* usually XmCR_VALUE_CHANGED */
     XEvent     *event;
     Boolean    set;         /* True for on, False for off */
     } XmToggleButtonCallbackStruct;
```

The set field indicates the new state of the callback, True or False. The reason field should be equal to XmCR_VALUE_CHANGED. Here's a sample toggle callback function:

```
void toggle_callback( widget, client_data, toggle_struct )

Widget                              widget;
caddr_t                             client_data;
XmToggleButtonCallbackStruct        *toggle_struct;

{          /* toggle_callback */

           /*
            * toggle_struct->set is the state.
            */
           if ( toggle_struct->set == True )
                 {
                 printf( "Ouch! Togglebutton changed to True (on)\n" );
                 }
           else
                 {
                 printf( "Ouch! Togglebutton changed to False (off)\n" );
                 }

}          /* toggle_callback */
```

A Function to Create a Toggle Button Widget

CreateToggle(), a convenience function, was used above in fileinfo.c to create toggle button widgets. CreateToggle () requires a parent widget, a name, a text message (which will be converted to an XmString type), an initial state (True or False), an indicator type (XmN_OF_MANY or XmONE_OF_MANY), and a callback function. Try this function with the indicatorOn resource set to True and then try False to see the difference:

```
Widget CreateToggle( parent, name, message, state, type,
callback_func )

Widget      parent;
char        name[];
char        message[]; /* text to appear next to toggle */
Boolean     state;              /* initial state */
int         type;               /*XmN_OF_MANY or XmONE_OF_MANY */
void        (*callback_func)(); /* state change callback */

{       /* CreateToggle */
        Widget          toggle_widget;
        Arg             args[10];
        int             n;
        XmString        motif_string;
        XmString        Str2XmString(); /* string.c */

        motif_string = Str2XmString( message );

        n = 0;
        XtSetArg( args[n], XmNlabelString, motif_string ); n++;
        XtSetArg( args[n], XmNindicatorType, type ); n++;

        /*
         * Try XmNindicatorOn with True and False
         */
        XtSetArg( args[n], XmNindicatorOn, True ); n++;
        /* XtSetArg( args[n], XmNindicatorOn, False ); n++; */

        XtSetArg( args[n], XmNset, state ); n++; /* on or off */

        toggle_widget = XmCreateToggleButton( parent,
                        name,
                        args,
                        n );

        XtManageChild( toggle_widget );

        /*
         * Add a callback
         * for when the value
         * is changed.
         */
        XtAddCallback( toggle_widget,
                        XmNvalueChangedCallback,
                        callback_func,
                        NULL );

        XmStringFree( motif_string );

        return( toggle_widget );

}       /* CreateToggle */
```

A group of toggle button widgets can all be set independently to True or False as the user desires. Sometimes, though, choices are mutually exclusive. You may want to allow only one toggle of a group to be set to True and want to force the rest of the toggle buttons to False, no matter what. These type of toggle buttons are often called radio buttons, since they act like buttons on old car radios—only one button can be in at a time.

To create radio buttons, group the toggle buttons together into a radio box.

Creating a Radio Box RowColumn Widget

The radio box is a RowColumn widget. To create a radio box RowColumn widget, set two resources to True: radioBehavior (XmNradioBehavior in C programs); and radioAlwaysOne (XmNradioAlwaysOne in C programs).

The radioBehavior resource tells the RowColumn that of all its toggle button (and toggle button gadget) children, only one can be set to True. The radioAlwaysOne makes sure that one of the toggle buttons (or toggle button gadgets) is always set to True. Together with the RowColumn widget, these two resources are all you need to set:

```
Widget CreateRadioBox( parent, name )

Widget     parent;
char       name[];

{      /* CreateRadioBox */
       Widget              radio;
       Arg                 args[10];
       int                 n;

       /*
        * Set up RowColumn to manage radio buttons.
        */
       n = 0;
       XtSetArg( args[n], XmNradioBehavior, True ); n++;
       XtSetArg( args[n], XmNradioAlwaysOne, True ); n++;

       radio = XmCreateRowColumn( parent,
                         name,
                         args,
                         n );

       XtManageChild( radio );

       return( radio );

}      /* CreateRadioBox */
```

Setting the State in a Toggle Button Widget

The state value of a toggle button widget is kept in the set resource (XmNset in C programs):

```
Arg    args[10];
int    n;

n = 0;
XtSetArg( args[n], XmNset, True ); n++; /* on */
/* create the toggle or call XtSetValues()... */
```

Motif also includes two functions for dealing with the set resource in toggle button widgets (there are corresponding gadget functions, too).

XmToggleButtonGetState() returns the value of the set resource—the "state" of the toggle button:

```
Boolean        state;
Widget         widget;

state = XmToggleButtonGetState( widget );
```

XmToggleButtonSetState() sets the state of a toggle button widget:

```
Boolean        state;
Boolean        notify;
Widget         widget;

XmToggleButtonSetState( widget,
              state,        /* True or False */
              notify );     /* Generate a callback? */
```

The notify parameter is set to True if you want to generate a callback—if you want the valueChangedCallback to be called. The notify parameter should be set to False if you don't want the valueChangedCallback function called. You can guess that a radio box RowColumn uses XmToggleButtonSetState() under the hood to force the state of the toggle button.

A Function to Set the State of a Toggle Widget

SetToggle() is a simple function to set the state of a toggle button widget. The only reason for this function is because there isn't always a nice True or False value. Instead, there often is a zero (0) or nonzero value (especially when masking struct stat flags for file information).

So, if the state does not equal zero (0), then set the toggle widget to True:

```
SetToggle( widget, state )

Widget          widget;
int             state;

{       /* SetToggle */
        Arg     args[10];
        int     n;

        if ( state != 0 )
                {
                n = 0;
                XtSetArg( args[n], XmNset, True ); n++; /* on */
                }
        else
                {
                n = 0;
                XtSetArg( args[n], XmNset, False ); n++; /* off */
                }
        XtSetValues( widget, args, n );

}       /* SetToggle */
```

Source Code for Toggle.c

The file toggle.c contains a number of utility functions for dealing with toggle button widgets, as shown in the following source code.

```
/*
 *      toggle.c
 *      Motif Toggle Button test
 *
 *      Written for Power Programming Motif
 */
#include         <X11/Intrinsic.h>
#include         <X11/StringDefs.h>
#include         <Xm/Xm.h>
#include         <Xm/RowColumn.h>
#include         <Xm/ToggleB.h>

Widget CreateToggle( parent, name, message, state, type,
callback_func )

Widget parent;
char            name[];
char            message[];          /* text to appear next to toggle */
Boolean state;  /* initial state */
int             type; /*            XmN_OF_MANY or XmONE_OF_MANY */
void            (*callback_func)(); /* state change callback */
```
continued...

...from previous page

```
/*
 *      Creates and manages a toggle button widget. The initial
 *      state of the toggle button is set to state. When the
 *      state changes, callback_func() will be called. The
 *      type specifies the radio button diamond XmONE_OF_MANY or the
 *      square XmN_OF_MANY shape for the toggle button.
 */

{       /* CreateToggle */
Widget          toggle_widget;
Arg             args[10];
int             n;
XmString motif_string;
XmString Str2XmString(); /* string.c */

        /*
         * Convert message to
         * an XmString.
         */
        motif_string = Str2XmString( message );

        n = 0;
        XtSetArg( args[n], XmNlabelString, motif_string ); n++;
        XtSetArg( args[n], XmNindicatorType, type ); n++;

        /*
         * Try XmNindicatorOn with True and False
         */
        XtSetArg( args[n], XmNindicatorOn, True ); n++;
        /*XtSetArg( args[n], XmNindicatorOn, False ); n++; */

        XtSetArg( args[n], XmNset, state ); n++; /* on or off */

        toggle_widget = XmCreateToggleButton( parent,
                                name,
                                args,
                                n );

        XtManageChild( toggle_widget );

        /*
         * Add a callback
         * for when the value
         * is changed.
         */
        XtAddCallback( toggle_widget,
                XmNvalueChangedCallback,
                callback_func,
                NULL );
```

continued...

...from previous page

```
        XmStringFree( motif_string );

        return( toggle_widget );

}       /* CreateToggle */

SetToggle( widget, state )

Widget widget;
int             state;

/*
 *      Sets the value of a toggle button to
 *      True of False, depending on the
 *      value of state. If state != 0,
 *      then the toggle is set to True.
 *      If state == 0, then the toggle is
 *      set to False.
 */

{       /* SetToggle */
        Arg     args[10];
        int     n;

        if ( state != 0 )
                {
                n = 0;
                XtSetArg( args[n], XmNset, True ); n++; /* on */
                }
        else
                {
                n = 0;
                XtSetArg( args[n], XmNset, False ); n++; /* off */
                }
        XtSetValues( widget, args, n );

}       /* SetToggle */

Widget CreateRadioBox( parent, name )

Widget parent;
char            name[];

/*
 *      Creates a RowColumn widget to oversee a group
 *      of radio buttons.
 */
```

continued...

...from previous page

```
{       /* CreateRadioBox */
        Widget      radio;
        Arg         args[10];
        int         n;

        /*
         * Set up RowColumn to manage radio buttons.
         */
        n = 0;
        XtSetArg( args[n], XmNradioBehavior, True ); n++;
        XtSetArg( args[n], XmNradioAlwaysOne, True ); n++;

        radio = XmCreateRowColumn( parent,
                    name,
                    args,
                    n );

        XtManageChild( radio );

        return( radio );

}       /* CreateRadioBox */

/* end of file */
```

THE DSTYLE PROGRAM

To test all these ideas, we've created a program, dstyle (for dialog style guide program).

The dstyle program picks up from the style program that was introduced in Chapter 14. We've added the code for a custom file information dialog on the File menu, accessed by the user through the new "File Info..." menu choice.

The widget hierarchy, especially for the file information dialog, is very complex. This hierarchy is listed below:

```
* Top-Level Shell
    * Main Window
        * Menu Bar
            * Cascade Button (File Menu)
                * Pushbutton Gadget ("New" Choice)
                * Pushbutton Gadget ("Open" Choice)
                * Separator Gadget
                * Pushbutton Gadget ("Save" Choice)
```

* Pushbutton Gadget ("Save As" Choice)
* Pushbutton Gadget ("Print" Choice)
* Separator Gadget
* Pushbutton Gadget ("File Info..." Choice)
* Separator Gadget
  Pushbutton Gadget ("Exit" Choice)
* Cascade Button (Edit Menu)
  * Pushbutton Gadget ("Undo" Choice)
  * Separator Gadget
  * Pushbutton Gadget ("Cut" Choice)
  * Pushbutton Gadget ("Copy" Choice)
  * Pushbutton Gadget ("Paste" Choice)
  * Separator Gadget
  * Pushbutton Gadget ("Clear" Choice)
  * Pushbutton Gadget ("Delete" Choice)
* Cascade Button (View Menu)
  * Pushbutton Gadget ("All" Choice)
  * Pushbutton Gadget ("Partial" Choice)
  * Separator Gadget
  * Pushbutton Gadget ("By Date" Choice)
  * Pushbutton Gadget ("By Name" Choice)
  * Pushbutton Gadget ("By Other" Choice)
* Cascade Button (Options Menu)
  * Pushbutton Gadget ("Colors" Choice)
* Cascade Button (Help Menu)
  * Pushbutton Gadget ("On Context" Choice)
  * Pushbutton Gadget ("On Help" Choice)
  * Pushbutton Gadget ("On Window" Choice)
  * Pushbutton Gadget ("On Keys" Choice)
  * Pushbutton Gadget ("Index" Choice)
  * Pushbutton Gadget ("Tutorial" Choice)
  * Pushbutton Gadget ("On Version" Choice)
  * Message Dialog (About box)
    * Pushbutton (OK on Message Dialog)
* Bulletin Board Dialog (File Information "fileinfo")
  * Label (for file name and size)
  * RowColumn (horizontal) for main dialog area ("mainrow")
    * Frame ("frame") for grouping
      * RowColumn (vertical, for owner "permissions")
      *Toggle Button ("Read")
      *Toggle Button ("Write")
      *Toggle Button ("Exec")
    * Frame ("frame") for grouping
      * RowColumn (vertical, for group "permissions")
      *Toggle Button ("Read")
      *Toggle Button ("Write")

>   *Toggle Button ("Exec")
>   * Frame ("frame") for grouping
>   * RowColumn (vertical, for world "permissions")
>   *Toggle Button ("Read")
>   *Toggle Button ("Write")
>   *Toggle Button ("Exec")
>   * RowColumn (vertical, radio box for "file_dir")
>   * Radio Toggle Button ("normal")
>   * Radio Toggle Button ("directory")
>   * Label ("owner")
>   * Label ("group")
>   * Label ("world")
>   * Separator Gadget ("fileinfosep")
>   * Pushbutton ("OK")—the default button
>   * Pushbutton ("Cancel")
>   * Pushbutton ("Help")—later made insensitive

Whew. When run, the File menu in the `dstyle` program adds a new menu choice to the style program: the "File Info..." choice. This choice launches the custom dialog (the whole reason for this program).

Figure 16-4 shows the file menu for the `dstyle` program.

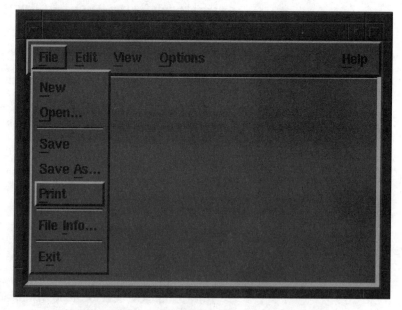

Figure 16-4 . The File Menu for the Dstyle Program.

Source Code for Dstyle.c

The file dstyle.c looks a lot like style.c. We've just added functions to create the file information dialog. If you don't have the separate source code diskette, start with style.c and just make the necessary changes—you'll save a lot of time typing.

For this example, we chose to display information on just one file, the file "dstyle.c" itself, with a call to FillFileInformation():

```
/*
 *      dstyle.c
 *      Custom dialog box program that follows
 *      the Motif Style Guide.
 *
 *      Written for Power Programming Motif
 *
 */

#include      <X11/Intrinsic.h>
#include      <X11/StringDefs.h>
#include      <Xm/Xm.h>
#include      <Xm/CascadeB.h>
#include      <Xm/MainW.h>
#include      <Xm/MessageB.h>
#include      <Xm/RowColumn.h>
#include      <Xm/ToggleB.h>

/*
 *      Message for about box
 */
#define MSG "Motif Style Guide Dialogs\nby Johnson and \
Reichard\nver. 1.0"

void quit_callback( widget, client_data, call_data )

Widget        widget;
caddr_t       client_data;
caddr_t       call_data;

/*
 *      Callback to quit program
 */

{       /* quit_callback */

        XtCloseDisplay( XtDisplay( widget ) );

        exit( 0 );

}       /* quit_callback */
```
continued...

...from previous page

```
void toggle_callback( widget, client_data, toggle_struct )

Widget                          widget;
caddr_t                         client_data;
XmToggleButtonCallbackStruct    *toggle_struct;

/*
 *      Callback for toggle widget. The
 *      XmToggleButtonCallbackStruct structure looks like:
 *
 *      typedef struct
 *              {
 *              int     reason;  -- usually XmCR_VALUE_CHANGED
 *              XEvent *event;
 *              Boolean set;    -- True for on, False for off
 *              } XmToggleButtonCallbackStruct;
 *
 */

{       /*  toggle_callback */

        /*
         * toggle_struct->reason should be
         * XmCR_VALUE_CHANGED.
         */

        /*
         * toggle_struct->set is the state.
         */
        if ( toggle_struct->set == True )
                {
                printf( "Ouch! Togglebutton changed to True (on)\n" );
                }
        else
                {
                printf( "Ouch! Togglebutton changed to False (off)\n" );
                }

}       /*  toggle_callback */

main( argc, argv )

int     argc;
char    *argv[];
```

continued...

...from previous page

```
{       /* main */
        Widget      parent;
        Widget      main_window;
        Widget      menu_bar;
        Widget      simple_menu();              /* menugad.c */
        Widget      simple_menu_item();         /* menugad.c */
        Widget      simple_menu_call(); /* menugad.c */
        Widget      file_menu, edit_menu, view_menu;
        Widget      options_menu, help_menu;
        Widget      FileInformationDialog();        /* filedial.c */
        void        fileinfo_callback(); /* filedial.c */
        Arg         args[10];
        int         n;

        parent = XtInitialize( argv[0],
                    "Dstyle",
                    NULL,
                    0,
                    &argc,
                    argv );

        n = 0;
        XtSetArg( args[n], XmNallowShellResize, True ); n++;
        XtSetValues( parent, args, n );

        /*
         * Create a main window without
         * setting too many resources.
         */
        n = 0;
        XtSetArg( args[n], XmNshadowThickness, 4 ); n++;
        XtSetArg( args[n], XmNshowSeparator, True ); n++;

        main_window = XmCreateMainWindow( parent,
                            "main",
                            args,
                            n );

        XtManageChild( main_window );

        /*
         * Create a file information dialog
         */
        (void) FileInformationDialog( main_window, "fileinfo",
                    toggle_callback );

        /*
         * For our test, we're choosing an
         * arbitrary file--this C file.
         */
```

continued...

...from previous page

```
        FillFileInformation( "dstyle.c" );

        /*
         * Create a menu bar
         */
        n = 0;
        menu_bar = XmCreateMenuBar( main_window,
                    "menu_bar",
                    args,
                    n );

        XtManageChild( menu_bar );

        /*
         * File menu
         */
        file_menu = simple_menu( menu_bar, "File", 'F' );

        simple_menu_item( file_menu, "New", 'N', False );
        simple_menu_item( file_menu, "Open...", 'O', False );
        simple_menu_item( file_menu, "Save", 'S', True );
        simple_menu_item( file_menu, "Save As...", 'A', False );
        simple_menu_item( file_menu, "Print", 'P', False );

        /*
         * Add in a menu choice to trigger
         * our custom file information
         * dialog.
         */
        simple_menu_call( file_menu, "File Info...", 'I',
                    True , fileinfo_callback );

        simple_menu_call( file_menu, "Exit", 'x', True,
                        quit_callback );

        /*
         * Edit menu
         */
        edit_menu = simple_menu( menu_bar, "Edit", 'E' );

        simple_menu_item( edit_menu, "Undo",   'U', False );
        simple_menu_item( edit_menu, "Cut",    't', True  );
        simple_menu_item( edit_menu, "Copy",   'C', False );
        simple_menu_item( edit_menu, "Paste",  'P', False );
        simple_menu_item( edit_menu, "Clear",  'l', True  );
        simple_menu_item ( edit_menu, "Delete", 'D', False );

        /*
         * View menu
         */
```

continued...

...from previous page

```
        view_menu = simple_menu( menu_bar, "View", 'V' );

        simple_menu_item( view_menu, "All", 'A', False );
        simple_menu_item( view_menu, "Partial...", 'P', False );
        simple_menu_item( view_menu, "By Date...", 'D', True );
        simple_menu_item( view_menu, "By Name...", 'N', False );
        simple_menu_item( view_menu, "By Other...", 'O', False );

        /*
         * Options menu
         */
        options_menu = simple_menu( menu_bar, "Options", 'O' );

        simple_menu_item( options_menu, "Colors...", 'O', False );

        /*
         * Help menu
         */
        help_menu = simple_menu( menu_bar, "Help", 'H' );

        simple_menu_item( help_menu, "On Context...", 'C', False );
        simple_menu_item( help_menu, "On Help...",    'H', False );
        simple_menu_item( help_menu, "On Window...",  'W', False );
        simple_menu_item( help_menu, "On Keys...",    'K', False );
        simple_menu_item( help_menu, "Index...",      'I', False );
        simple_menu_item( help_menu, "Tutorial...",   'T', False );

        /*
         * On version box
         */
        AboutBox( help_menu, MSG );

        XmMainWindowSetAreas( main_window,
                    menu_bar,
                    (Widget) NULL,
                    (Widget) NULL,
                    (Widget) NULL,
                    (Widget) NULL );

        XtRealizeWidget( parent );
        XtMainLoop();

}       /* main */

/* end of file */
```

Compiling and Linking the Dstyle Program

The `dstyle` program needs the following C source files:

```
about.c   (from Chapter 14)
bulletin.c  (from Chapter 15)
dstyle.c
fileinfo.c
label.c (from Chapter 2)
menugad.c (from Chapter 14)
push.c (from Chapter 3)
string.c (from Chapter 2)
toggle.c
```

You can compile and link the `dstyle` program with a UNIX command like:

```
cc -o dstyle about.c bulletin.c dstyle.c fileinfo.c label.c \
      menugad.c push.c string.c toggle.c -lXm -lXt -lX11
```

With `Makefile` in Appendix C, you can use:

```
make dstyle
```

or

```
make all
```

A Resource File for the Dstyle Program

The file `Dstyle.ad` contains a few resource definitions for the `dstyle` program. Feel free to change the definitions as much as you like.

Rename this file to `Dstyle` and then place in your home directory ($HOME in UNIX parlance) or in a place where other application default files go, such as `/usr/lib/X11/app-defaults`. See Chapter 13 for more information on where resource files can be placed.

If you want a radically different file information dialog, you can munge the locations in the `Dstyle.ad` resource file. Have fun.

The Contents of the File Dstyle.ad

The following is the file `Dstyle.ad`.

```
!
!          Dstyle.ad (note capital "D"),
!          a Motif resource file for the
!          dstyle program in chapter 16.
!
dstyle*fontList: variable
!dstyle*fontList:       -adobe-helvetica-bold-r-normal--12-120-75-75-p-70-iso8859-1

dstyle.width:                  400
dstyle.height:                 200


!
!          FileInfo Custom Dialog Resources
!
!
!          size of the dialog
!
dstyle*fileinfo.width:         450
dstyle*fileinfo.height:        160
!
!          default title for the dialog
!
dstyle*fileinfo.dialogTitle: File Information
!
!          file name and size label location
!
dstyle*label.x:                0
dstyle*label.y:                0
dstyle*label.width:            450
!
!          mainrow is the main row column widget

dstyle*mainrow.x:              0
dstyle*mainrow.y:              32
!
!          Set up the separator gadget line.
!          The width should match the width of
!          the file info dialog.
!
dstyle*fileinfosep.x:          0
dstyle*fileinfosep.y:          150
dstyle*fileinfosep.width:      450
!
!          OK push button
!
dstyle*OK.x:                   30
dstyle*OK.y:                   160
!
!          Cancel push button
```
continued...

...from previous page

```
!
dstyle*Cancel.x:                     190
dstyle*Cancel.y:                     165
!
!         Help push button
!
dstyle*Help.x:                       370
dstyle*Help.y:                       165
!
!         RowColumn for owner file permissions
!
dstyle*owner.x:                      35
dstyle*owner.y:                      125
!
!         RowColumn for group file permissions
!
dstyle*group.x:                      130
dstyle*group.y:                      125
!
!         RowColumn for world file permissions
!
dstyle*world.x:                      235
dstyle*world.y:                      125
!
!         end of file !
```

Running the Dstyle Program

Figure 16-5 shows the `dstyle` program.

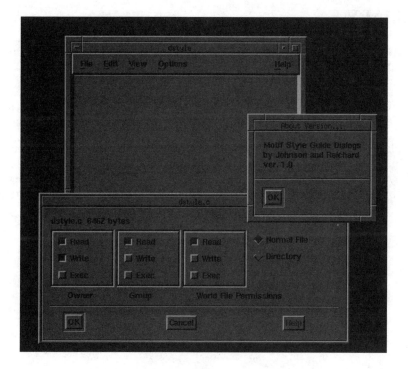

Figure 16-5 . The Dstyle Program.

Choose the "Exit" choice in the File menu to quit.

MOTIF FUNCTIONS AND MACROS INTRODUCED IN THIS CHAPTER

The following is a list of Motif functions and macros introduced in this chapter.

```
XmCreateToggleButton()
XmToggleButtonGetState()
XmToggleButtonSetState()
```

You should be familiar with these functions and macros before going on to Chapter 17.

SUMMARY

Creating a dialog by hand is a tough task, but most Motif applications will need to do this at one time or another. The file `fileinfo.c` can be used as an example for whenever you want to roll your own dialogs.

The toggle button widget is used a lot in dialogs. Create a toggle button widget with `XmCreateToggleButton()`.

If you place a toggle button widget in a `RowColumn` widget and want only one toggle button to be set to on (`True`) at any time, that is, to enforce a radio button behavior, set the `radioAlwaysOne` and the `radioBehavior` resources to `True` in the `RowColumn` widget. Make sure all the toggle buttons have a diamond shape with an `indicatorType` resource set to `XmONE_OF_MANY`.

Wrapping it All Up

I n Section V, we'll try to tie together the many threads of Motif programming. Chapter 17 presents a full-blown Motif application, based mostly on the concepts of the last half of this book.

The X File Browser application will list the files in a directory and allow you to view the contents of text files. You'll also get a chance to work with menu choices, dialogs, and a whole host of Motif widgets working together in one application.

Chapter **17**

A File Browser Application

T his chapter puts together a Motif application using most of the techniques discussed in this book. The bulk of the chapter will be devoted to the source code for this application. We assume that by now you're rather familiar with Motif sources, so we won't waste a lot of space explaining things in great detail.

You'll get the most out of this chapter by examining the source code and then trying out the application. As with most graphical applications, you shouldn't have a lot of problems figuring out what to do when you run the application.

Figure 17-1 shows the X Window File Browser (or xfb for short). It displays the files and subdirectories within a given directory. You can view the contents of text files, as well as the file permissions of any file by using the file information dialog presented in the dstyle program.

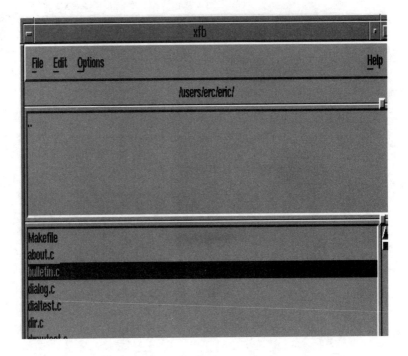

Figure 17-1. The X Window File Browser Application.

Two scrolled lists are kept: one that displays the subdirectories; and one that lists the files in the current directory. When the user clicks on a directory name, the files in that directory are listed in the file scrolled list (with the subdirectories listed in the subdirectory scrolled list). When the user clicks on a file name, that file is loaded into a scrolled text widget. Information on the file is also placed into the file-information dialog used in the dstyle program which was explained in Chapter 16.

Most of what we're doing in the xfb program is pulling together the lessons from the rest of this book with the addition of some new features. One of the things you need to be able to do is reload text into a text widget and list the contents of a directory.

VIEWING A TEXT FILE

The X file browser program needs to be able to load up a text file into a scrolled text widget to view the file. We've already covered most of this in Chapter 7, but now you'd like to replace the contents of the text widget each time the user selects a new file.

The file `viewfile.c` contains routines to manage a scrolled text widget and a label widget (the label contains the file name). Again, we're using the technique of having a global widget variable for the label and the scrolled text. Other than that, this code is fairly straightforward.

Source Code for Viewfile.c

The following is the source code for `viewfile.c`.

```
/*
 * viewfile.c
 * Motif routines to manage a scrolled text window.
 *
 * Written for Power Programming Motif
 *
 */

#include <X11/Intrinsic.h>
#include <X11/StringDefs.h>
#include <X11/Shell.h>
#include <Xm/Xm.h>
#include <Xm/MessageB.h>

/*
 * Globals for the viewfile widget
 */
Widget    viewfile_widget;         /* scrolled text for viewing file */
Widget    viewerror_widget;        /* error dialog */
Widget    viewlabel_widget;        /* name of file */
Boolean   viewerror_up = False;    /* is error dialog managed? */

void unviewerror_callback( widget, client_data, call_data )

Widget    widget;
caddr_t   client_data;
caddr_t   call_data;

/*
 * Callback to unmanage viewerror_widget error dialog.
 * If the viewerror_widget is managed, then unmanage
 * it (to make the dialog disappear), and set
 * a global status.
 */
```

continued...

...from previous page

```
{ /* unviewerror_callback */

   if( viewerror_up == True )
                {
                XtUnmanageChild( viewerror_widget );
                viewerror_up = False;
                }

} /* unviewerror_callback */

Widget   CreateViewText( parent )

Widget   parent;

/*
 *   CreateViewText() creates a scrolled text widget
 *   and caches the widget ID in a global variable,
 *   viewfile_widget. This routine also creates
 *   an error dialog in case loading a file fails.
 */

{   /* CreateViewText */
    Widget    CreateLabelWidget();      /* label.c */
    Widget    CreateScrolledText();     /* text.c */
    Arg       args[20];
    int       n;

    /*
     * Create a label widget to hold the file name.
     */
    n = 0;
    viewlabel_widget = CreateLabelWidget( parent,
                                "filename",
                                "View File",
                                args,
                                n );

    /*
     * Create the scrolled text widget.
     */
    viewfile_widget = CreateScrolledText( parent, "viewfile" );

    /*
     * Create error dialog in case we cannot load the file.
     */
    n = 0;
    XtSetArg( args[n], XmNautoUnmanage, False ); n++;

    viewerror_widget = XmCreateErrorDialog( parent,
                                "viewerror",
```

continued...

...from previous page

```
                                        args,
                                        n );

        /*
         * Callback to unmanage dialog
         */
        XtAddCallback( viewerror_widget,
                XmNokCallback,
                unviewerror_callback,  NULL );

        /*
         * Get rid of unwanted
         * push buttons.
         */
        XtUnmanageChild( XmMessageBoxGetChild( viewerror_widget,
                        XmDIALOG_HELP_BUTTON ) );

        XtUnmanageChild( XmMessageBoxGetChild( viewerror_widget,
                        XmDIALOG_CANCEL_BUTTON ) );

        return( viewfile_widget );

}    /* CreateViewText */

FillViewText( filename )

char filename[];

{    /* FillViewText */
    Boolean         status;
    Arg             args[10];
    int             n;
    char        string[400];
    XmString         motif_string;
    XmString         Str2XmString();    /* string.c */

    /*
     * Fill in the text widget
     * with the contents of
     * the text file.
     */
    status = FillWidgetWithFile( viewfile_widget, filename );

    /*
     * If we failed to load the file,
     * put up the error dialog.
     */
    if ( status == False )
                {
                /*
                 * Build the proper message.
```

continued...

...from previous page

```
                 */
                sprintf( string, "Error in loading [%s]",
                                        filename );

        motif_string = Str2XmString( "Error in loading file" );

        n = 0;
        XtSetArg( args[n], XmNmessageString, motif_string ); n++;

        XtSetValues( viewerror_widget, args, n );

        XmStringFree( motif_string );

        /*
         * Make dialog appear
         */
        if ( viewerror_up == False )
            {
            XtManageChild( viewerror_widget );
            viewerror_up = True;
            }

        /*
         * Also display message in label.
         */
        SetLabel( viewlabel_widget, string );
        }
    else
        {
        /*
         * If successful
         */
        SetLabel( viewlabel_widget, filename );
        }

}   /* FillViewText */

/* end of file */
```

READING THE FILE NAMES IN A DIRECTORY

In addition to viewing files, you need to list the files and subdirectories within a directory. Much of the code to do this is UNIX-specific, so you may have to port this to your version of UNIX or to whatever other operating system you may be running (such as VMS or AmigaDOS).

We've tested the file dir.c on a number of UNIX boxes so you shouldn't have too much trouble. The file dir.c uses the list functions from Chapter 8 (in the file list.c) to place the file names into scrolled list widgets.

Source Code for Dir.c

The file dir.c has routines to read the files in a given directory and to place the file names and subdirectory names into list widgets. If you are not running the UNIX operating system, you will probably have to port the functions in this file.

This file needs at least one symbol defined. If your system uses a struct dirent for reading directories, define DIRENT. If your system uses a struct direct, then define DIRECT. If you are running under Hewlett-Packard's HP-UX, or just need to include the file ndir.h, then also define hpux.

The following is the source code for dir.c.

```
/*
 *   dir.c
 *   UNIX directory-reading routines
 *   for the X File Browser program.
 *
 *   You may have to port this to
 *   your operating system.
 *
 *   Written for Power Programming Motif
 *
 *   Define:
 *        DIRENT (-DDIRENT) for using struct dirent
 *        DIRECT (-DDIRECT) for using struct direct
 *        hpux   (-Dhpux) for ndir.h
 *
 */

#include <stdio.h>
#include <sys/types.h>
#include <sys/stat.h>

#ifdef DIRENT
#include <dirent.h>
#endif

#ifdef hpux
#include <ndir.h>
#endif
```

continued...

...from previous page

```c
#include <X11/Intrinsic.h>
#include <X11/StringDefs.h>
#include <Xm/Xm.h>

/*
 *  Define file types
 */
#define NORMAL_FILE    0
#define DIRECTORY      1
#define EXECUTABLE     2

FillInFileNames( file_widget, dir_widget, path, max_files )

Widget    file_widget;  /* where file names go */
Widget    dir_widget;   /* where directory names go */
char      path[];       /* name of the directory we're looking at */
int       max_files;    /* max we allow in a list widget */

/*
 *  Fills in two list widgets with file names
 *  and subdirectory names from the given path.
 */

{   /* FillInFileNames */
    int      file_type;
    int      first_file = True, first_dir = True;
    int      total_count = 0;
    int      file_count = 0, dir_count = 0;

#ifdef DIRENT
    DIR      *opendir(), *dirp;
    struct   dirent  *dp, *readdir();
#endif

#ifdef DIRECT
    DIR      *opendir(), *dirp;
    struct   direct  *dp;
#endif

    /*
     *  Open the directory
     */
    dirp     = opendir( path );

    if ( dirp == NULL )
        {
        return( file_count );
        }
```

continued...

...from previous page

```
/*
 *   In Unix, the first two directory entries are
 *   "." and ".." -- current dir and parent dir:
 *    Skip current dir.
 */
dp = readdir( dirp );

/*
 * For all directories, except the
 * root, we want "..", the parent
 * directory, so users can jump up
 * a level, too.
 */
if ( strcmp( path, "/" ) == 0 )
    {
    dp = readdir( dirp );
    }

/*
 *   Read through the directory.
 *   Check each file, is it a
 *   directory or a normal file?
 *
 */
while( ( dp = readdir( dirp ) ) != NULL )
    {
    total_count++;

    /*
     * Check for file type match
     */
    file_type = CheckFileType( path, dp->d_name );

    if ( file_type == DIRECTORY )
        {
        dir_count++;

        if ( dir_count < max_files )
            {
            if ( first_dir == True )
                {
                AddToList( dir_widget,
                      dp->d_name, 1 );
                first_dir = False;
                }
            else
                {
                AddToList( dir_widget,
```

continued...

...from previous page

```
                                  dp->d_name, 0 );
                   }
              }
         }
       else
         {
             /*
              * Not a directory
              */
             file_count++;

             if ( file_count < max_files )
                 {
                 if ( first_file == True )
                     {
                     AddToList( file_widget,
                         dp->d_name, 1 );
                     first_file = False;
                     }
                 else
                     {
                     AddToList( file_widget,
                         dp->d_name, 0 );
                     }
                 }
         }

    }

    /*
     *   Close the directory "file"
     */
    closedir( dirp );

    /*
     * Check if there were no files
     */
    if ( first_file == True )
        {
        AddToList( file_widget, "No Files...", 1 );
        }

    /*
     * return number of files
     */
    return( total_count );

}   /* FillInFileNames */
```

continued...

...from previous page
```
CheckFileType( path, filename )

charpath[];
charfilename[];

/*
 *   Returns EXECUTABLE, DIRECTORY or NORMAL_FILE,
 *   based on the type of the file returned by
 *   the stat() function. may have to port
 *   this to your operating system.
 */

{   /* CheckFileType */
    int             length, file_type;
    char            full_name[ 300 ];
    struct stat     stat_buffer;

    /*
     *   Build up full path
     */
    strcpy( full_name, path );

    length = strlen( path );

    if ( path[length-1] != '/' )
        {
        strcat( full_name, "/" );
        }

    strcat( full_name, filename );

    /*
     *   Get information on the file
     */
    stat( full_name, &stat_buffer );

    /*
     *   Check if a directory
     */
    file_type = NORMAL_FILE; /* default */

    if ( stat_buffer.st_mode & S_IFDIR )
        {
        file_type = DIRECTORY;
        }
    else
        {
        if ( stat_buffer.st_mode & S_IEXEC )
            {
```
continued...

...from previous page
```
            file_type = EXECUTABLE;
            }
        else
            {
            file_type = NORMAL_FILE;
            }
        }

    return( file_type );

}   /* CheckFileType */

FillFileLists( file_list, dir_list, label_widget,
current_path )

Widget   file_list;            /* list that holds file names */
Widget   dir_list;             /* list that holds subdirectory names */
Widget   label_widget; /* holds current_path name */
char     current_path[];       /* which directory to examine */

/*
 * Fills in the directory and the file list with the
 * names of the directories and files in a given
 * directory (current_path). The label_widget is updated
 * with the current_path.
 */

{   /* FillFileLists */

    /*
     * Clear out lists
     */
    ClearList( file_list );
    ClearList( dir_list );

    /*
     * Read directory and fill
     * in the file names found
     * there.
     */
    FillInFileNames( file_list, dir_list, current_path, 200 );

    /*
     * Fill in label widget with
     * current path name
```
continued...

...from previous page
```
        */
    SetLabel( label_widget, current_path );

}    /* FillFileLists */

ChangeToParent( path )

charpath[];

/*
 *   Changes a path name to the name of
 *   that path's parent, e.g., changes
 *        /foo1/foo2/foo3/
 *   to
 *        /foo1/foo2/
 *
 *   This function does not deal with
 *   symbolic links very well.
 */

{    /* ChangeToParent */
    int  i;

    i = strlen( path ) - 2;

    while( ( i > 0 ) && ( path[i] != '/' ) )
        {
        path[i] = '\0';
        i--;
        }

}    /* ChangeToParent */

GetCurrentDirectory( path )

charpath[];      /* RETURN */

/*
 *   GetCurrentDirectory() fills path with the
 *   current directory name, or with "/" for the
 *   root dir on failure. On success, a "/"
 *   is appended to the path.
 */

{    /* GetCurrentDirectory */
    int      length;
    char     *getcwd();

        /*
```
continued...

...from previous page
```
 * Set up current path. If your system
 * doesn't have getcwd(), then you can
 * either port this or set it to start
 * at an arbitrary directory. Note that
 * we use UNIX-style file names throughout
 * this program.
 */
path[0] = '\0';

(void) getcwd( path, 200 );
length  = strlen( path );

if ( path[length - 1] != '/' )
    {
    strcat( path, "/" );
    }

}   /* GetCurrentDirectory */

/* end of file */
```

THE XFB PROGRAM

The xfb program displays the files and directories within a given directory and allows you to view the contents of text files in that directory. A paned window widget is used to separate the various parts of the display. As you can see below, its widget hierarchy is rather involved.

```
* Top-Level Shell
  * Main Window
    * Menu Bar
      * Cascade Button (File Menu)
      * Pulldown Menu (File)
        * Pushbutton Gadget ("Get File Info..." Choice)
        * Pushbutton Gadget ("Exit" Choice)
      * Cascade Button (Edit Menu)
      * Pulldown Menu (Edit)
        * Pushbutton Gadget ("Undo" Choice)
        * Separator Gadget
        * Pushbutton Gadget ("Cut" Choice)
        * Pushbutton Gadget ("Copy" Choice)
        * Pushbutton Gadget ("Paste" Choice)
        * Separator Gadget
        * Pushbutton Gadget ("Clear" Choice)
        * Push Button Gadget ("Delete" Choice)
      * Cascade Button (Options Menu)
      * Pulldown Menu (Options)
```

* Push Button Gadget ("Go To Home Dir" Choice)
* Push Button Gadget ("Go To Parent Dir" Choice)
* Push Button Gadget ("Go To Root Dir" Choice)
* Cascade Button (Help Menu)
* Pulldown Menu (Help)
  * Push Button Gadget ("On Files..." Choice)
  * Push Button Gadget ("On Directories..." Choice)
  * Push Button Gadget ("On Viewing Files.." Choice)
  * Push Button Gadget ("On Version..." Choice)
  * Message Dialog (About box)
    * Push Button (OK on Message Dialog)
* Bulletin Board Dialog (File Information "fileinfo")
 * Label (for file name and size)
 * RowColumn (horizontal) for main dialog area ("mainrow")
  * Frame ("frame") for grouping
   * RowColumn (vertical, for owner "permissions")
    *Toggle Button ("Read")
    *Toggle Button ("Write")
    *Toggle Button ("Exec")
  * Frame ("frame") for grouping
   * RowColumn (vertical, for group "permissions")
    *Toggle Button ("Read")
    *Toggle Button ("Write")
    *Toggle Button ("Exec")
  * Frame ("frame") for grouping
   * RowColumn (vertical, for world "permissions")
    *Toggle Button ("Read")
    *Toggle Button ("Write")
    *Toggle Button ("Exec"
  * RowColumn (vertical, radio box for "file_dir")
   * Radio Toggle Button ("normal")
   * Radio Toggle Button ("directory")
 * Label ("owner")
 * Label ("group")
 * Label ("world")
 * Separator Gadget ("fileinfosep")
 * Push Button ("OK") -- the default button
 * Push Button ("Cancel")
 * Push Button ("Help") -- later made insensitive
* Paned Window ("pane")
 * Label Widget ("pathlabel")
 * Scrolled List ("dirlist")
 * Scrolled List ("filelist")
 * Label Widget ("filename")
 * Scrolled Text ("viewfile")
 * Error Dialog ("viewerror")

Source Code for xfb.c

The file xfb.c contains the meat of the xfb application and most of the code that creates the widgets listed previously:

```
/*
 *   xfb.c
 *   Motif X Window File Browser
 *
 *   Written for Power Programming Motif
 *
 */

#include  <stdio.h>
#include  <X11/Intrinsic.h>
#include  <X11/StringDefs.h>
#include  <Xm/Xm.h>
#include  <Xm/List.h>
#include  <Xm/MainW.h>
#include  <Xm/PanedW.h>
#include  <Xm/RowColumn.h>

/*
 *    Globals for xfb
 */
static Widget    file_list;          /* list of normal files */
static Widget    dir_list;           /* list of subdirectories */
static Widget    label_widget;       /* Shows current path */
static char      current_path[ 1025 ];   /* current directory path name */
static char      current_file[ 1025 ];   /* current selected file name */

#define MSG "X File Browser\nversion 1.0\nby Johnson and Reichard"

void generic_callback( widget, client_data, call_data )

Widget     widget;
caddr_t    client_data;
caddr_t    call_data;

/*
 *    Does nothing.
 */

{    /* generic_callback */
}    /* generic_callback */
```

continued...

...from previous page

```
void quit_callback( widget, client_data, call_data )

Widget     widget;
caddr_t    client_data;
caddr_t    call_data;

/*
 *    Quits our program
 */

{    /* quit_callback */

    XtCloseDisplay( XtDisplay( widget ) );

    exit( 0 );

}    /* quit_callback */

void file_callback( widget, client_data, list_data )

Widget                    widget;
caddr_t                   client_data;
XmListCallbackStruct      *list_data;

/*
 *    Callback to set up file information.
 *    The XmListCallbackStruct looks like:
 *
 *        typedef struct
 *                {
 *                int                 reason;
 *                XEvent        *event;
 *                XmString      item;
 *                int                 item_length;
 *                int                 item_position;
 *                XmString      *selected_items;
 *                int                 selected_item_count;
 *                int                 selection_type;
 *                } XmListCallbackStruct;
 */

{    /* file_callback */
    char fullpath[ 1024 ];
    char *string;

    XmStringGetLtoR( list_data->item,
            XmSTRING_DEFAULT_CHARSET,
            &string );
```

continued...

...from previous page

```
      strcpy( current_file, string );
      XtFree (string);
      /*
       * Only set up file info if we have files
       */
      if ( ( strlen( current_file ) > 0 ) &&
           ( strcmp( current_file, "No Files..." ) != 0 ) )
                  {
                  strcpy( fullpath, current_path );
                  strcat( fullpath, current_file );

                  FillFileInformation( fullpath );

                  /*
                   * Adjust view file window, too.
                   */
                  FillViewText( fullpath );
                  }

}            /* file_callback */

void dir_callback( widget, client_data, list_data )

Widget                          widget;
caddr_t                         client_data;
XmListCallbackStruct            *list_data;

/*
 *    Callback function to load up the files in
 *    a new directory.
 */

{    /* dir_callback */
    char *string;

    XmStringGetLtoR( list_data->item,
        XmSTRING_DEFAULT_CHARSET,
        &string );

    if ( strcmp( string, ".." ) == 0 )
            {
            ChangeToParent( current_path );
            }
    else
            {
            /*
             * Build up new path
             */
            strcat( current_path, string );
```

continued...

...from previous page

```
          strcat( current_path, "/" );
          }

     /*
      * Since we just changed
      * directories, clear
      * selected file name.
      */
     current_file[0] = '\0';

     /*
      * Clear lists,
      * then fill in
      * with file names.
      */
     FillFileLists( file_list, dir_list, label_widget, current_path );
     XtFree (string);
}    /* dir_callback */

go_home_callback( widget, name, call_data )

Widget    widget;
char      *name;
caddr_t   call_data;

/*
 *    Switches to display user's home directory.
 *    This uses the function getenv() and assumes
 *    UNIX-style file names.
 */

{    /* go_home_callback */
     char *home_path, *getenv();
     int  length;

     home_path = getenv( "HOME" );

     if ( home_path != (char *) NULL )
          {
          strcpy( current_path, home_path );

          length = strlen( current_path );

          if ( current_path[length-1] != '/' )
                {
                strcat( current_path, "/" );
                }
```

continued...

...from previous page

```
            /*
             * Since we just changed
             * directories, clear
             * selected file name.
             */
            current_file[0] = '\0';

            FillFileLists( file_list, dir_list,
                        label_widget, current_path );
            }

    }    /* go_home_callback */

go_parent_callback( widget, name, call_data )

Widget    widget;
char      *name;
caddr_t   call_data;

{   /* go_parent_callback */
    if ( strcmp( current_path, "/" ) != 0 )
        {
        ChangeToParent( current_path );

        /*
         * Since we just changed
         * directories, clear
         * selected file name.
         */
        current_file[0] = '\0';

        /*
         * Clear lists,
         * then fill in
         * with file names.
         */
        FillFileLists( file_list, dir_list,
                    label_widget, current_path );
        }

    }    /* go_parent_callback */

go_root_callback( widget, name, call_data )

Widget    widget;
char      *name;
caddr_t   call_data;

{    /* go_root_callback */
```
continued...

...from previous page

```
      strcpy( current_path, "/" );

      /*
       * Since we just changed
       * directories, clear
       * selected file name.
       */
      current_file[0] = '\0';

      /*
       * Clear lists,
       * then fill in
       * with file names.
       */
      FillFileLists( file_list, dir_list, label_widget, current_path
);

}     /* go_root_callback */

main( argc, argv )

int  argc;
char *argv[];

{     /* main */
      Widget          main_window;
      Widget          parent, menu_bar;
      Widget          go_menu, file_menu;
      Widget          pane_widget;
      Widget          CreateLabelWidget(); /* label.c */
      Widget          CreateViewText();    /* viewfile.c */
      Arg             args[20];
      int             n;

      /*
       * Set up current path.
       */
      GetCurrentDirectory( current_path );

      parent = XtInitialize( argv[0],
                             "XFb",
                             NULL,
                             0,
                             &argc,
                             argv );

      n = 0;
      XtSetArg( args[n], XmNallowShellResize, True ); n++;
```
continued...

...from previous page

```
    XtSetValues( parent, args, n );

    main_window = XmCreateMainWindow( parent,
                            "main",
                            args,
                            n );

    XtManageChild( main_window );

    /*
     * Create a menu bar
     */
    n = 0;
    menu_bar = XmCreateMenuBar( main_window,
                            "menu_bar",
                            args,
                            n );

    XtManageChild( menu_bar );

    /*
     * Set up file information dialog
     */
    (void) FileInformationDialog( main_window, "fileinfo",
                            generic_callback );

    /*
     * File, Options and Help menu
     */
    SetUpMenus( menu_bar );

    /*
     * Create paned window to
     * hold label and list widgets.
     */
    n = 0;
    XtSetArg( args[n], XmNallowResize, True ); n++;
    XtSetArg( args[n], XmNseparatorOn, True ); n++;

    pane_widget = XtCreateManagedWidget( "pane",
                            xmPanedWindowWidgetClass,
                            main_window,
                            args, n );

    n = 0;
    label_widget = CreateLabelWidget( pane_widget,
                            "pathlabel",
                            current_path,
                            args, n );
```

continued...

...from previous page

```
    /*
     * Create scrolled lists for files
     * and directories.
     */
    CreateFileDirLists( pane_widget, current_path );

    /*
     * Create scrolled text window to view file contents
     */
    (void) CreateViewText( pane_widget );

    XmMainWindowSetAreas( main_window,  /* main window */
                  menu_bar,           /* menu bar */
                  (Widget) NULL,      /* command area */
                  (Widget) NULL,      /* horiz scroll */
                  (Widget) NULL,      /* vert scroll */
                  pane_widget );      /* work area */

    XtRealizeWidget( parent );
    XtMainLoop();

}    /* main */

SetUpMenus( menu_bar )

Widget    menu_bar;

{    /* SetUpMenus */
    Widget        file_menu, edit_menu, go_menu, help_menu;
    Widget        simple_menu_call();  /* menugad.c */
    Widget        simple_menu_item();  /* menugad.c */
    Widget        simple_menu();       /* menugad.c */
    extern void   fileinfo_callback();

    file_menu = simple_menu( menu_bar, "File", 'F' );

    simple_menu_call( file_menu, "Get File Info...", 'I',
        False, fileinfo_callback );

    simple_menu_call( file_menu, "Exit", 'x',
        False, quit_callback );

    /*
     * Edit menu
     */
    edit_menu = simple_menu( menu_bar, "Edit", 'E' );

    simple_menu_item( edit_menu, "Undo",     'U', False );
```

continued...

417

...from previous page

```
    simple_menu_item( edit_menu, "Cut",    't', True  );
    simple_menu_item( edit_menu, "Copy",   'C', False );
    simple_menu_item( edit_menu, "Paste",  'P', False );
    simple_menu_item( edit_menu, "Clear",  'l', True  );

    /*
     * Options menu
     */
    go_menu = simple_menu( menu_bar, "Options", 'O' );

    simple_menu_call( go_menu, "Go To Home Dir", 'H',
        False, go_home_callback );

    simple_menu_call( go_menu, "Go To Parent Dir", 'P',
        False, go_parent_callback );

    simple_menu_call( go_menu, "Go To Root Dir", 'R',
        False, go_root_callback );

    /*
     * Help menu
     */
    help_menu = simple_menu( menu_bar, "Help", 'H' );

    simple_menu_item( help_menu, "On Files...",
                                 'F', False );
    simple_menu_item( help_menu, "On Directories...",
                                 'D', False );
    simple_menu_item( help_menu, "On Viewing Files...",
                                 'V', False );

    /*
     * Create About Version menu choice and dialog
     */
    AboutBox( help_menu, MSG );

}   /* SetUpMenus */

CreateFileDirLists( parent, path )

Widget    parent;
char      path[];

/*
 *    Creates two scrolled
 *    lists, placed into
 *    globals dir_list and file_list.
 */

{   /* CreateFileDirLists */
    Widget        CreateScrolledList();    /* list.c */
```
continued...

...from previous page

```
      Arg           args[10];
      int           n;

      /*
       * Create Scrolled lists
       */
      n = 0;
      dir_list      = CreateScrolledList( parent,
                      "dirlist",
                      args, n,
                      dir_callback );

      n = 0;
      file_list     = CreateScrolledList( parent,
                      "filelist",
                      args, n,
                      file_callback );

      /*
       * Fill in scrolled lists
       * with file and dir names
       */
      FillInFileNames( file_list, dir_list, path, 200 );

}     /* CreateFileDirLists */

/* end of file */
```

Compiling and Linking the xfb Program

The xfb program needs the following C files:

about.c (from Chapter 14)
bulletin.c (from Chapter 15)
dir.c
fileinfo.(from Chapter 16)
label.c (from Chapter 2)
list.c (from Chapter 8)
menugad.c (from Chapter 14)
push.c (from Chapter 3)
string.c (from Chapter 2)
text.c (from Chapter 7)
toggle.c (from Chapter 16)
viewfile.c
xfb.c

As we stated above, the file dir.c needs at least one symbol defined. If your system uses a struct dirent for reading directories, define DIRENT. If your system uses a struct direct, then define DIRECT. If you are running under Hewlett-Packard's HP-UX, or just need to include the file ndir.h, then also define hpux.

You can compile and link this program using a UNIX command like:

```
cc -o xfb -DDIRENT about.c bulletin.c dir.c fileinfo.c \
   label.c list.c menugad.c push.c string.c text.c \
   toggle.c viewfile.c xfb.c -lXm -lXt -lX11
```

or, using Makefile in Appendix C:

```
make xfb
```

or

```
make all
```

A Resource File for the xfb Program

The file XFb.ad contains a few resource definitions for the dstyle program. Feel free to change the definitions as much as you like. Much of this file sets up resources for the file information custom dialog, so if you are typing this in by hand, start out with the file Dstyle.ad and go from there.

Rename this file to XFb and then place in your home directory ($HOME in UNIX parlance) or in a place where other application default files go, such as /usr/lib/X11/app-defaults. See Chapter 13 for more information on where resource files can be placed.

If you want to change the way the xfb program looks, munge the XFb.ad resource file.

Contents of the File XFb.ad

Here are the contents of the file XFb.ad:

```
!
!  XFb.ad (note capital "XF"),
!  a Motif resource file for the
!  xfb program in chapter 17.
!
xfb*foreground: black
xfb*background: grey
!
xfb*fontList:  variable
!xfb*fontList: -adobe-helvetica-bold-r-normal--12-120-75-
!75-p-70-iso8859-1

xfb.width:                      430
xfb.height:                     560


!
!  Scrolled Lists
!
xfb*pathlabel.height:           15
xfb*filename.height:            15
xfb*pathlabel.width:            430
xfb*filelist.height:            50
xfb*filelist.visibleItemCount:  8
xfb*dirlist.height:             100
xfb*dirlist.visibleItemCount:   6
!
!  View File
!
xfb*viewfile.fontList:          fixed
xfb*viewfile.height:            180
!
!
!  FileInfo Custom Dialog Resources
!
!
!  size of the dialog
!
xfb*fileinfo.width:             450
xfb*fileinfo.height:            160
!
!  default title for the dialog
!
xfb*fileinfo.dialogTitle:  File Information
!
!  file name and size label location
!
```

continued...

421

...from previous page

```
xfb*label.x:                        0
xfb*label.y:                        0
xfb*label.width:                    430
!
! mainrow is the main row column widget

xfb*mainrow.x:          0
xfb*mainrow.y:          32
!
! Set up the separator gadget line.
! The width should match the width of
! the file info dialog.
!
xfb*fileinfosep.x:                  0
xfb*fileinfosep.y:                  150
xfb*fileinfosep.width:              450
!
! OK push button
!
xfb*OK.x:                           30
xfb*OK.y:                           160
!
! Cancel push button
!
xfb*Cancel.x:           190
xfb*Cancel.y:           165
!
! Help push button
!
xfb*Help.x:                         370
xfb*Help.y:                         165
!
! RowColumn for owner file permissions
!
xfb*owner.x:                        35
xfb*owner.y:                        125
!
! RowColumn for group file permissions
!
xfb*group.x:                        130
xfb*group.y:                        125
!
! RowColumn for world file permissions
!
xfb*world.x:                        235
xfb*world.y:                        125
!
! end of file
!
```

Running the xfb Program

The xfb program in action is shown in Figure 17-2.

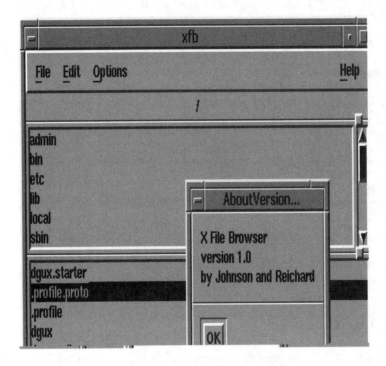

Figure 17-2. The Xfb Program in Action.

Enhancing the xfb Program

As it stands, the xfb program is not a complete application ready for commercial distribution. We wanted to provide a fairly complex Motif application which you can enhance.

There are a number of things you could do to flesh out and enhance the xfb program including:

> 1) Providing help for the application. The help menu lists help choices for:
> On Files...
> On Directories...
> On Viewing Files..
> None of these choices do anything—they should
> provide help, as should the file information dialog.

> 2) Reading in a large directory takes a lot of time. You could try unmanaging the scrolled list widgets and then remanaging them when the list is filled up again. If you have Motif 1.1, you could use the function XmListDeleteAllItems(), and see if this improves the performance.

> 3) The file information dialog could allow users to set file permissions, as well as viewing them.

> 4) The xfb program does not handle symbolic links very well.

This just about concludes learning how to program Motif. There are only a few final topics to discuss.

MOTIF TRADEOFFS

With the Motif toolkit a single function encapsulates a lot of code. This makes the job of the software developer easier, but leads to very large programs.

With Motif 1.0 on a Hewlett-Packard 375, the first program from Chapter 1 (first.c, which merely put up a push-button widget) led to an executable file that was 580072 bytes. On an HP 825 this was 763904 bytes. Under SCO Open Desktop 1.0, the first program took up 605344 bytes on disk. Not only will you soon fill up your hard disk with Motif programs, but these programs use similarly large amounts of RAM as well.

The general rule of thumb is that Motif programs are large and use up a lot of system resources. If you have a low-end system, Motif will not do you a lot of good. There is some hope in that Motif 1.1 uses shared libraries if available on your operating system. This should dramatically improve the problem with large programs.

The other problem with Motif programs is performance. Motif programs are slow and access the disk far too much. Part of this problem is that Motif sits on top of the Xt Intrinsics, which have their own overhead, and then on top of the X library which also has its own overhead.

With each widget, you generally have a window in X, which means that low-end X servers (like X terminals or low-memory PCs turned into X terminals) will have a hard time, since X terminals usually don't have the memory necessary to run a good number of complex Motif applications. Other improvements in Motif 1.1 should help performance, though. In any event, don't be surprised to see very large sizes for Motif applications.

OTHER ADVANCED MOTIF TOPICS

In order to concentrate on introducing Motif applications programming, we had to leave out a lot of the more advanced areas of Motif. We did this on purpose,because we believe that with enough examples to get you started, you will be able to pick up a Motif reference and make sense of most of the other topics.

Some of the topics we didn't go into, and that you'll now probably want to look up, include: translation tables: the Motif clipboard; the UIL prototyping language; and writing your own widgets. All of these topics are too advanced to be placed in a beginning Motif book.

Translation tables use resource files and functions to customize the actions that are executed when users input events into a Motif program. You can modify what is done for mouse button and keyboard events to customize an interface to your own style. Most reference pages on Motif widgets include a section on the default translation table for the widget.

The Motif clipboard provides a means for exchanging data between programs. Under the hood, much of the clipboard uses the X Window concept of selections which is a very advanced topic. We devoted a whole chapter to it in *Advanced X Window Applications Programming* (MIS:Press, 1990). Some Motif widgets support cut and paste in their default configurations, including the text widget you used in the `xfb` application, above. For more information on the Motif clipboard, take a look at the functions starting with "`XmClipboard`", such as `XmClipboardCopy()`, in the *OSF/Motif Programmer's Reference*.

The UIL (for User Interface Language) protyping language came from Motif's root in the DECwindows XUI widget set. UIL, which is not available on all Motif-based systems, allows you to prototype the interface—the Motif portion—of a program. UIL statements read something akin to C statements. The Motif toolkit includes a set of functions for accessing UIL data and widgets from a Motif C program. UIL is interpreted, so it is often easier to use UIL to prototype an interface and then translate the UIL file into C.

Finally, writing your own widgets is a daunting task. If a Motif widget doesn't offer exactly what you want, you can use the drawing-area widget introduced in Chapter 11. Or, you can write your own widget. Then your widget will become a first-class citizen in the Motif toolkit. This is a very useful feature, but rather advanced for a beginning book.

SUMMARY

This chapter introduced our last Motif program—a UNIX file browser. The xfb application uses most of the techniques discussed in this book in a working example and provides plenty of room for improvement.

Section VI

Appendices

The appendices provide helpful information on Motif. Appendix A explains exactly what you need to run Motif, including: software, cpus, monitors, hard drives, and networking cards. Appendix B lists addresses for ordering Motif. Appendix C provides a Unix `Makefile` for compiling. Appendix D lists additional Motif reading materials.

What You Need to Run Motif

T o run Motif, you first need to get the X Window System up and running. If you cannot get that far, you will never have much luck with Motif, since Motif applications are really X Window applications under the hood.

People commonly acquire X by purchasing a UNIX system that bundles the X Window System. Unfortunately, there are no shrink-wrap X packages on the market, where you simply throw a diskette in the drive and—voila—X appears on your screen. In these cases, it's simply not a matter of learning X but it's a matter of learning UNIX at the same time. This isn't an insurmountable task by any stretch—but be warned that an inexperienced computer user will put in a lot of work before ever reaching the X level.

For those of us without a Cray or a DEC VAX in our office, it's a matter of obtaining a workstation or PC with the firepower to run X. There are three basic paths to an X system: get a UNIX workstation, an X terminal, or software to turn a personal computer (Amiga, Macintosh or PC) into an X terminal. If you go the X terminal route, you'll also need another computer on a network that can run X and Motif applications (X terminals just provide the X server—not the most interesting of applications).

If your budget allows, the most simple solution is to purchase a workstation. (Our personal budgets, alas, don't allow this, but our employers' budgets do.) Workstations from Data General, IBM, Hewlett-Packard, Motorola, DEC, and others all come bundled with X, and most include Motif. Such a workstation (equipped with hard disk) will set you back about $10,000 at the low end, but it's an invaluable tool if you're a professional software developer, analyst, or designer. Our experience shows that a workstation is beyond the reach of a good portion of potential users. A lower-priced (and a lower-performing) alternative is to configure a PC to run X by turning it into an X terminal or running X under UNIX. This can be a simple solution, but not every PC is equipped to run X.

First of all, you'll want to configure a PC as an X server. In theory, according to some vendors and magazines, you can use an 80286, 80386 or 80486 system equipped with 640K of RAM, a monochrome display, a networking card, and X software. Theory, though, doesn't work as well when it comes to performance. Reality dictates at least an 80386 or 80486 with eight megs of RAM, a large-screen color display, and, a mondo hard drive—80MB is OK, 120MB better, 300+ great—if you're running UNIX. When running graphics-intensive programs on top of UNIX, the more power the better. With hardware prices (particularly in the RAM and 80386 fields) dropping rapidly, you're looking at a speed demon for just under $10,000.

SOFTWARE

The software you choose dictates your ultimate hardware configuration. For a PC, there are two software routes: X server software running under DOS, or UNIX configurations that support X and Motif. The truth is, we haven't played with the DOS X servers like PC Xview from Graphic Software Systems or Locus's PC Xsight. In theory, you can run Xview or Xsight in 640K on a PC AT. This software essentially turns your DOS PC into an X terminal. You'll still need another computer on the network to run X applications. You'll also want as much extended or expanded RAM as possible.

Our experience on PCs has been with versions of UNIX from Interactive Systems (386/ix) and SCO (Open Desktop). Other vendors supporting X under UNIX for PCs are Everex (Esix), IBM (AIX), and Intel. Since X draws some features (in part) from the operating system underneath, it seems like a good idea to use the power of UNIX if it's available.

CPUS

We're experienced with PCs, workstations, and Macintoshes. Again, more is better—more megahertz and more RAM. The amount of RAM needed will depend on the software—some PC versions of UNIX require a minimum of two megs, while others (like AIX) require four. If you can afford it, buy much more than the minimum—buy as much RAM as your checkbook allows. Eight megabytes is a realistic minimum for a system that runs UNIX and X, and since Motif puts more demands on the system, sixteen megs is a lot better. Release 4 of the X Window System requires less RAM and provides much better performance. Unfortunately, few vendors have upgraded their X offerings to Release 4 as of this writing.

Using a 386 or a 486 as an X server also allows the users to run DOS applications. While we're not huge fans of DOS, there are some applications in DOS that don't have counterparts in the X world. In addition, there's a version of X that runs under AmigaDOS from GfxBase while the new Amiga 3000UX has an X Window option. We can't recommend it or argue against them, but they're worth checking out.

MONITORS

Since X is a graphic windowing product, your monitor's resolution is important. Again, the more power the better. You'll need a minimum of 640-by-480 resolution (VGA). This is probably the minimum usable for X. Better yet is a Super VGA (800-by-600 or 1024-by-768) or 8514/A (1024-by-768). High-end monitors cost more—you'll need to pay extra for both the monitor and graphics card—but they can increase performance because part of the X server can be loaded onto the card's limited memory. Your CPU doesn't have to work as hard which speeds up your system.

HARD DRIVES

There's only one rule to remember about hard drives: the bigger the better. (This is a typical male attitude, isn't it?) An 80MB drive is the minimum—especially with UNIX—while 120MB or 330MB is better. If you can afford that high-performance Wren drive, go for it.

NETWORKING CARD

Most DOS X implementations won't work without a networking card of some sort. What you choose will ultimately depend on your networking needs.

Where You Can Order Motif

M otif is a software product of the Open Software Foundation, also called OSF. You can order a source code license from the OSF for $1,000 (at least as of this writing).

Open Software Foundation
11 Cambridge Center
Cambridge, MA 02142
U.S.A.
Phone: (617) 621-8700

In addition to the OSF, a number of computer vendors offer all or part of Motif with their versions of the UNIX operating system. Vendors such as Hewlett-Packard and Data General include Motif along with the X Window System. SCO's Open Desktop product includes Motif, and you can order Motif as an add-on for most 386 versions of UNIX, including Interactive UNIX and Esix.

If your computer vendor, such as Sun Microsystems, doesn't sell Motif, then you can order Motif from the OSF or from a third party, such as ICS:

Integrated Computer Solutions
163 Harvard Street
Cambridge, MA 02139
U.S.A.
Phone: (617) 547-0510

Your best bet is to contact your system vendor and ask for Motif. If that fails, then call up the Open Software Foundation or a third-party vendor.

Appendix C

A UNIX Makefile

Since all Motif programs need to link in at least three libraries, we put together a Makefile to help take care of all the special options in compiling. In Makefile four steps are needed.

STEP 1

Determine what C compiler options you need. First, figure out the command sequence to start your C compiler. On most UNIX systems, this is "cc", but if you use the GNU C compiler, this may be "gcc". If you are compiling C programs on your system, you have to know this one.

Next, decide what kind of command-line options you need to pass to the C compiler.

On SCO's Open Desktop, for example, you may need to pass the following when compiling any X Window-based application (remember that Motif programs are also X Window programs under the hood):

435

```
cc -Dsysv -DLAI_TCP -Di386 -DSYSV
```

Determine the flags needed to properly invoke your C compiler and place these in the make variable CC.

STEP 2

Determine what you need to do to link Motif programs. On most systems, the LIBS make variable should be set to:

```
LIBS = -lXm -lXt -lX11
```

If your X Window and Motif libraries are in a nonstandard location, you may need to use the -L option for the linker. The Data General Aviion, for example, usually places the X Window libraries in the /usr/opt/X11/lib directory, a nonstandard location (the standard is in /usr/lib). In such a case, you'd need a LIBS make variable set to:

```
LIBS = -L/usr/opt/X11/lib -lXm -lXt -lX11
```

On SCO's Open Desktop, you need to link in a number of other libraries, and therefore need a LIBS make variable set to:

```
LIBS = -lXm -lXt -lX11 -ltlisock -lsocket -lnsl_s
```

This is because networking is often considered an add-on for 386 versions of UNIX. If you're running Interactive, Intel, or Esix for the 386, you will probably need special link options as well.

STEP 3

Determine the flags necessary to compile dir.c, a file that reads the file names in a directory. This is somewhat UNIX-specific, so you may need to port dir.c anyway. Most UNIX variants need a definition of DIRENT, and so set the DIR_FLAGS make variable to:

```
DIR_FLAGS=      -DDIRENT
```

On Hewlett-Packard machines, you may need to set the DIR_FLAGS make variable to:

```
DIR_FLAGS=      -Dhpux -DDIRECT
```

See Chapter 17 for more information on the file dir.c.

STEP 4

Determine the flags to link in the PW library. On most UNIX variants, you'll need to link in the PW library to compile `dialog.c` (from Chapter 4). If so, set the `PW_LIB` make variable to:

```
PW_LIB= -lPW
```

On SCO's Open Desktop 1.0, as discussed in Chapter 4, you want to clear this make variable and should not link in the PW library:

```
PW_LIB=
```

The whole idea of this `Makefile` is to speed up the compiling and linking for the example programs in this book. If `Makefile` causes problems, you're probably best off skipping this `Makefile` entirely and rolling your own. We tried to make this as portable as possible, but we cannot cover all machines and all custom installations. Good luck.

To compile any of the programs, type:

```
make program_name
```

`Program_name` is the name of the program as we introduced it in the text, such as

```
make dialtest
```

This is used to make the `dialtest` program in Chapter 4.

To compile and link all the example programs, you can type in:

```
make all
```

MAKEFILE

The code for `Makefile` is as follows:

```
#
#   Programming Motif source code examples.
#
#   To compile all the Programming Motif sources,
#   follow STEPS 1 to 4 below to customize this
#   Makefile for your system. Then, type
#         make all
#   and away you go.
#
#-----------------------------------------------------------
#
```

continued...

437

...from previous page

```
#   STEP 1: CC is the C compiler command you need to
#   invoke, plus whatever flags are necessary. Some
#   samples are below.
#
#   SCO OpenDesktop 1.0 needs the following definitions:
#CC= cc -g -Dsysv -DLAI_TCP -Di386 -DSYSV
#
#   On most systems, this will suffice:
#CC= cc -g
#
#   Or, to optimize:
#CC= cc -O
#
CC= cc -O
#
#------------------------------------------------------------ #
#   STEP 2: LIBS are the libraries needed to link a
#   Motif program. You may need to specify where
#   the linker should look for the Motif and X
#   libraries, using the -L option.
#
#   On SCO Open Desktop, you'll need a LIBS something like:
#LIBS = -lXm -lXt -lX11 -ltlisock -lsocket -lnsl_s
#
#   On Interactive UNIX 2.2, you'll need something like:
#LIBS = -lXm -lXt -lX11 -linet
#
#   On most UNIX boxes, you'll need something like:
#LIBS = -lXm -lXt -lX11
#
#   If your X Window and Motif libraries are in a
#   non-standard place, like /usr/opt/X11, use something
#   like the following:
#LIBS = -L/usr/opt/X11/lib -lXm -lXt -lX11
#
#
LIBS = -L/usr/opt/X11/lib -lXm -lXt -lX11
#
#------------------------------------------------------------
#
#   STEP 3: DIR_FLAGS holds the flags needed to compile dir.c,
#   which reads directories.
#
#   On Hewlett-Packard HP-UX systems, use:
#DIR_FLAGS= -Dhpux -DDIRECT
#
#   On most System V-style systems (including SunOS,
#   even though it has BSD roots), use:
#DIR_FLAGS= -DDIRENT
#
DIR_FLAGS= -DDIRENT
```

continued...

...from previous page

```
#
#
#---------------------------------------------------------- #
#   STEP 4: On most systems, the PW library is
#   needed to compile the file selection dialog
#   widget. Place the proper flags in PW_LIB.
#
#PW_LIB= -lPW
#
PW_LIB= -lPW
#
#
#---------------------------------------------------------- #
#   Compile all the sample programs with make all.
#

all:      dialtest drawtest dstyle first formtest hello listtest \
          menubar menu panetest restest scale style text \
          toptest worktest xfb

#
#   Chapter 1
#
first:    first.c
    $(CC) -o first first.c $(LIBS)

#
#   Chapter 2
#
hello.o:        hello.c
    $(CC) -c hello.c

label.o:        label.c
    $(CC) -c label.c

string.o:       string.c
    $(CC) -c string.c

hello:   hello.o label.o string.o
    $(CC) -o hello hello.o label.o string.o $(LIBS)

#
#   Chapter 3: Widgets that Hold Other Widgets...
#
formtest.o: formtest.c
    $(CC) -c formtest.c

push.o:         push.c
    $(CC) -c push.c
```

continued...

439

...from previous page

```
formtest:      formtest.o label.o push.o string.o
   $(CC) -o formtest formtest.o label.o push.o string.o $(LIBS)

panetest.o:    panetest.c
   $(CC) -c panetest.c

panetest:      panetest.o label.o push.o string.o
   $(CC) -o panetest panetest.o label.o push.o string.o $(LIBS)

#
#   Chapter 4: Dialogs
#
dialog.o: dialog.c
   $(CC) -c dialog.c

dialtest.o:    dialtest.c
   $(CC) -c dialtest.c

dialtest:      dialtest.o dialog.o push.o string.o
   $(CC) -o dialtest dialtest.o dialog.o push.o string.o \
                                  $(LIBS) $(PW_LIB)

#
# Chapter 5:   Menu bars
#
mainwind.o:    mainwind.c
   $(CC) -c mainwind.c

menubar.o:     menubar.c
   $(CC) -c menubar.c

mtest.o: mtest.c
   $(CC) -c mtest.c

MENU_OBJS=     mainwind.o menubar.o string.o dialog.o

menubar: mtest.o dialog.o mainwind.o menubar.o string.o
   $(CC) -o menubar mtest.o dialog.o mainwind.o \
      menubar.o string.o $(LIBS) $(PW_LIB)

#
#
#   Chapter 6: Pull-down Menus
#
menu.o:  menu.c
   $(CC) -c menu.c

mtest2.o:      mtest2.c
   $(CC) -c mtest2.c
```

continued...

440

...from previous page
```
MAIN_OBJS=      $(MENU_OBJS) menu.o label.o

menu:      dialog.o label.o mainwind.o menu.o menubar.o mtest2.o string.o
    $(CC) -o menu  dialog.o label.o mainwind.o menu.o menubar.o \
       mtest2.o string.o $(LIBS) $(PW_LIB)


#
#   Chapter 7: Scrolled text widget
#
text.o:  text.c
    $(CC) -c text.c

texttest.o:     texttest.c
    $(CC) -c texttest.c

text:    dialog.o label.o mainwind.o menubar.o menu.o string.o \
                    texttest.o text.o
    $(CC) -o text dialog.o label.o mainwind.o menubar.o menu.o \
         string.o texttest.o text.o $(LIBS) $(PW_LIB)


#
#   Chapter 8: Scrolled Lists
#
list.o: list.c
    $(CC) -c list.c

listtest.o:    listtest.c
    $(CC) -c listtest.c

listtest:     listtest.o list.o string.o
    $(CC) -o listtest listtest.o list.o string.o $(LIBS)


#
#   Chapter 9: Top-Level shell test
#
toptest.o:     toptest.c
    $(CC) -c toptest.c

toptest: dialog.o mainwind.o menubar.o string.o toptest.o
    $(CC) -o toptest dialog.o mainwind.o menubar.o string.o \
         toptest.o $(LIBS) $(PW_LIB)


#
#   Chapter 10: Scale Widget
#
scale.o:       scale.c
    $(CC) -c scale.c
```

continued...

...from previous page
```
scale:    scale.o push.o string.o
    $(CC) -o scale scale.o push.o string.o $(LIBS)


#
#   Chapter 11: Xlib calls from Motif Programs
#
drawtest.o:    drawtest.c
    $(CC) -c drawtest.c

drawtest:        drawtest.o push.o string.o
    $(CC) -o drawtest  drawtest.o push.o string.o  $(LIBS)


#
# Chapter 12, Background Processing With Xt
#
worktest.o: worktest.c
    $(CC) -c worktest.c

worktest:        worktest.o push.o string.o
    $(CC) -o worktest  worktest.o push.o string.o  $(LIBS)


#
#   Chapter 13, Resources
#
restest.o: restest.c
    $(CC) -c restest.c

restest: restest.o push.o
    $(CC) -o restest restest.o push.o $(LIBS)


#
# Chapter 14,  Motif Style Guide Menus
#
about.o: about.c
    $(CC) -c about.c

menugad.o:     menugad.c
    $(CC) -c menugad.c

style.o: style.c
    $(CC) -c style.c

style:    about.o menugad.o string.o style.o
    $(CC) -o style about.o menugad.o string.o style.o $(LIBS)


#
# Chapter 16,  Motif Style Guide Dialogs
#
bulletin.o: bulletin.c
```
continued...

...from previous page
```
    $(CC) -c bulletin.c

dstyle.o:       dstyle.c
    $(CC) -c dstyle.c

fileinfo.o:    fileinfo.c
    $(CC) -c fileinfo.c

toggle.o:       toggle.c
    $(CC) -c toggle.c

DSTYLE_OBJS=   about.o bulletin.o dstyle.o fileinfo.o label.o \
    menugad.o push.o string.o toggle.o

dstyle:   $(DSTYLE_OBJS)
    $(CC) -o dstyle $(DSTYLE_OBJS) $(LIBS)


#
# Chapter 17: A File browser Application (xfb)
#
xfb.o:   xfb.c
    $(CC) -c xfb.c

dir.o:   dir.c
    $(CC) $(DIR_FLAGS) -c dir.c

viewfile.o:    viewfile.c
    $(CC) -c viewfile.c

XFB_OBJS=      about.o bulletin.o dir.o fileinfo.o label.o \
        list.o menugad.o push.o string.o text.o \
        toggle.o viewfile.o xfb.o

xfb:      $(XFB_OBJS)
    $(CC) -o xfb $(XFB_OBJS) $(LIBS)


#
#   end of file
#
```

443

Additional Reading

C ontrary to what people may tell you, if you want to write commercial-grade Motif applications, you really should get a thorough grounding in both the X library (Xlib) and the X Toolkit Intrinsics (Xt), as well as in the Motif toolkit. Motif depends a lot on the Intrinsics and the underlying Xlib, you may want to take a look at some of the books listed below. Since new X Window and Motif books seem to appear on a daily basis, you'll also want to check your local bookstore.

MOTIF DOCUMENTATION

The official documentation on Motif from the Open Software Foundation is listed below. Your implementation of the Motif toolkit should come with these manuals. You will use these all the time, especially the programmer's reference. These manuals can also be purchased from Prentice Hall.

OSF/Motif Programmer's Guide, Open Software Foundation, Cambridge, MA, 1989.

OSF/Motif Programmer's Reference Manual, Open Software Foundation, Cambridge, MA, 1989.

OSF/Motif Style Guide, Open Software Foundation, Cambridge, MA, 1989.

OTHER MOTIF BOOKS

These books are not part of the official documentation, but they will probably help out in writing Motif applications.

Rost, Randi J., *X and Motif Quick Reference Guide*, Digital Press, Bedford, MA, 1990 (distributed by Prentice Hall). ISBN (Digital Press) 1-55558-052-1, (Prentice Hall) 0-13-972209-2.

Young, Douglas A., *The X Window System: Programming and Applications with Xt, OSF/Motif Edition*, Prentice Hall, Englewood Cliffs, NJ , 1990. ISBN 0-13-497074-8.

Young, Douglas A., *OSF/Motif Reference Guide*, Prentice Hall, Englewood Cliffs, NJ, 1990. ISBN 0-13-642786-3.

X TOOLKIT INTRINSICS BOOKS

Asente, Paul J. and Ralph R. Swick, *X Window System Toolkit*, Digital Press, Bedford, MA, 1990 (distributed by Prentice Hall). ISBN (Digital Press) 1-55558-051-3, (Prentice Hall) 0-13-972191-6.

McCormack, Joel, Paul Asente and Ralph R. Swick, *X Toolkit Intrinsics: C Language Interface, X11 Release 4 Version*, 1989, MIT X Consortium. This document comes with the X Window System Release 4, from MIT.

Nye, Adrian and Tim O'Reilly, *X Toolkit Intrinsics Programming Manual*, O'Reilly and Assoc., Sebastopol, CA, 1990. ISBN 0-937175-33-1 .

O'Reilly, Tim (editor), *X Toolkit Intrinsics Reference Manual*, O'Reilly and Assoc., Sebastopol, CA, 1990. ISBN 0-937175-35-8.

X LIBRARY BOOKS

Johnson, Eric F. and Kevin Reichard, *X Window Applications Programming*, MIS: Press, Portland, OR, 1989. ISBN 1-55828-016-2.

446

Johnson, Eric F. and Kevin Reichard, *Advanced X Window Applications Programming*, MIS: Press, Portland, OR, 1990. ISBN 1-55828-029-4.

Jones, Oliver, *Introduction to the X Window System*, Prentice Hall, Englewood Cliffs, NJ, 1989. ISBN 0-13-499997-5.

Nye, Adrian, Xlib Programming Manual, vol. 1, 2nd ed., O'Reilly and Assoc., Sebastopol, CA, 1990. ISBN 0-937175-11-0.

Nye, Adrian (ed.), *Xlib Reference Manual*, vol. 2, 2nd ed., O'Reilly and Assoc., Sebastopol, CA, 1990. ISBN 0-937175-12-9.

Scheifler, Robert W. and James Gettys, with Jim Flowers, Ron Newman and David Rosenthal, 2nd ed., *X Window System: The Complete Reference to Xlib, X Protocol, ICCCM, XLFD*, Digital Press, Bedford, MA, 1990. ISBN (Digital Press) 1-5558-050-5, (Prentice Hall) 0-13-97 2050-2.1

Index

Italicized listings are programs and functions created by the authors.

A

about.c, 316-317, 331, 388, 419-420, 442
AboutBox, 314-316, 318-319, 331, 387, 418
activateCallback, 18, 62, 122, 126, 164
AddToList, 188, 193, 197, 403-404
allowResize, 63
AmigaDOS, 3-4, 21, 161, 230, 361, 400, 430, 431
Apple Macintosh, 3, 21, 305, 312, 430, 431
application defaults file, 292, 298, 333 See also resource files
Athena widgets, 10, 271 See also Xaw
autoUnmanage, 339-340

B

background processing, 253, 268, 442
BadValue, 68
borderWidth, 292, 294-295, 299
bottomAttachment, 51
bottomPosition, 53
browse selection, 182
browseSelectionCallback, 183
bulletin-board dialog, 338-345, 348-350, 353, 359
bulletin-board widget, 336, 339-340, 343-344 See also XmBulletinBoard
bulletin.c, 345, 348, 353, 364, 388, 419-420, 442-443
BulletinB.h include file, 31, 339, 345
BulletinBoardDialog, 72
BulletinDefaultButton, 343-346, 356, 366
BulletinDialogTitle, 344-346, 362, 368
ButtonPress events, 232, 239, 245, 251, 259-260, 263
ButtonRelease events, 232, 239, 245, 251

C

callback function, 17-19, 21, 61-62, 74, 79, 81, 88, 91, 93-94, 103, 105-106, 126,
 129-130, 138-139, 148, 184, 186, 197, 216, 219-220, 229, 234, 238, 241-242,
 254-255, 257, 260, 267, 314-315, 322-323, 326, 339, 372-373, 412
       creating, 17
       defined, 17
       passing data to, 19
       writing, 18
cancelCallback, 78
cancelLabelString, 77
cascade button widgets, 122, 137 See also XmCascadeButton
cascaded menus, 147

G

H

I

K

L